the blot

by tom neely

i will destroy you
los angeles, california

i will destroy you
p.o. box 39963
los angeles, ca 90039

www.iwilldestroyyou.com

first edition printed in canada, may 2007

ISBN 978-0-9742715-8-3

for mom, dad, blake & pamela

"i hear nothing but your voice..."
                                    -james joyce

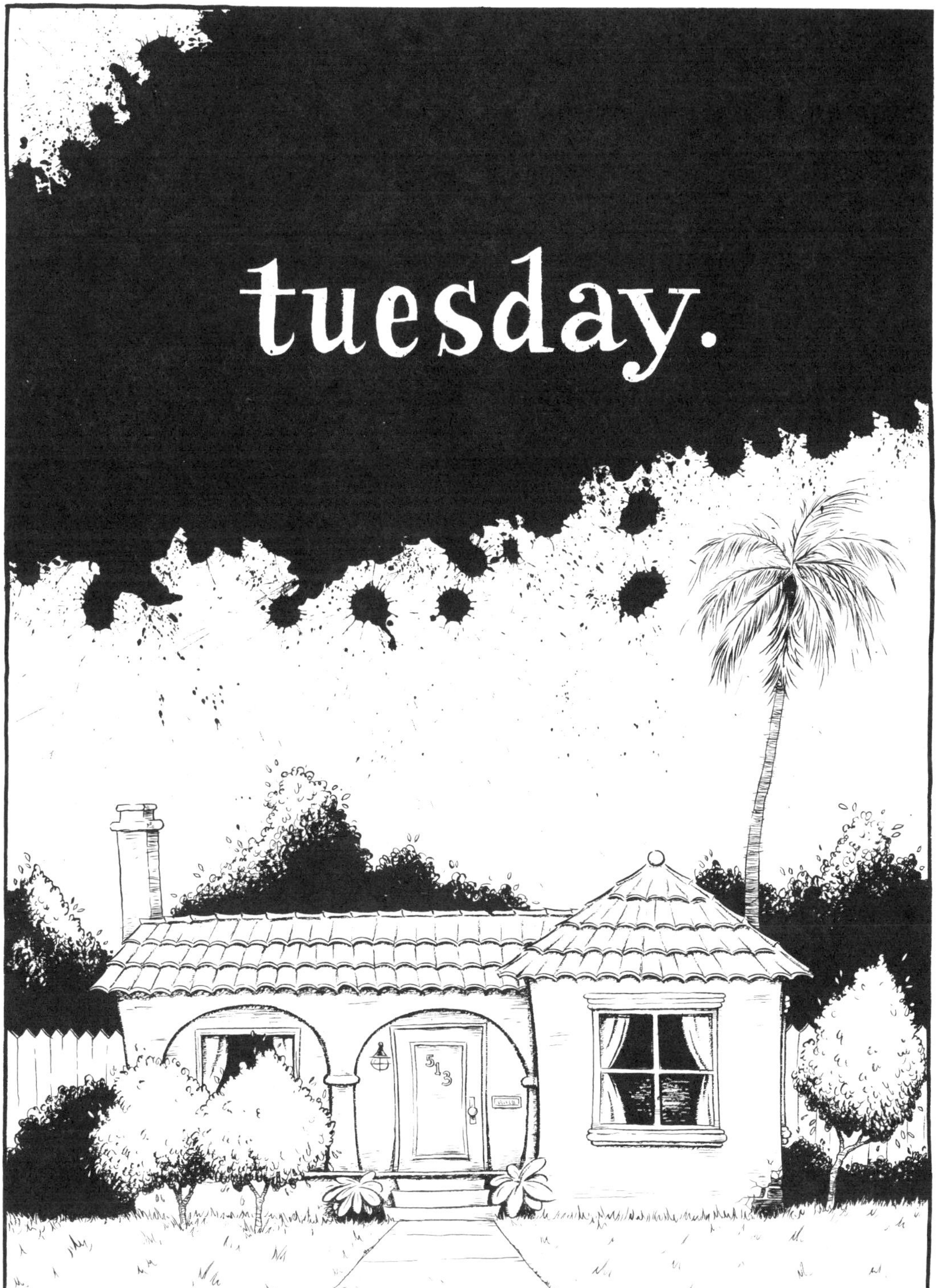
tuesday.
513

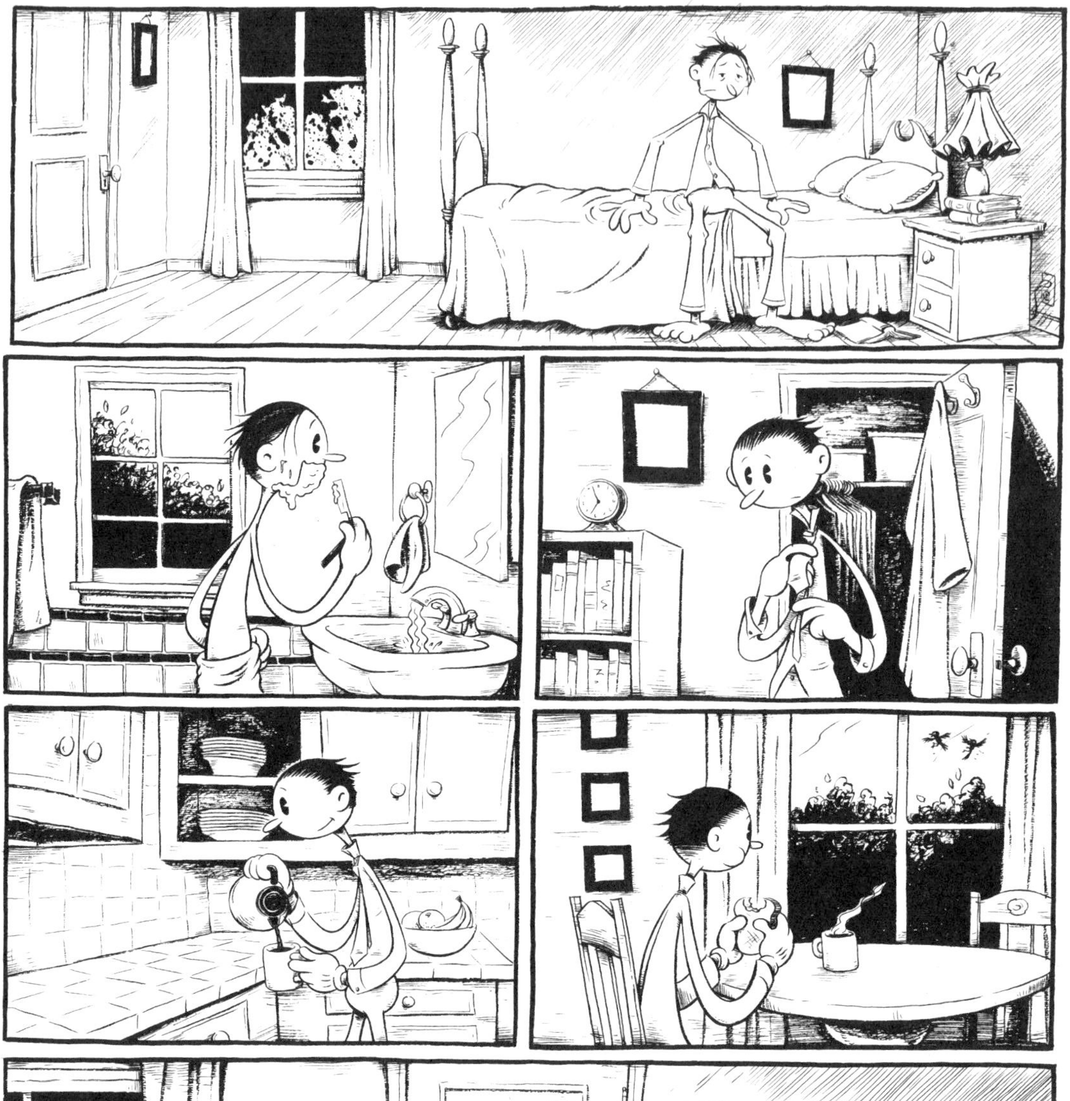

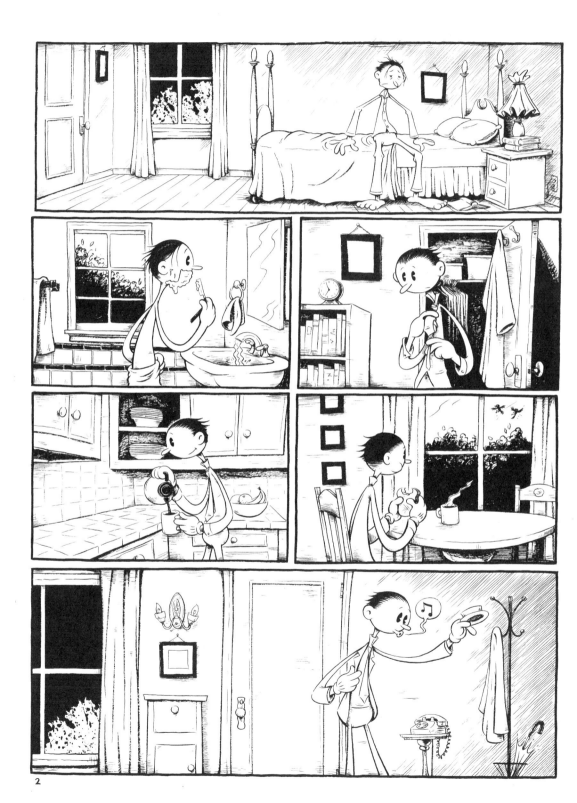

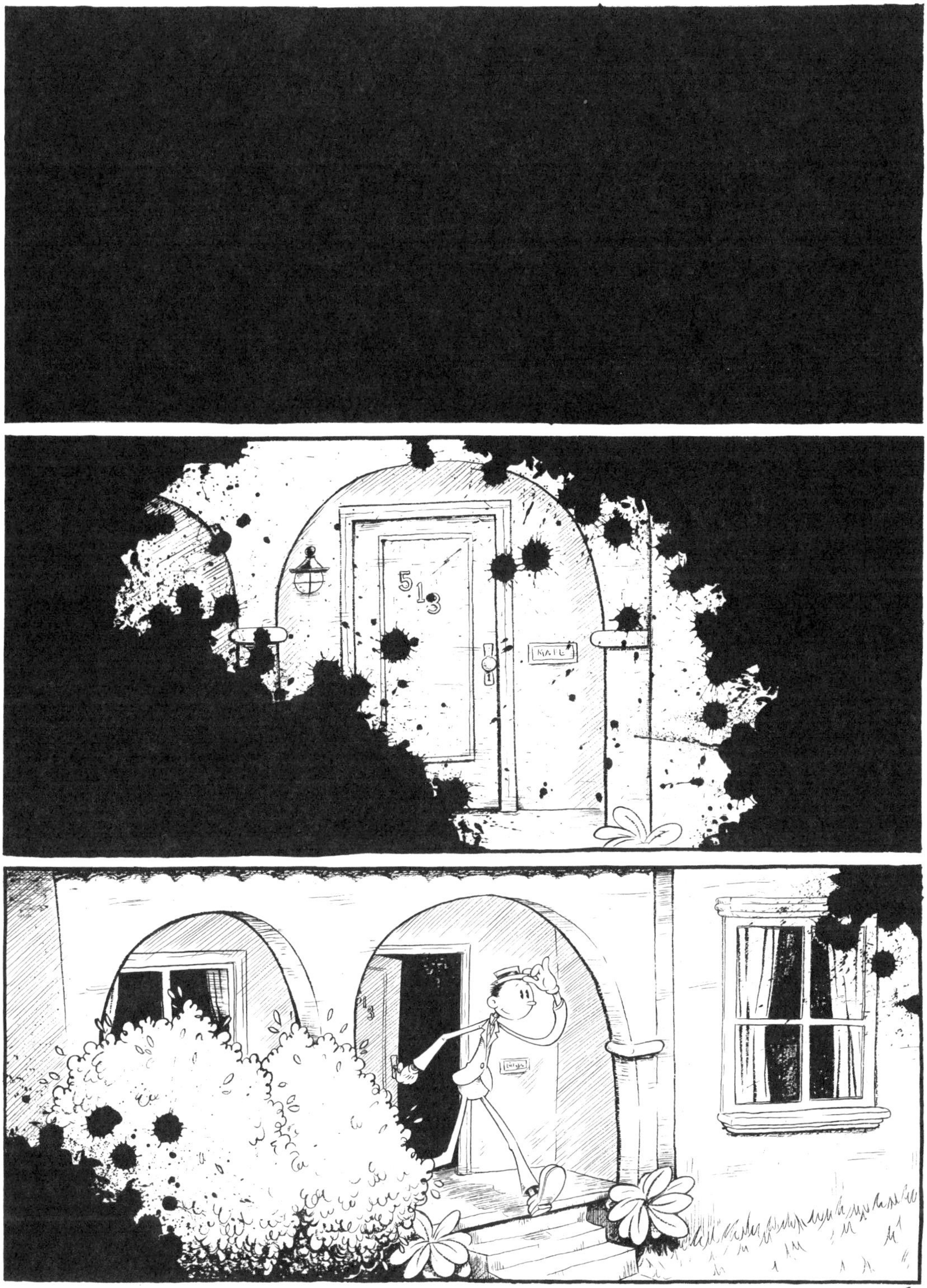
513

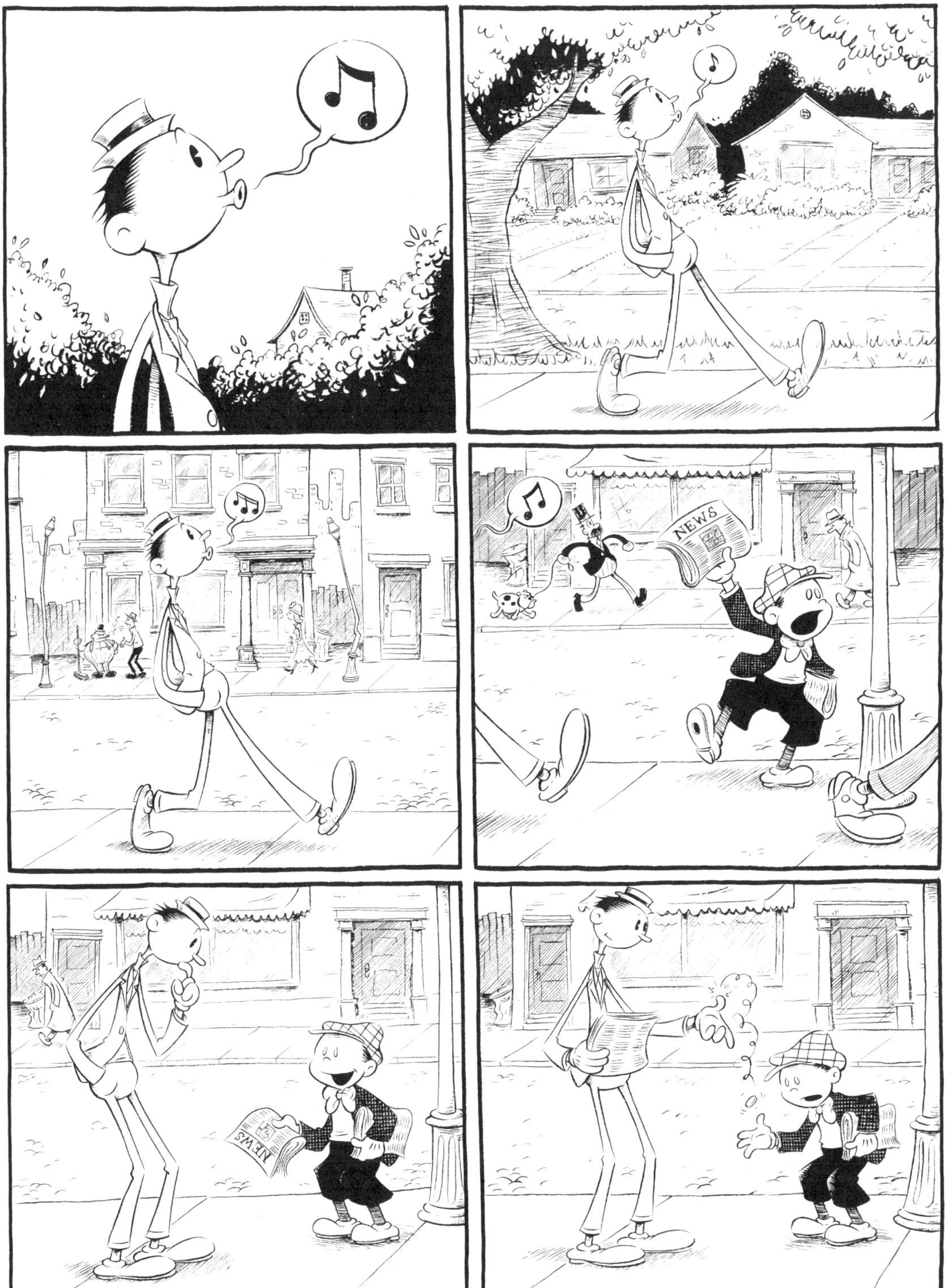
NEWS
NEWS

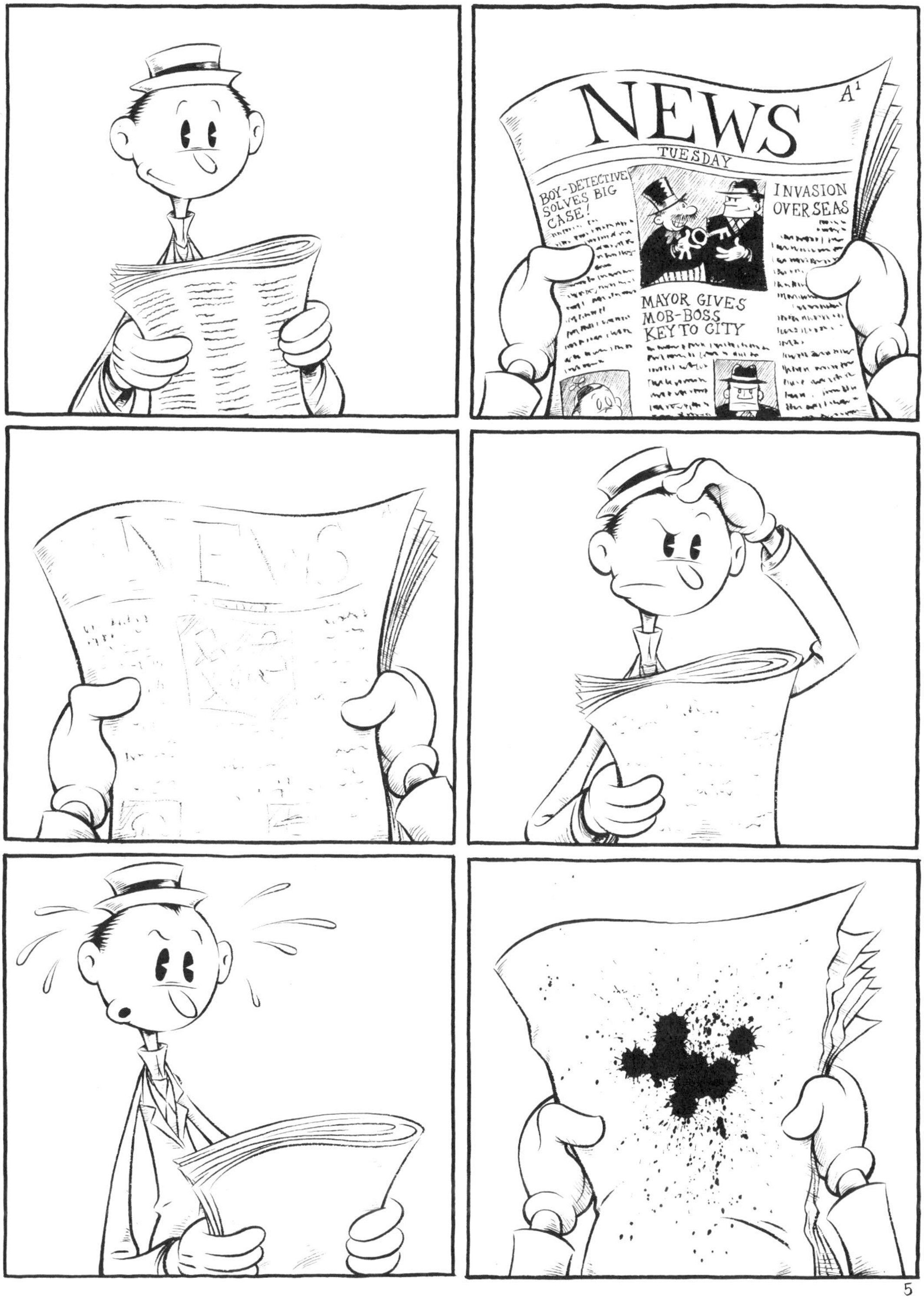
NEWS
A1
TUESDAY
BOY-DETECTIVE SOLVES BIG CASE!
INVASION OVER SEAS
MAYOR GIVES MOB-BOSS KEY TO CITY

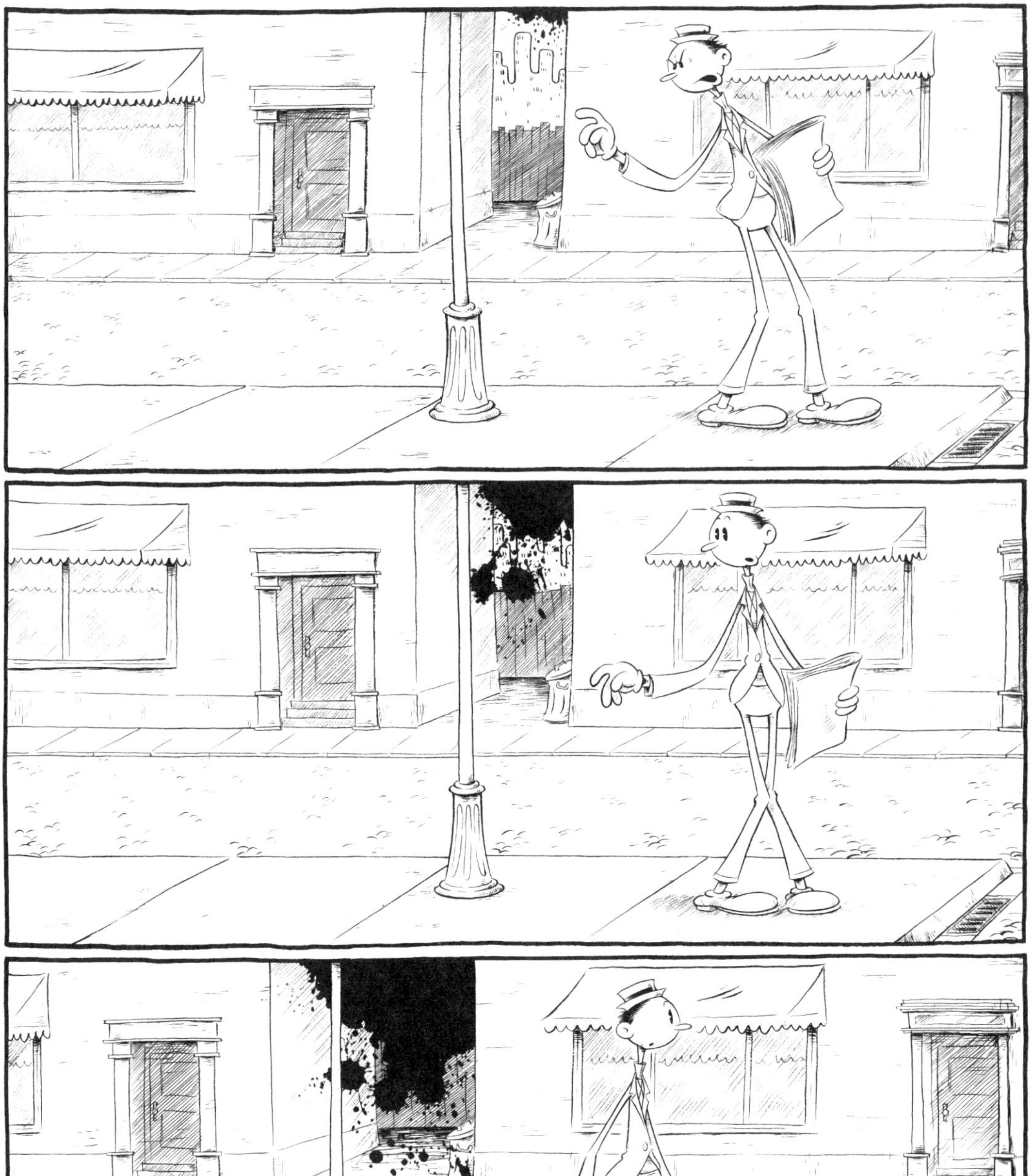

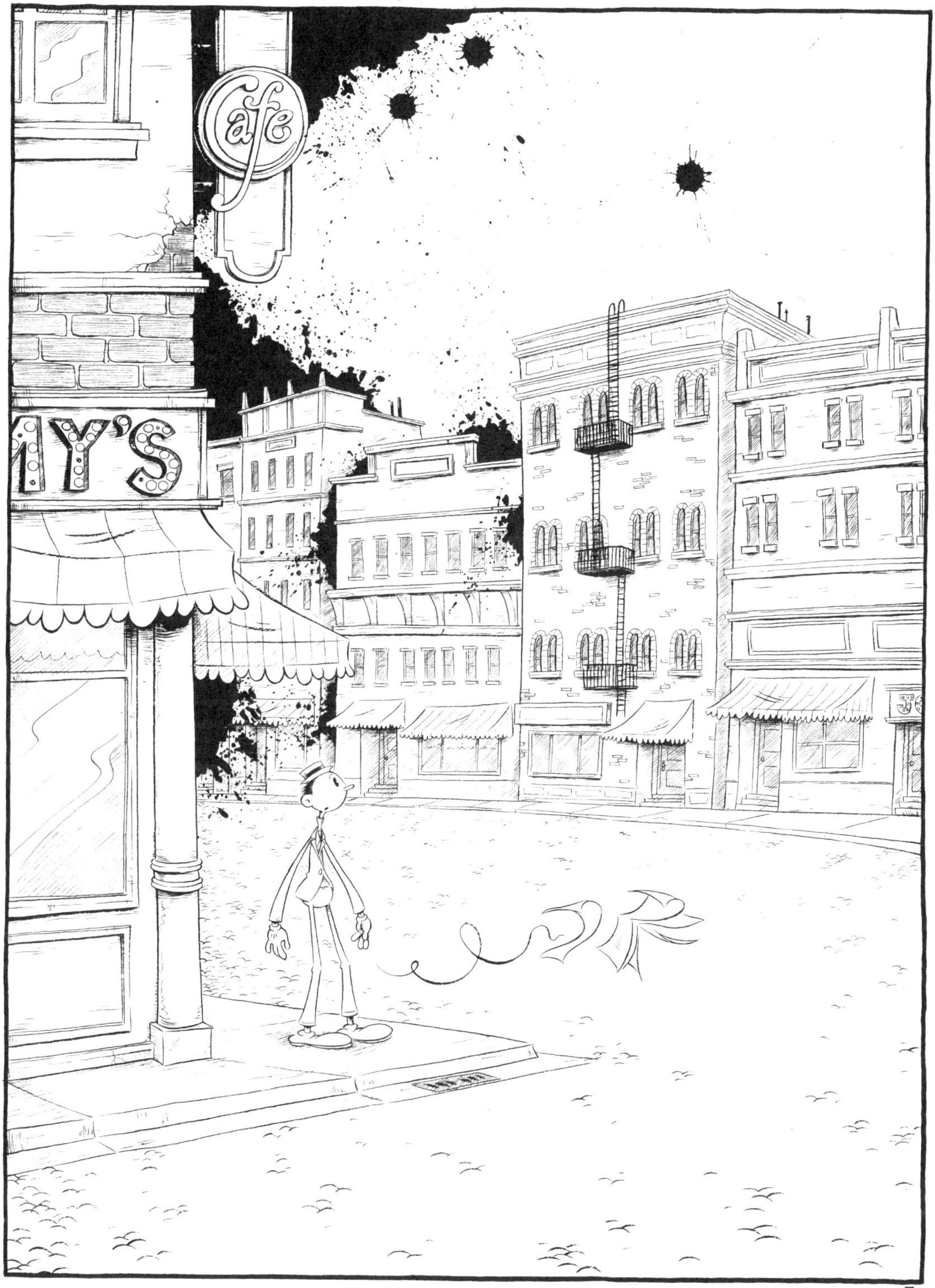
Cafe
MY'S

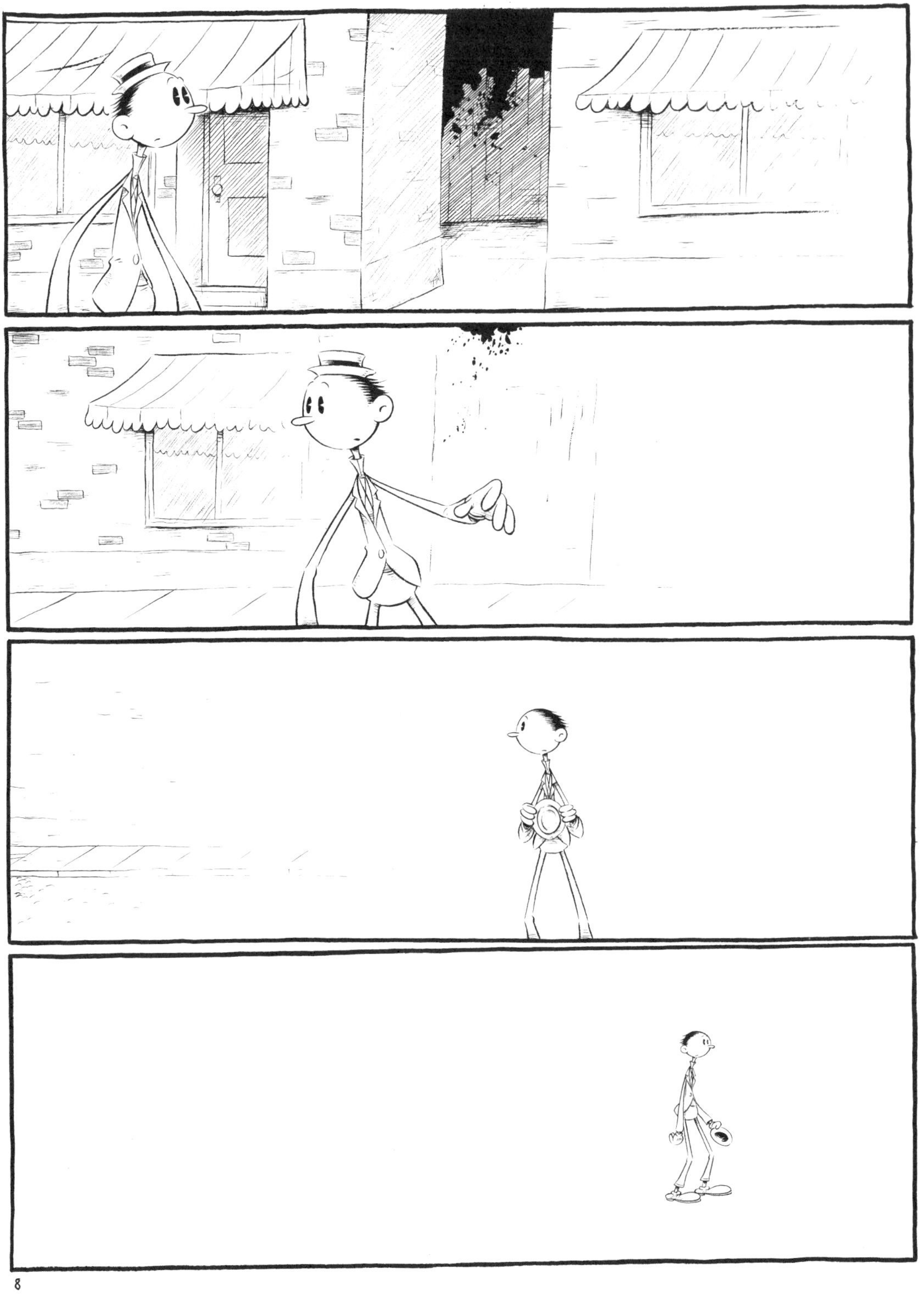

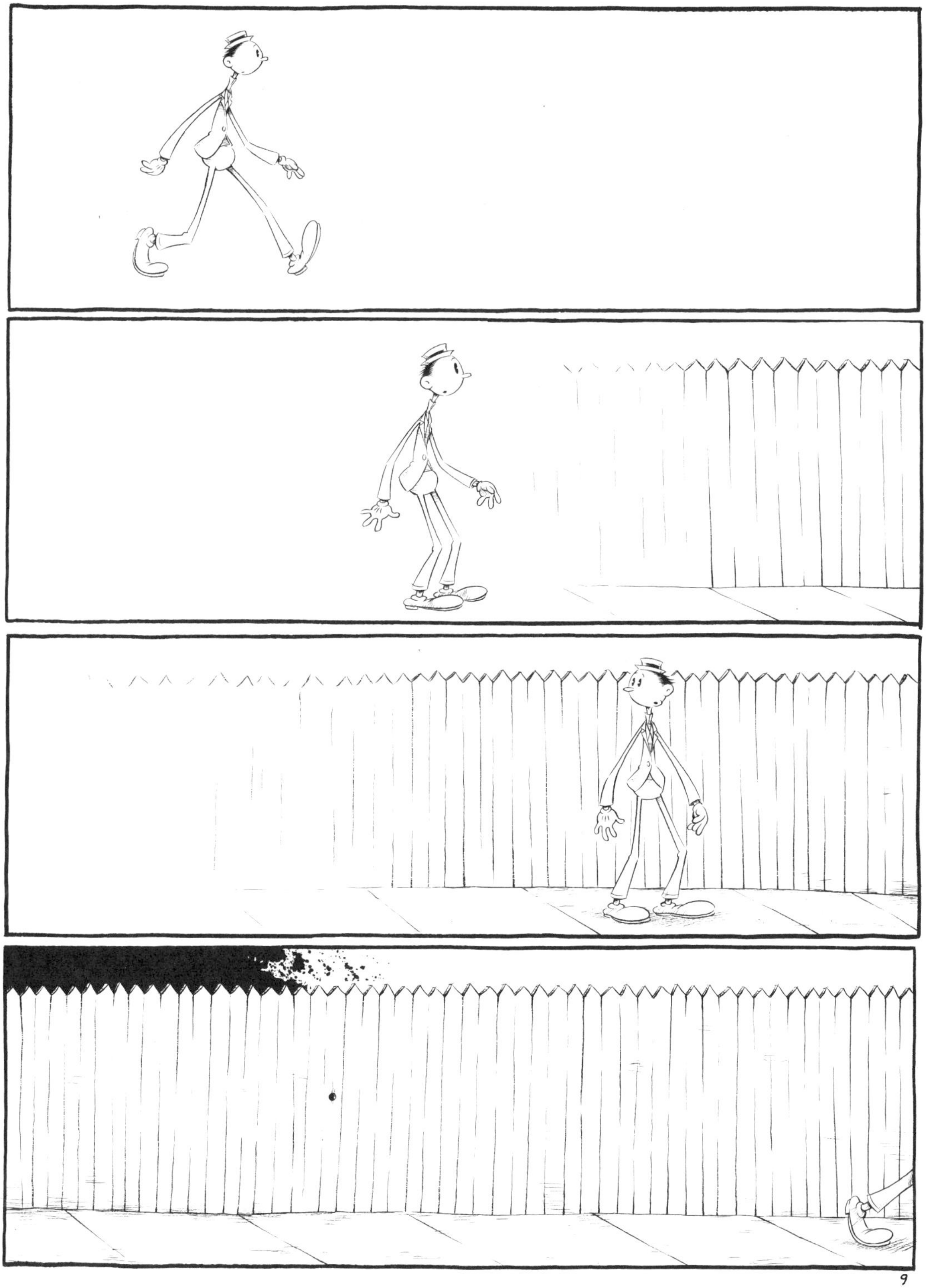

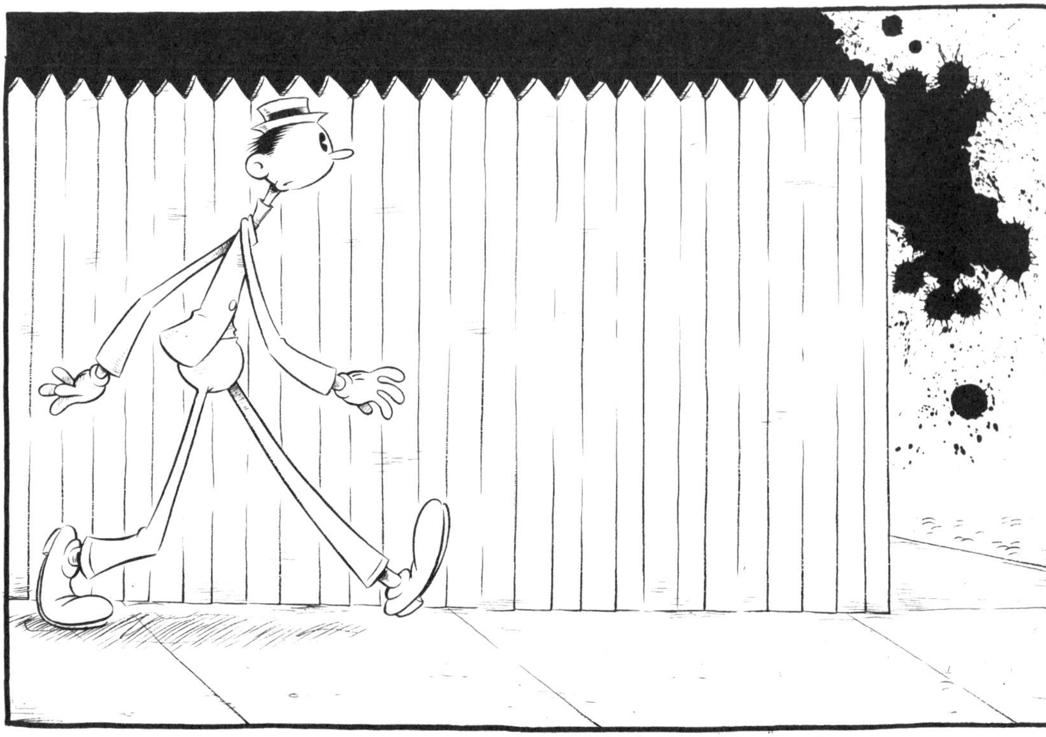

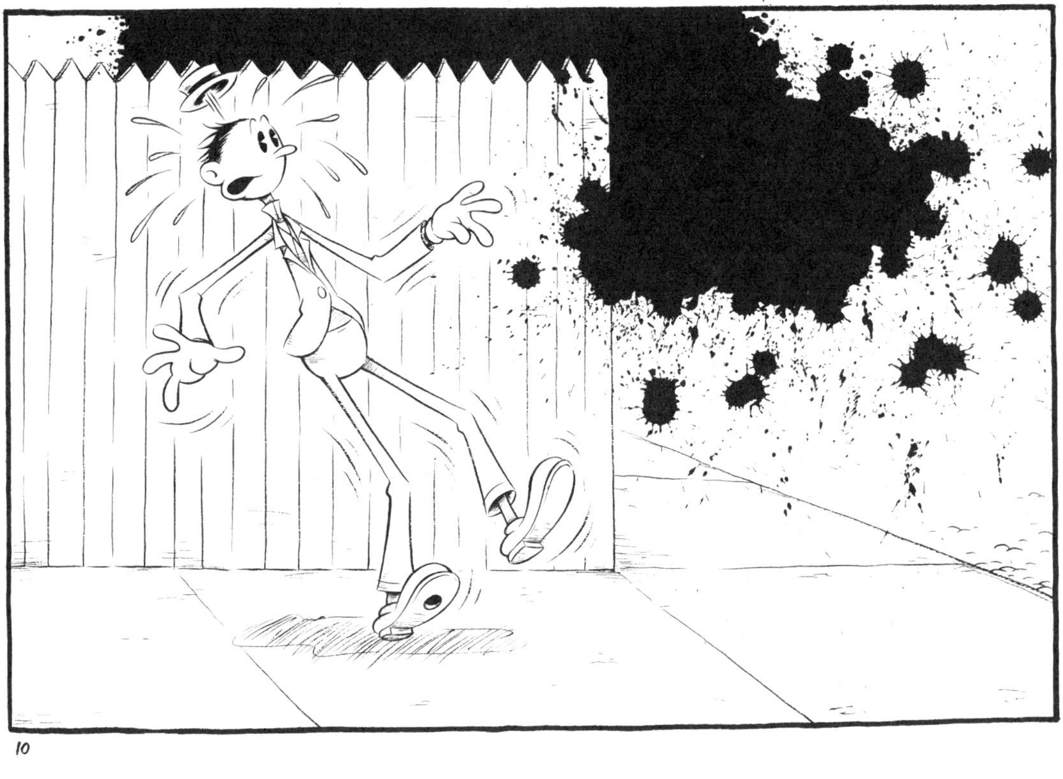

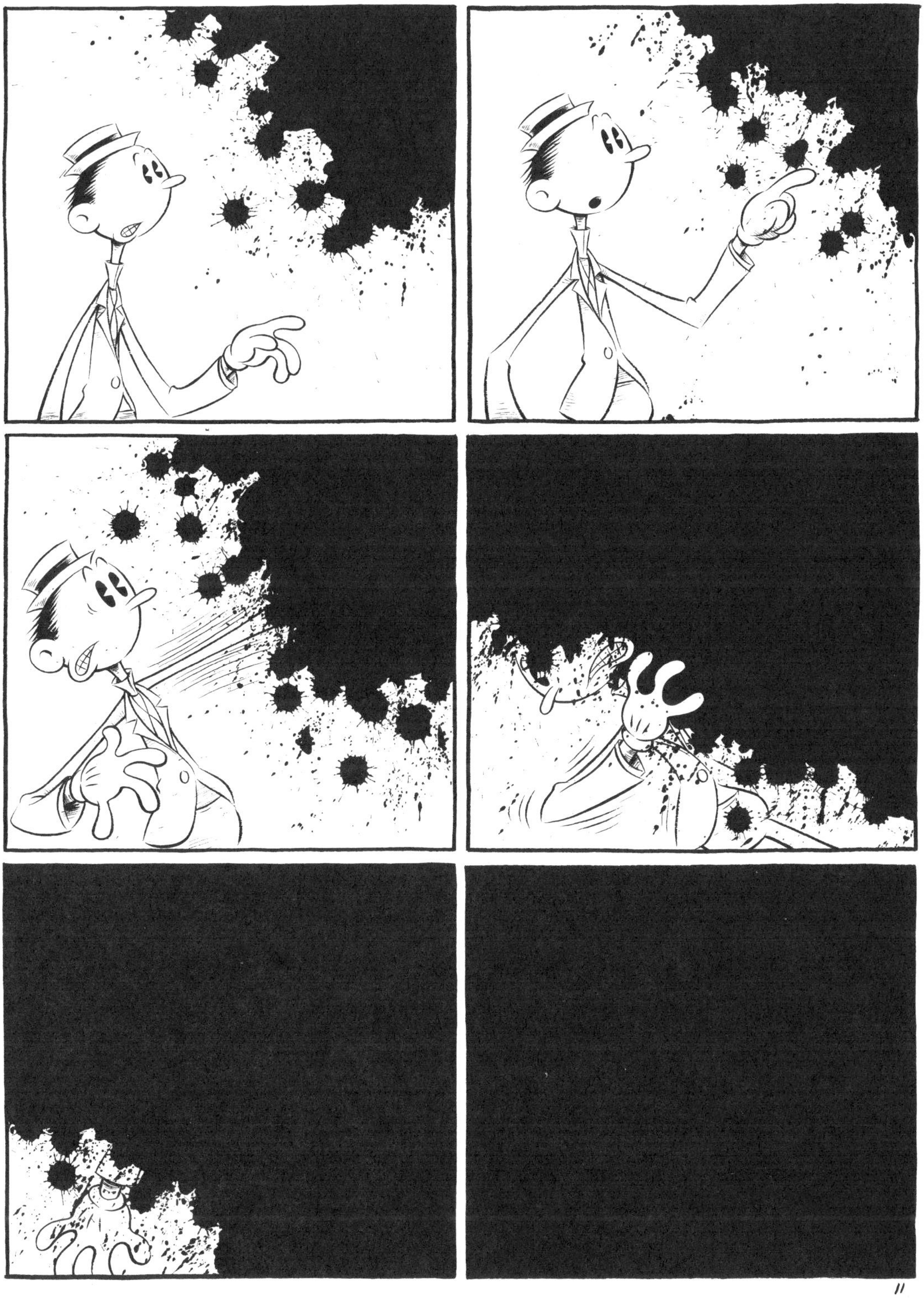

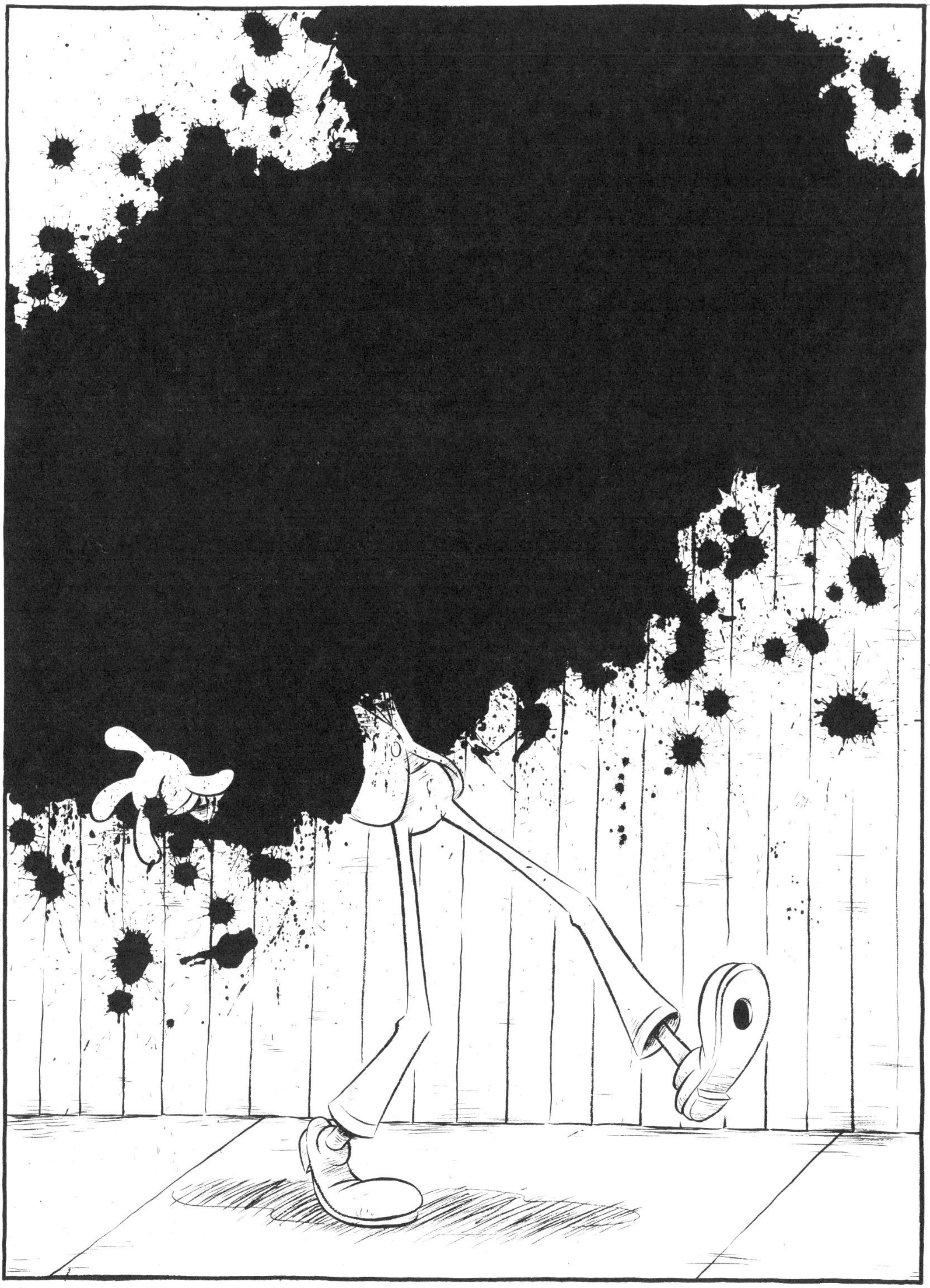

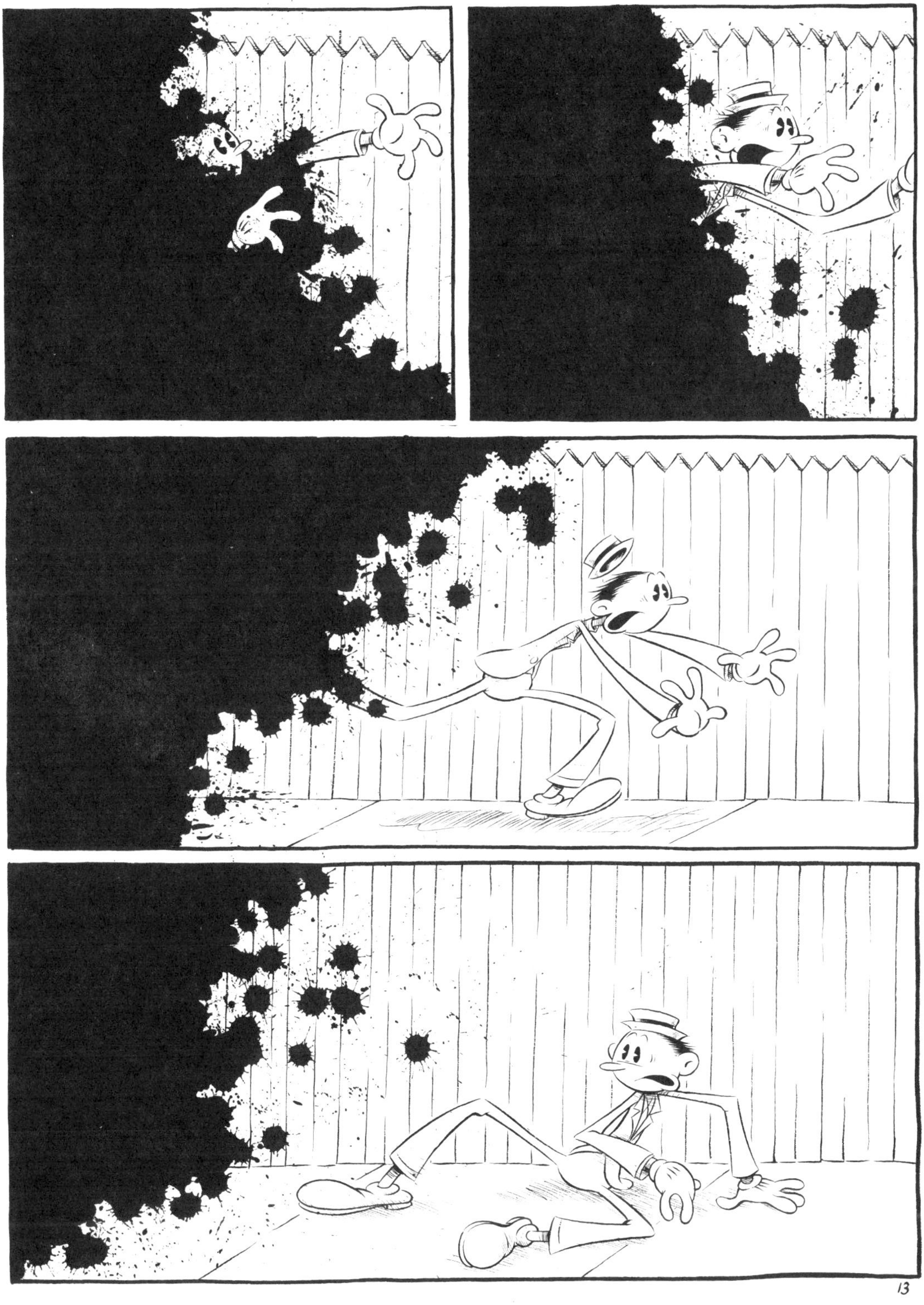

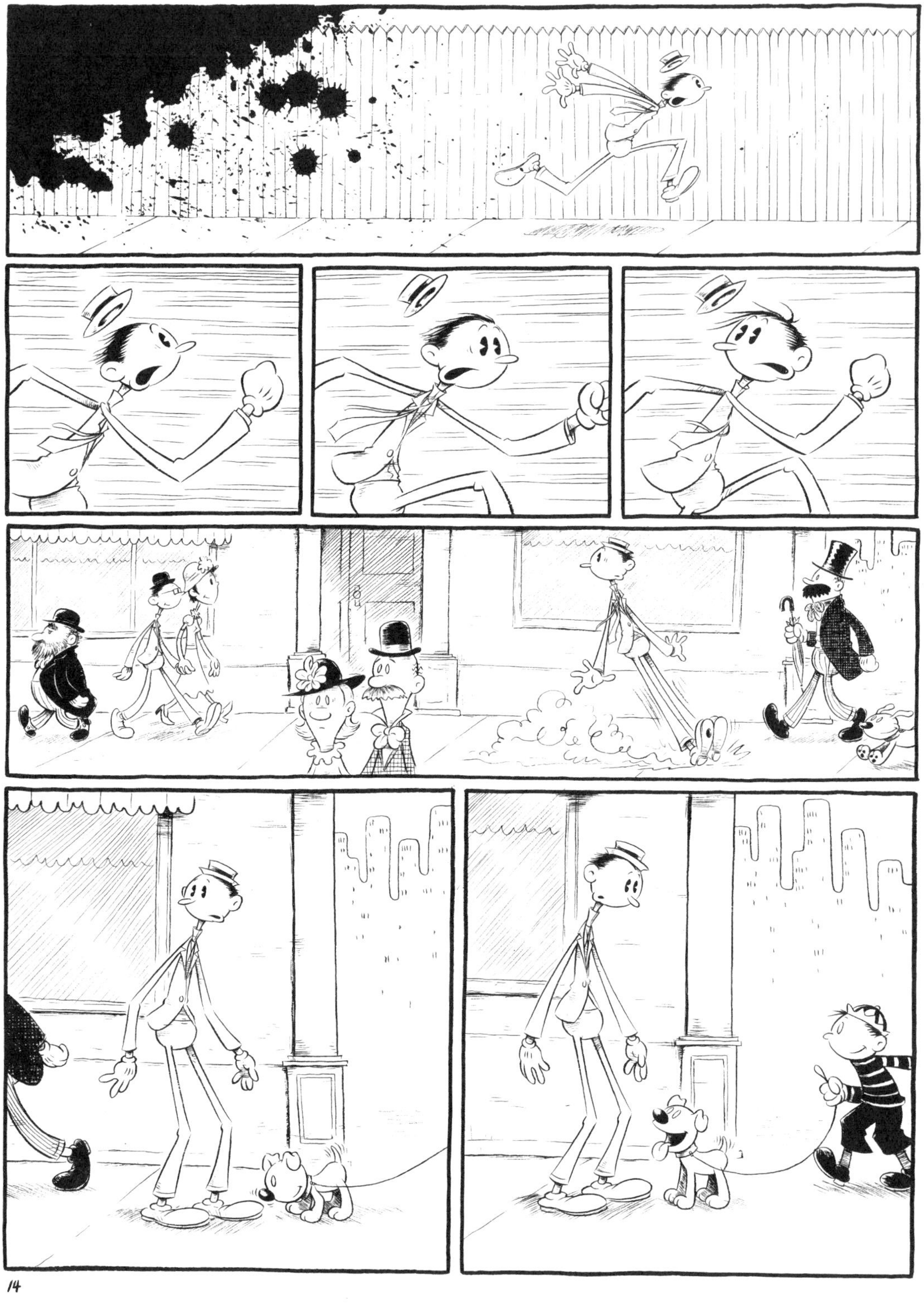

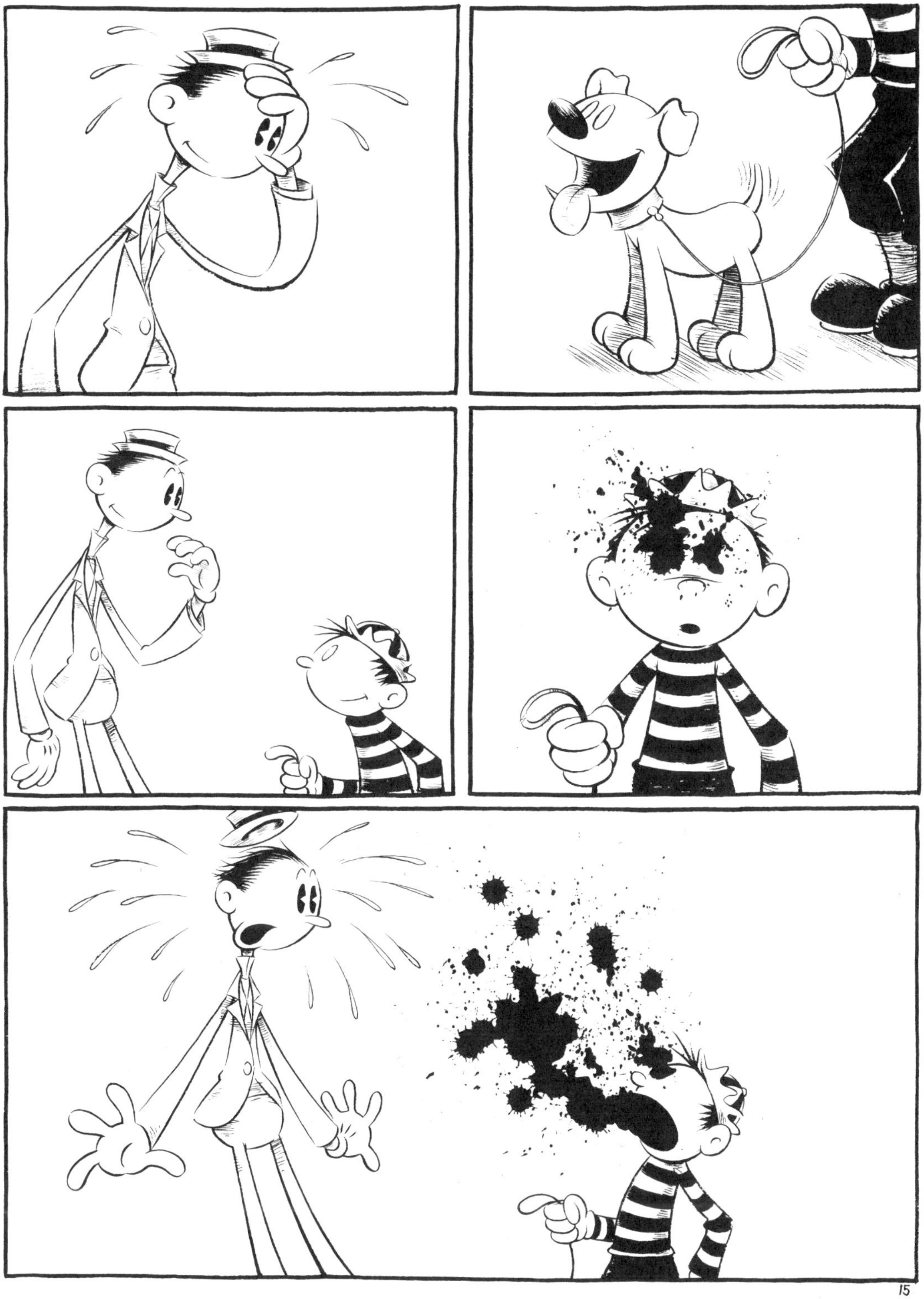

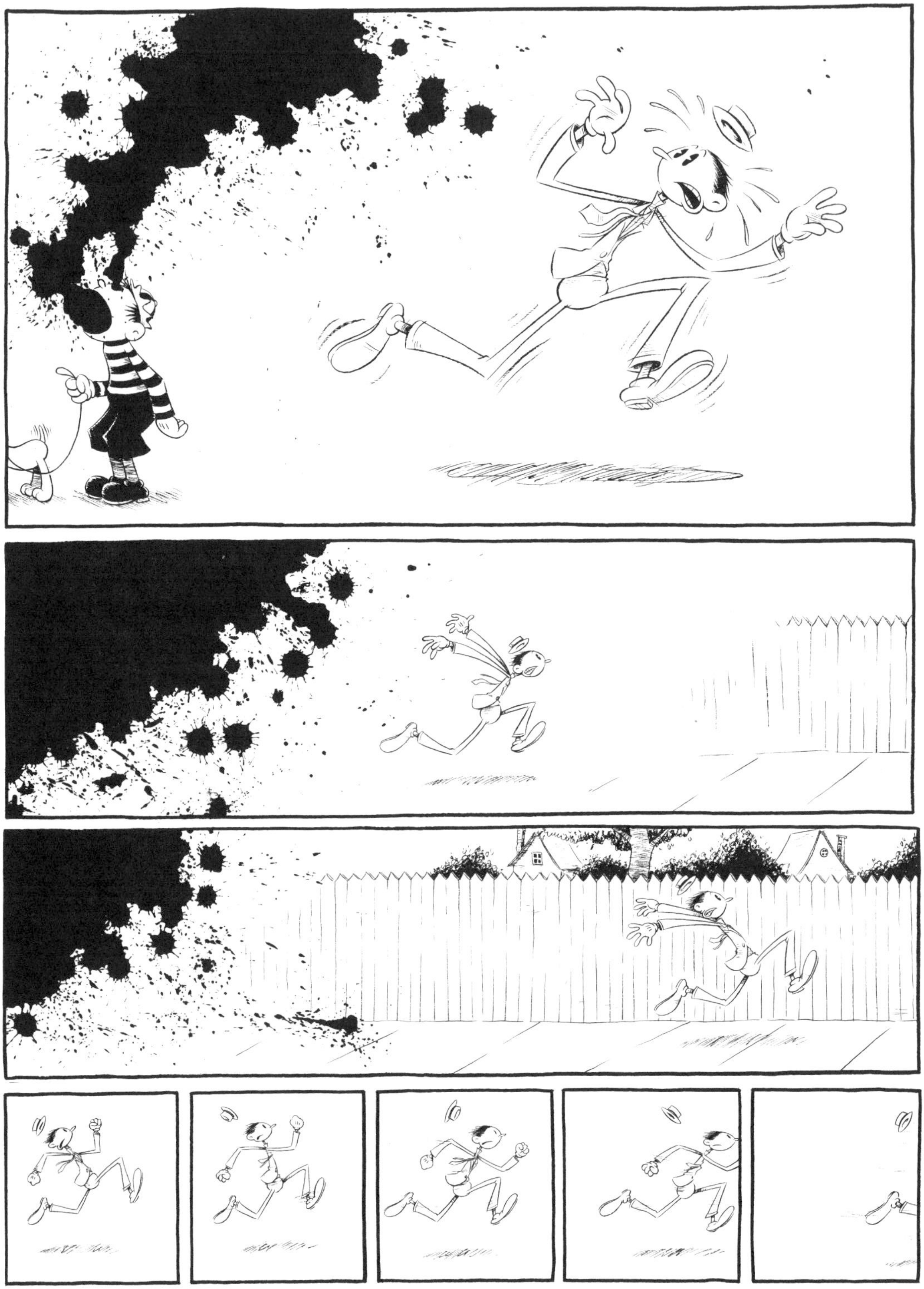

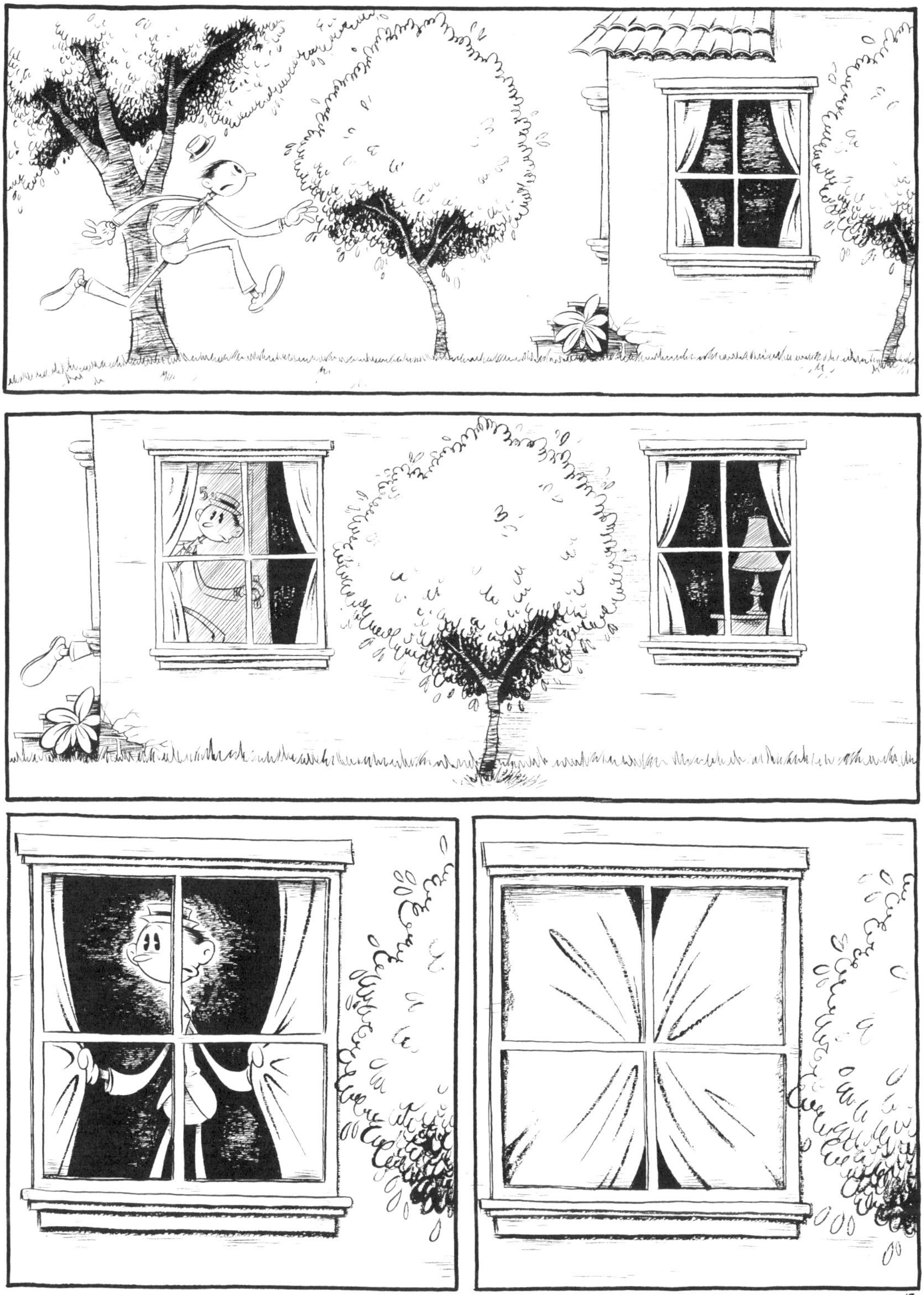

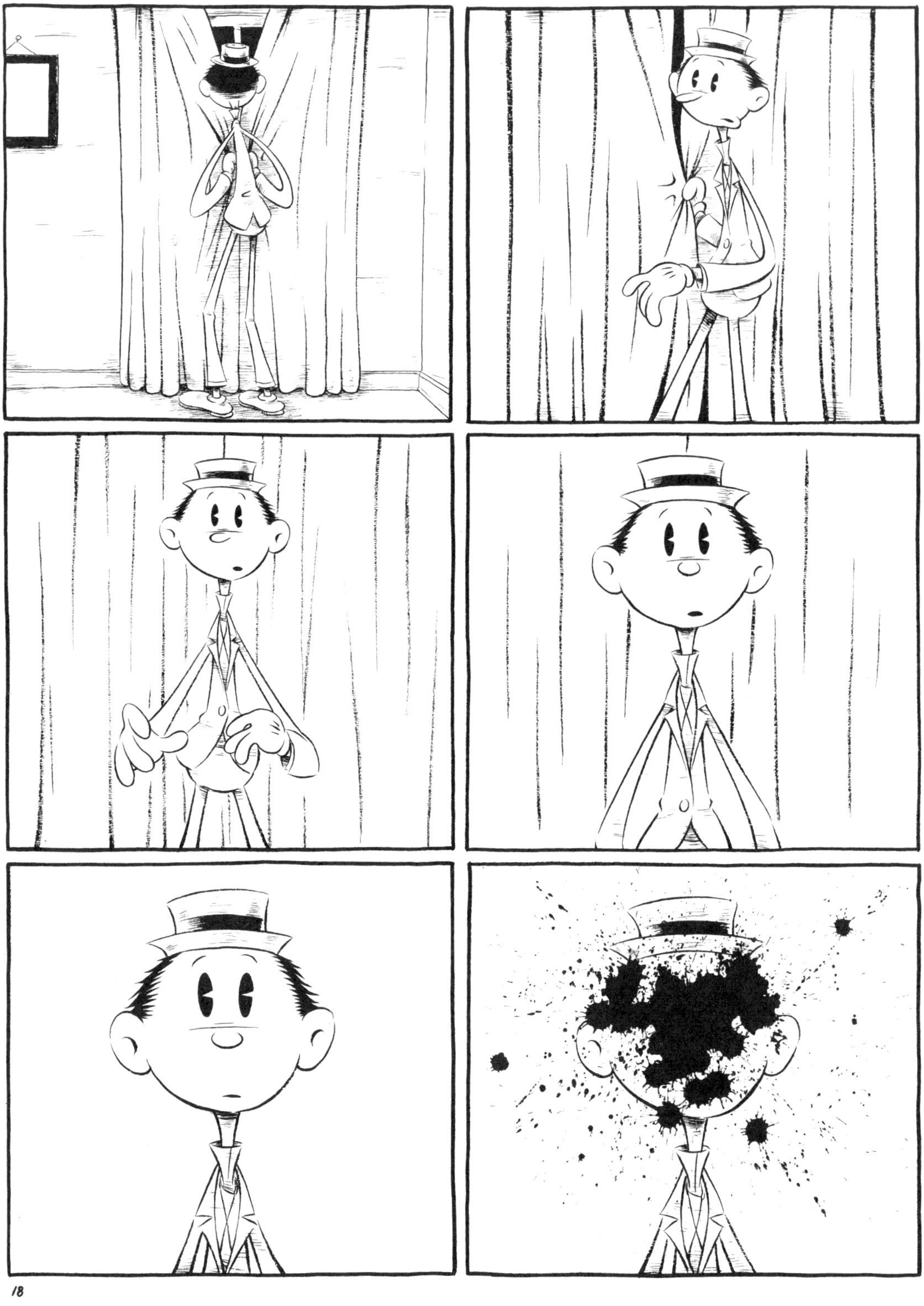

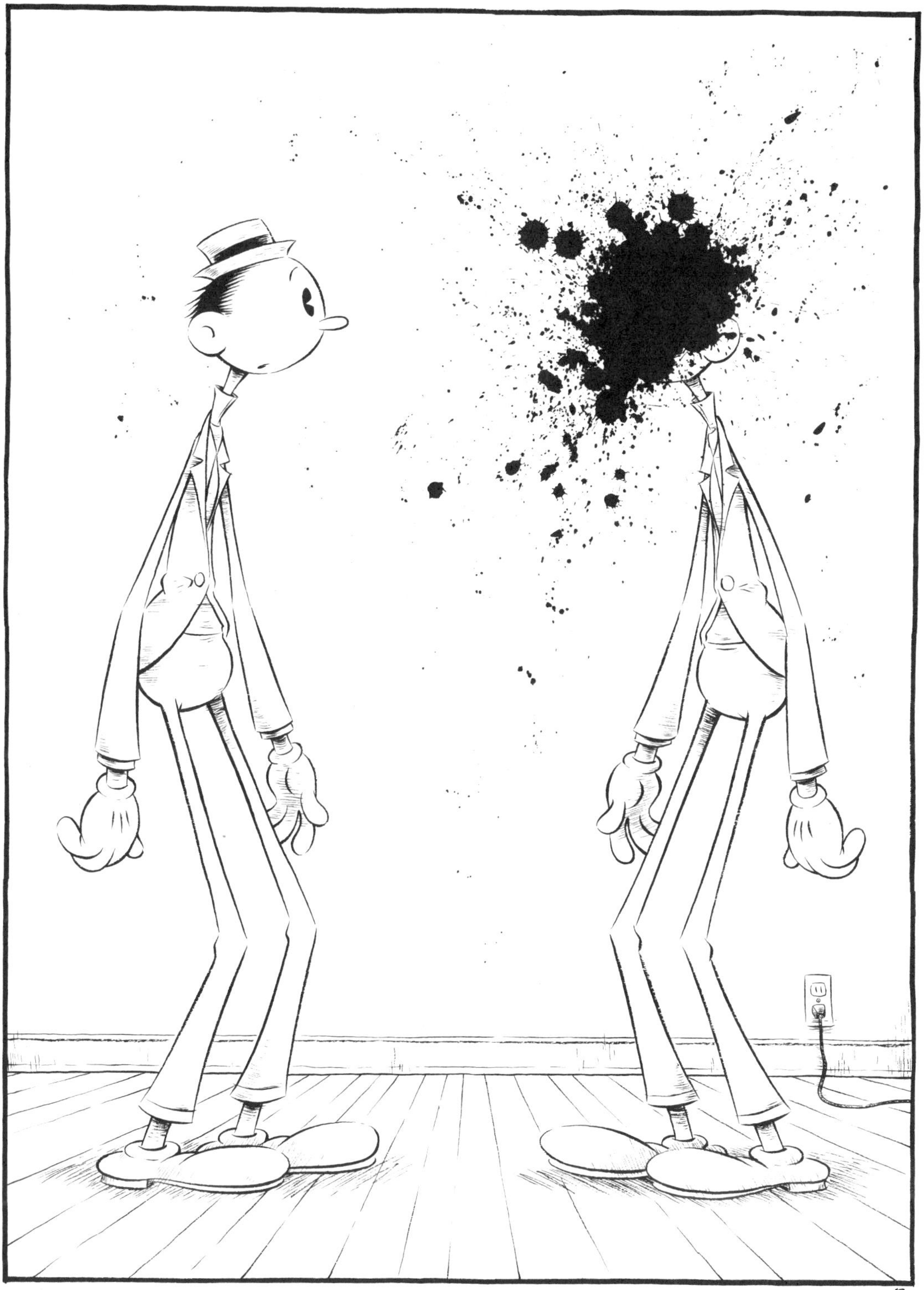

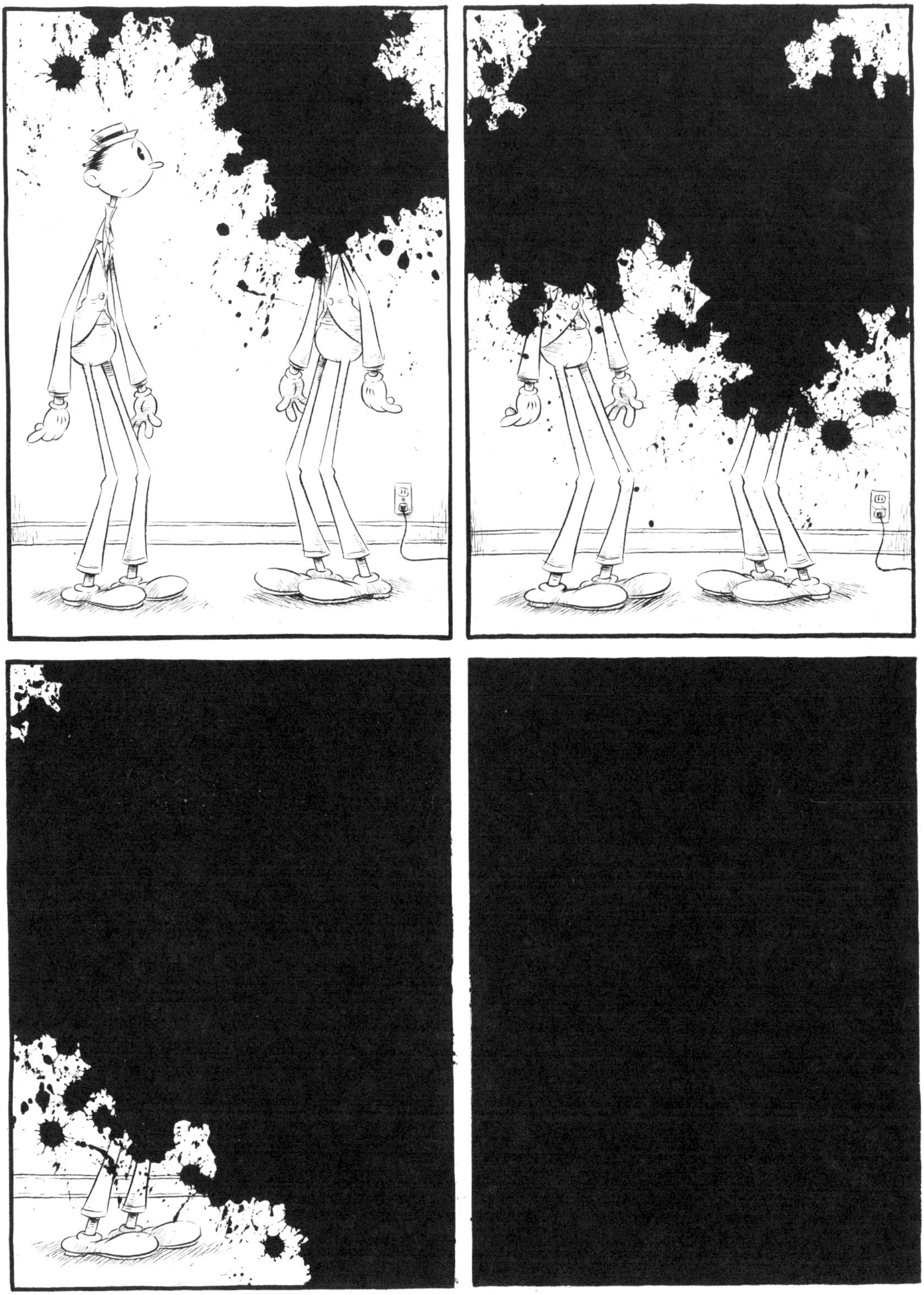

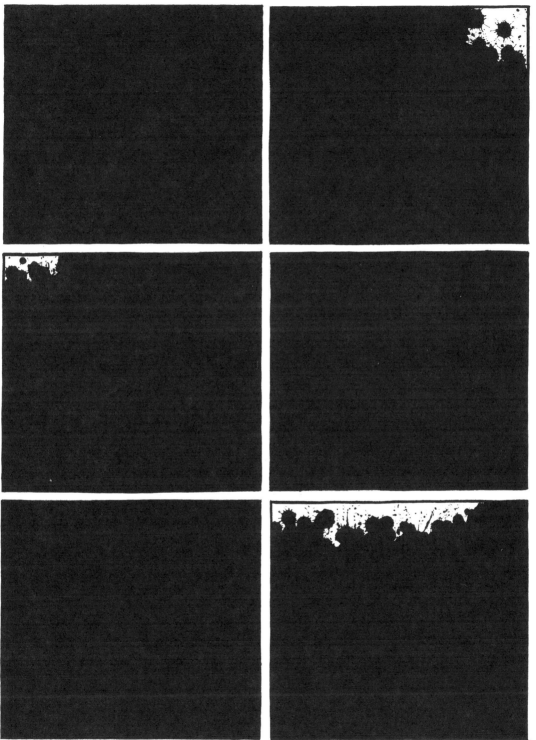

21

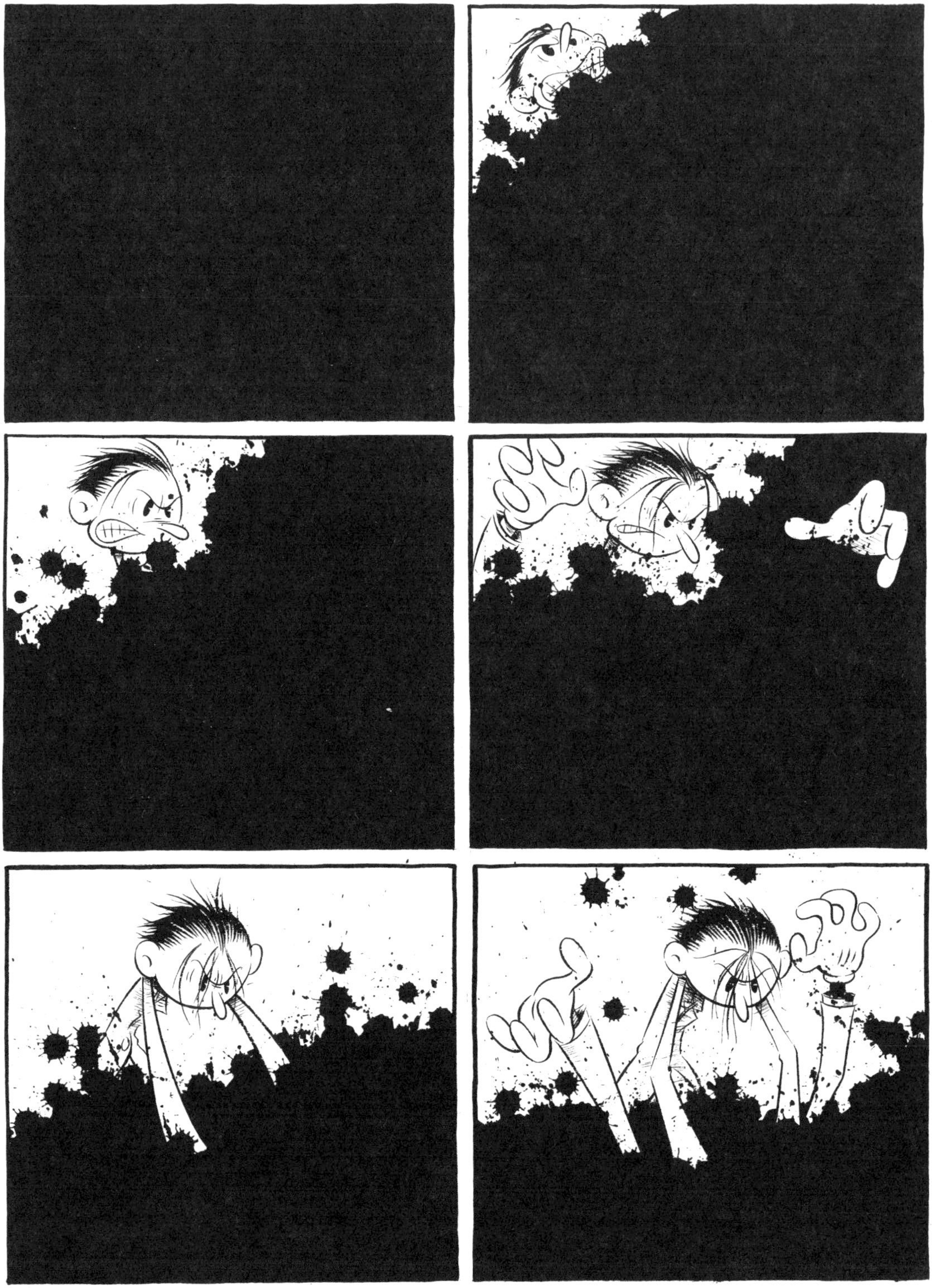

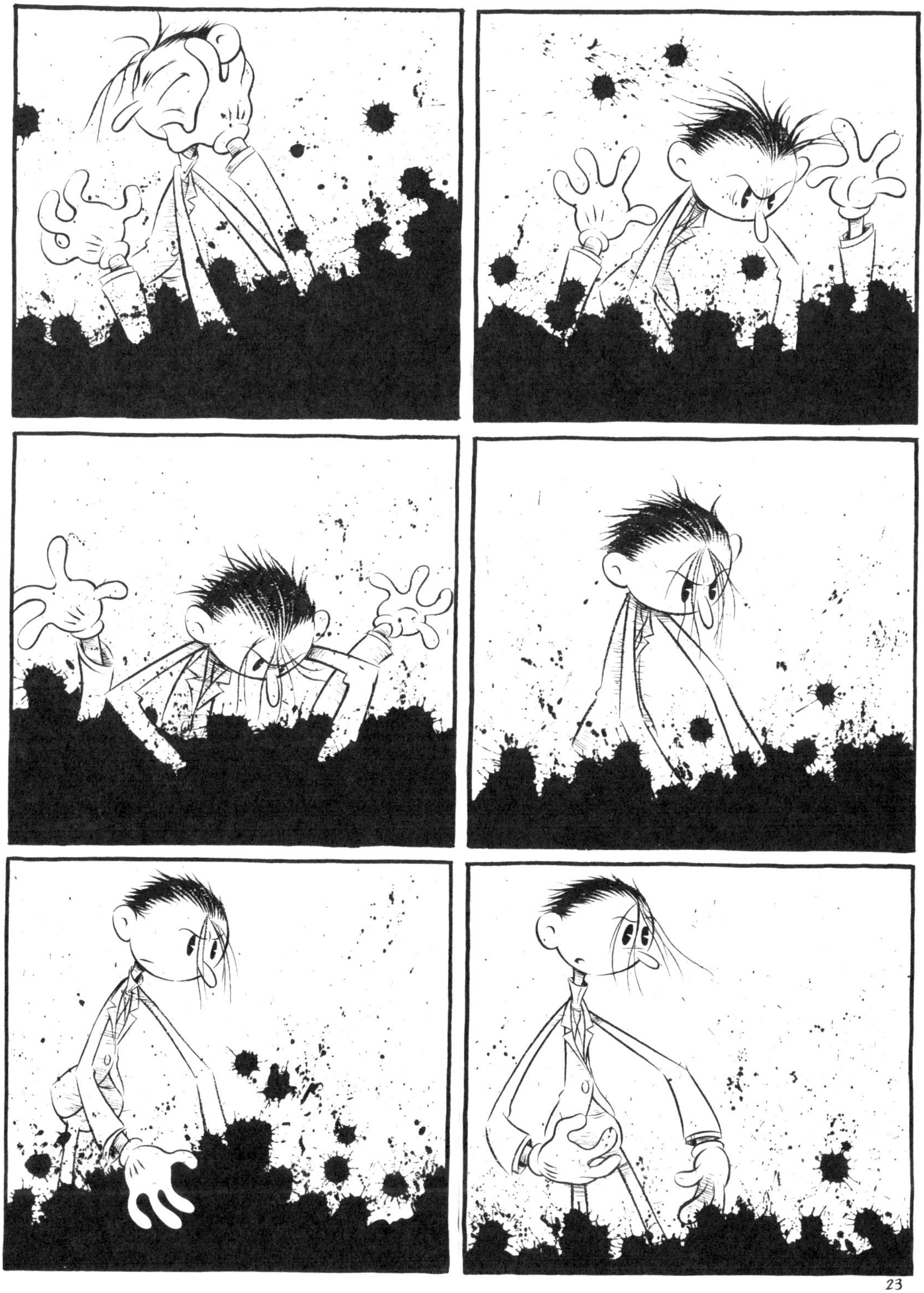

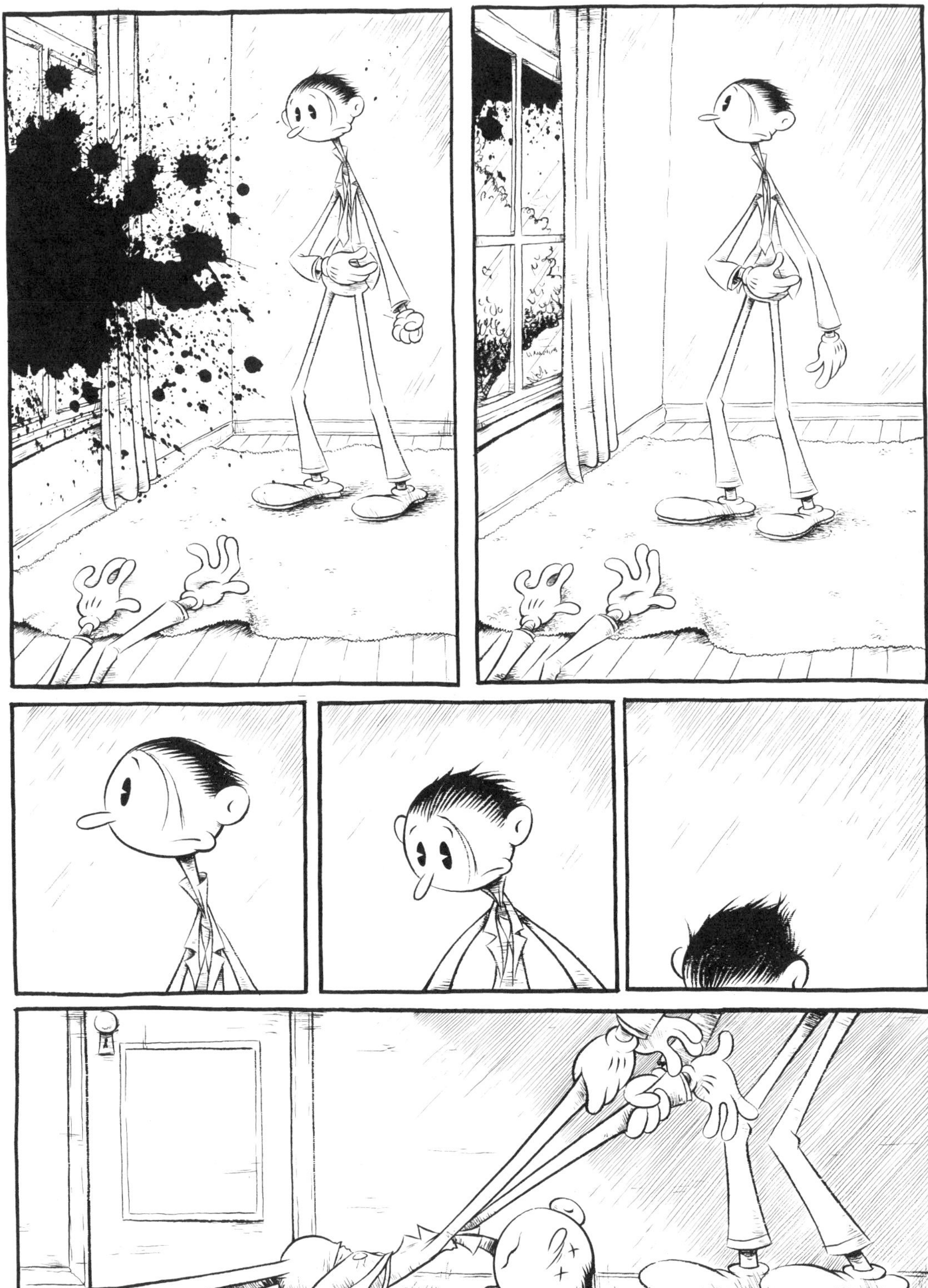

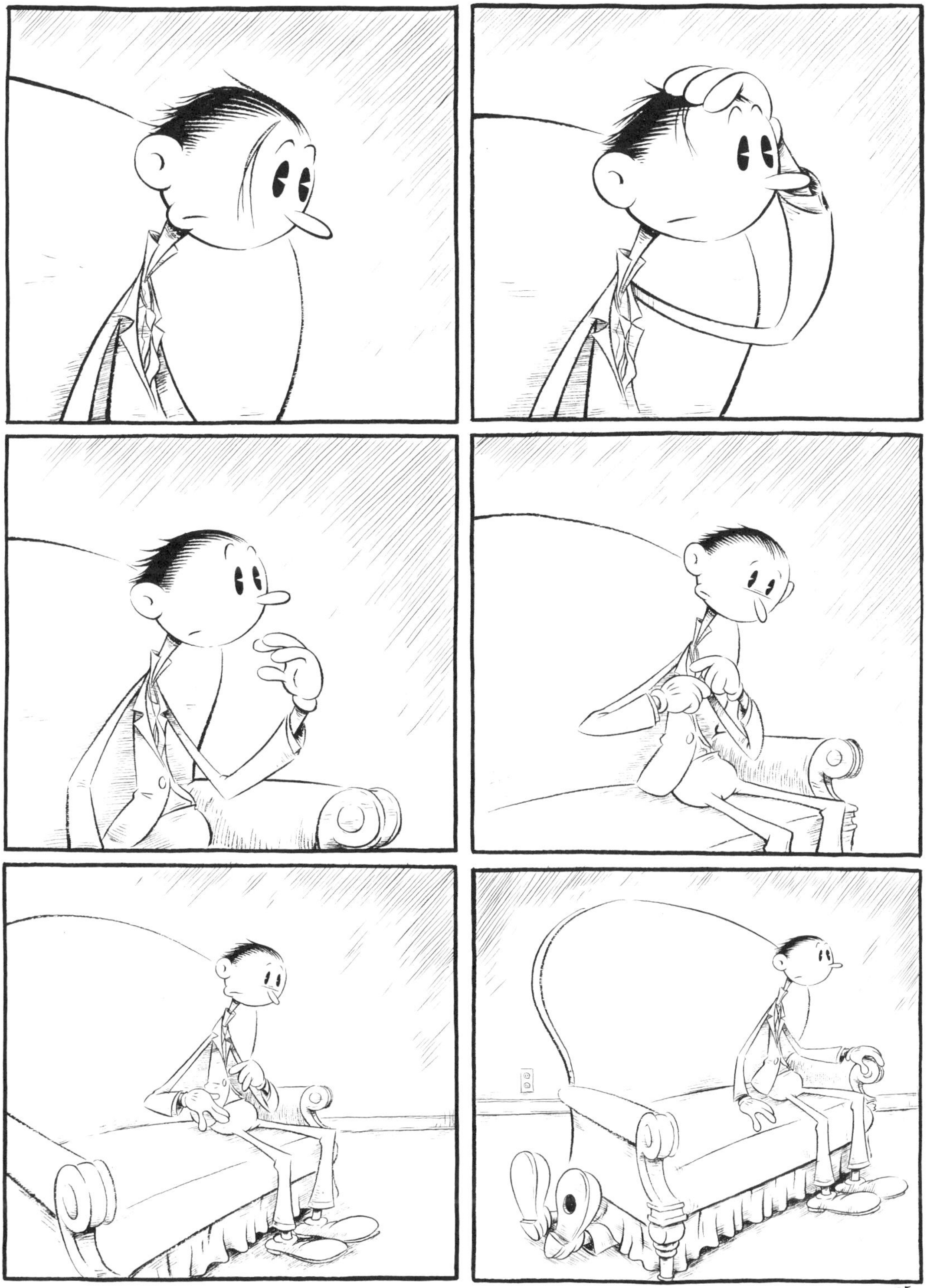

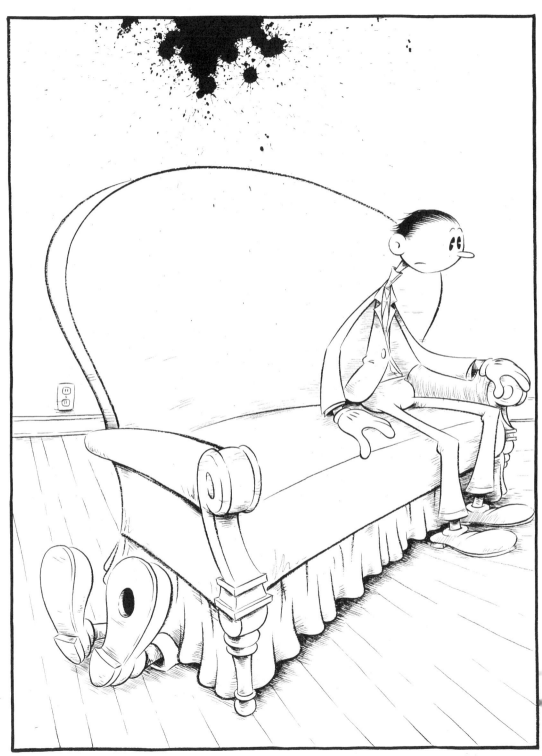

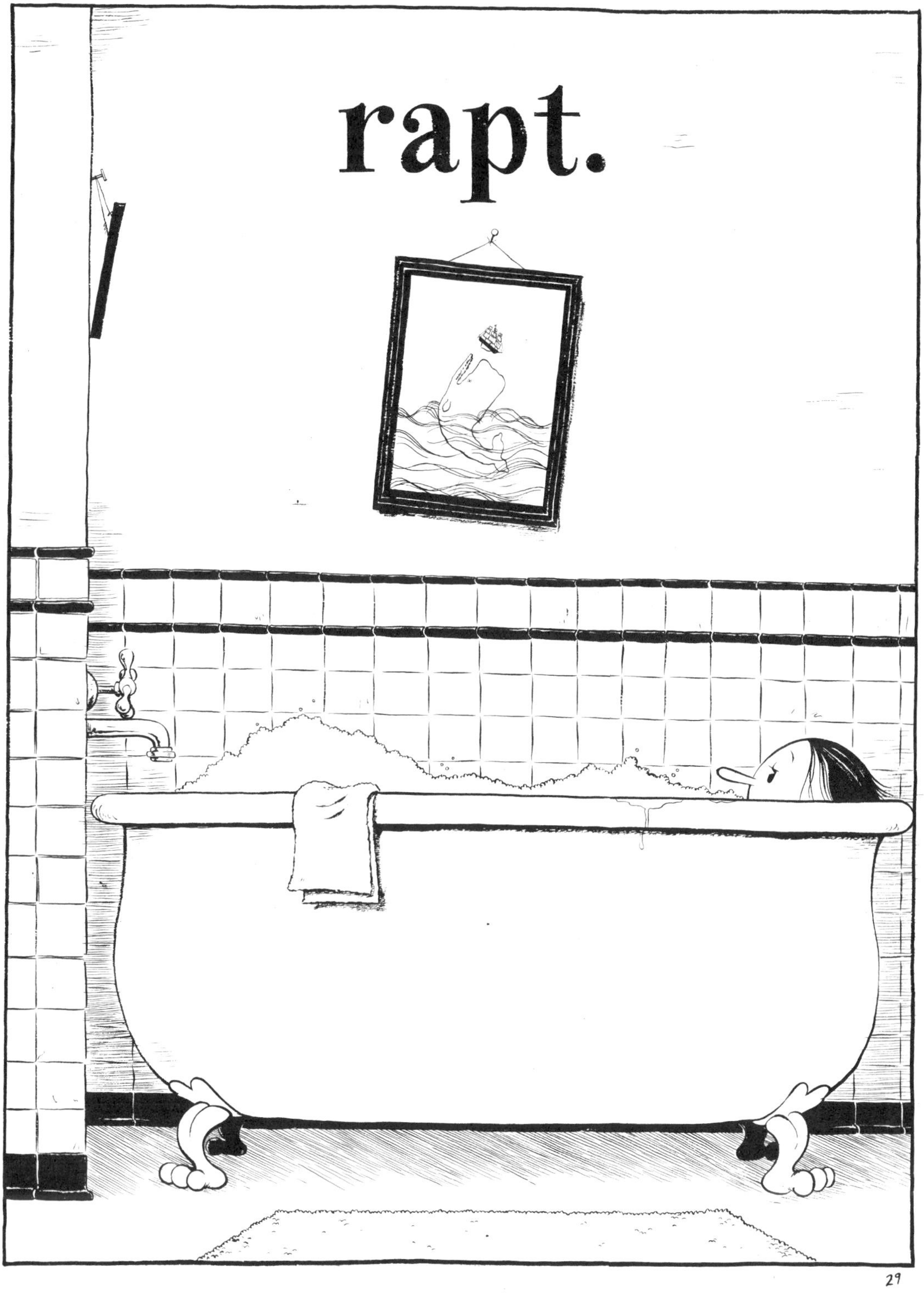
rapt.

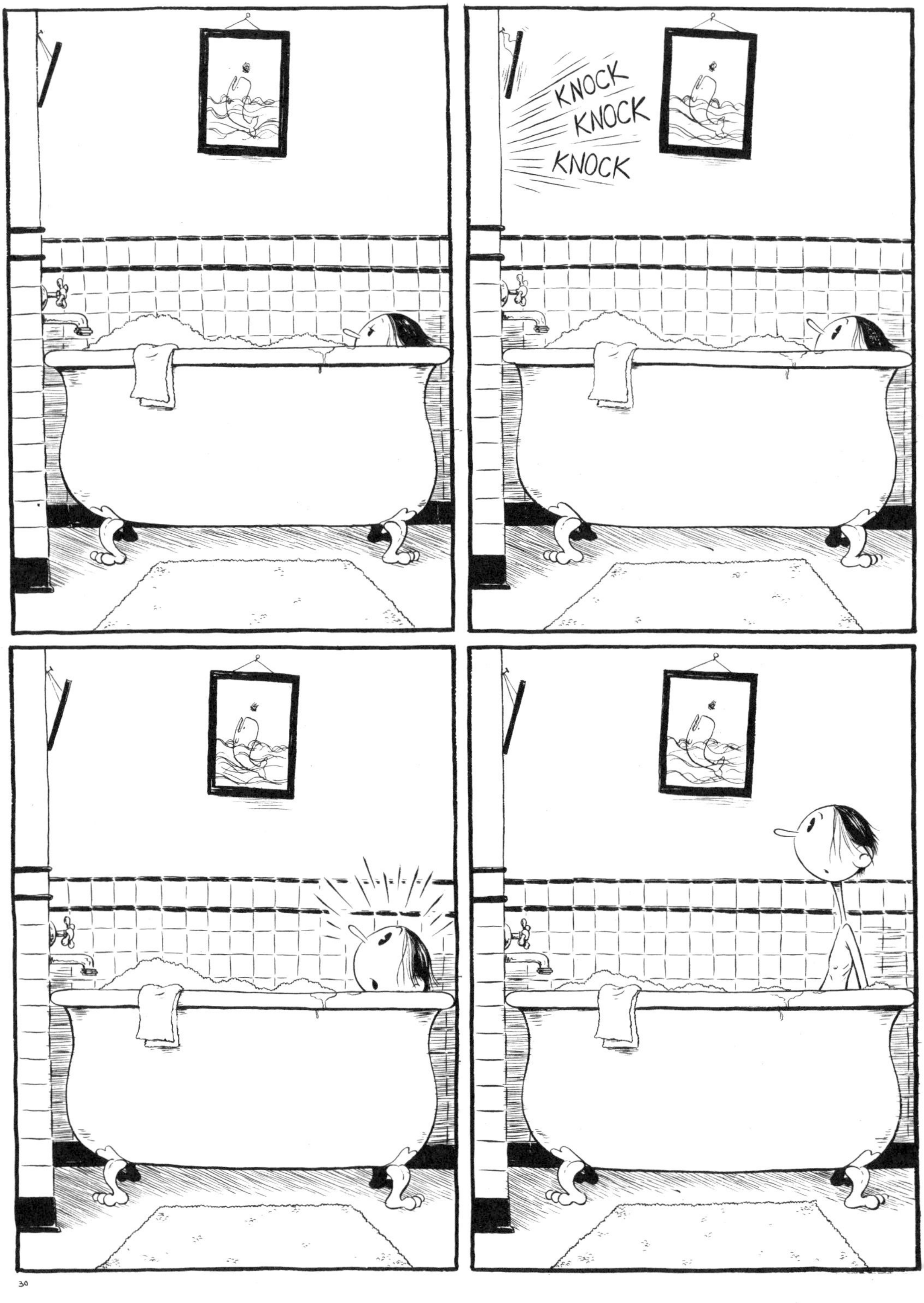
KNOCK
KNOCK
KNOCK

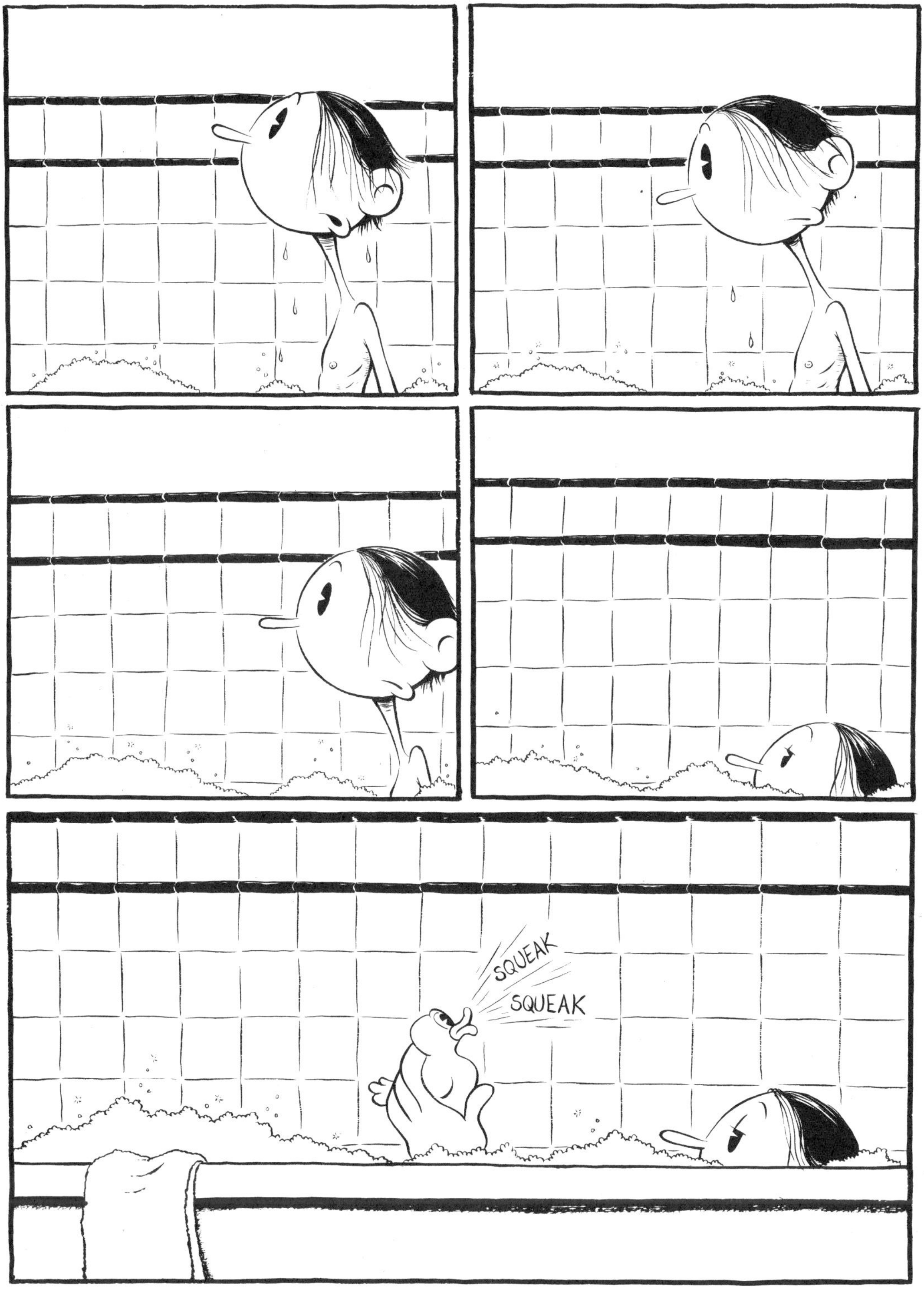
SQUEAK
SQUEAK

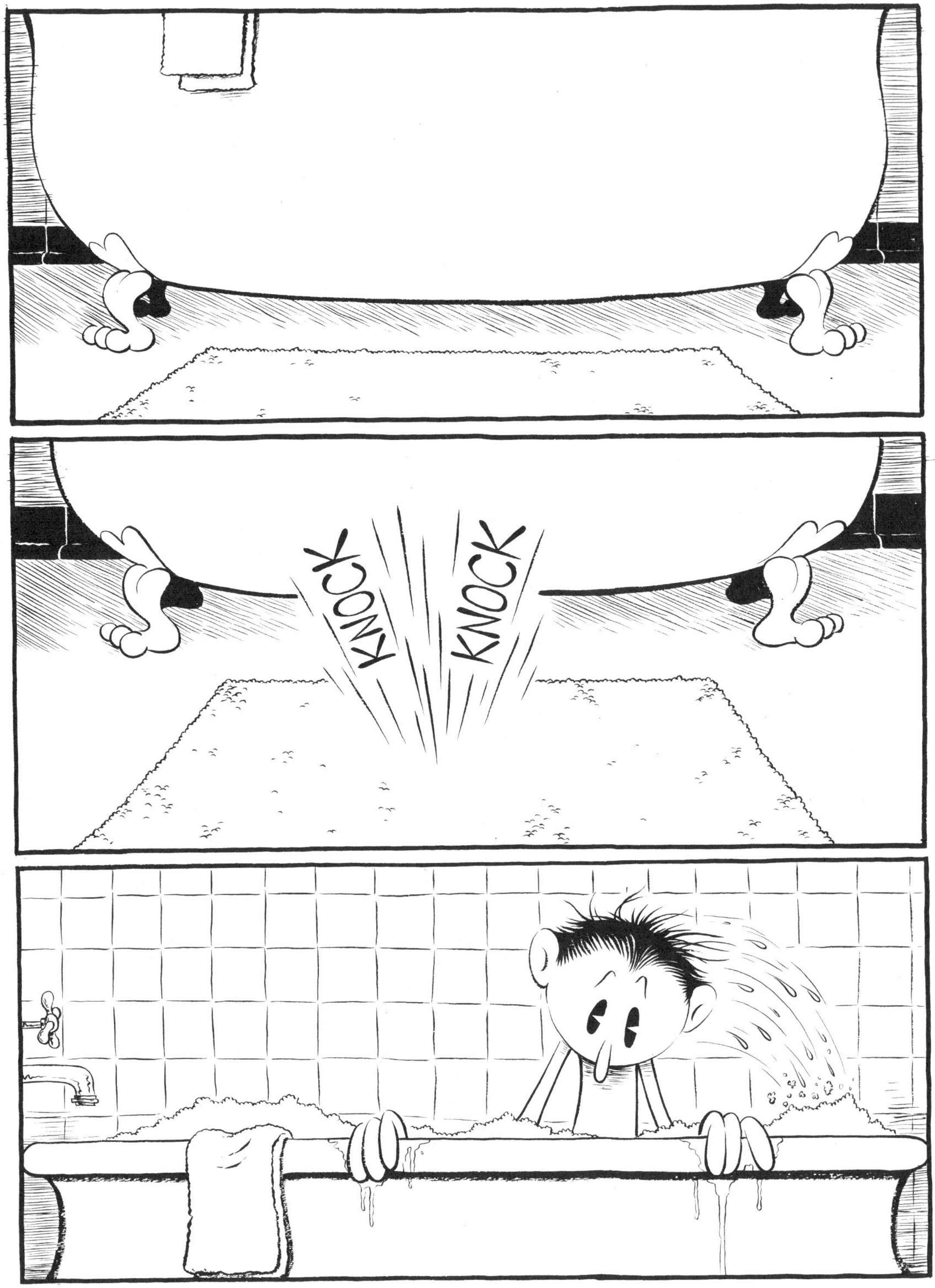
KNOCK
KNOCK

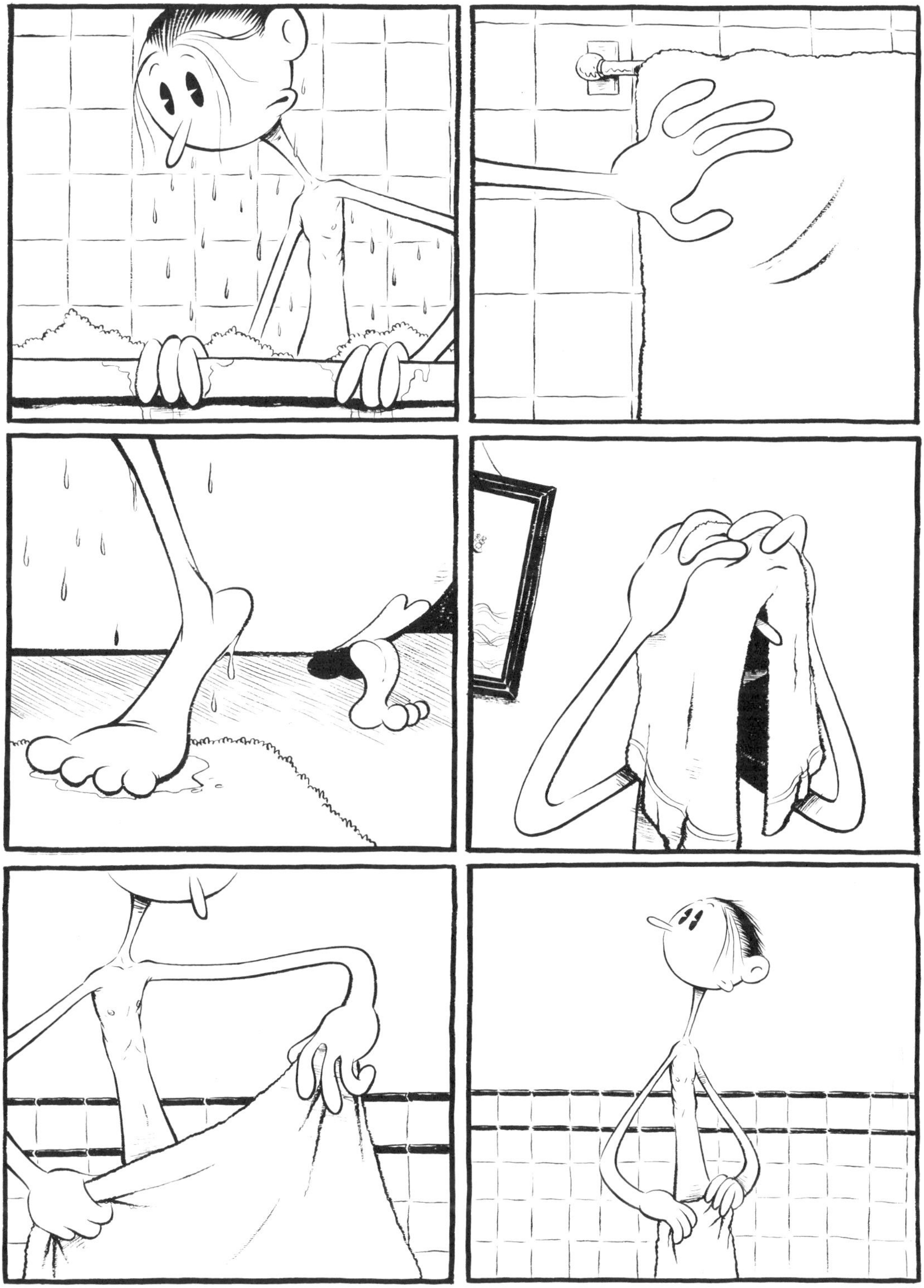

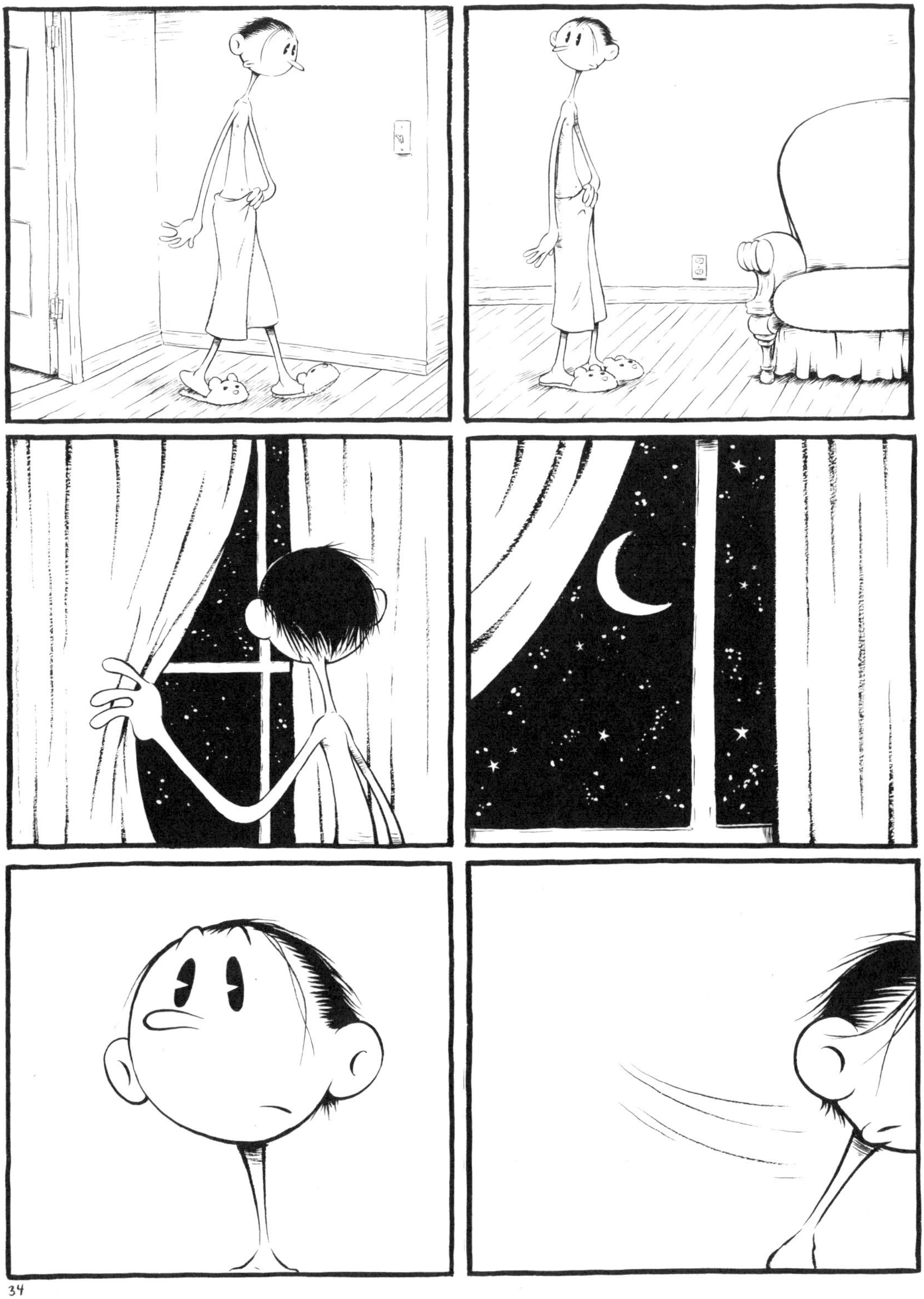

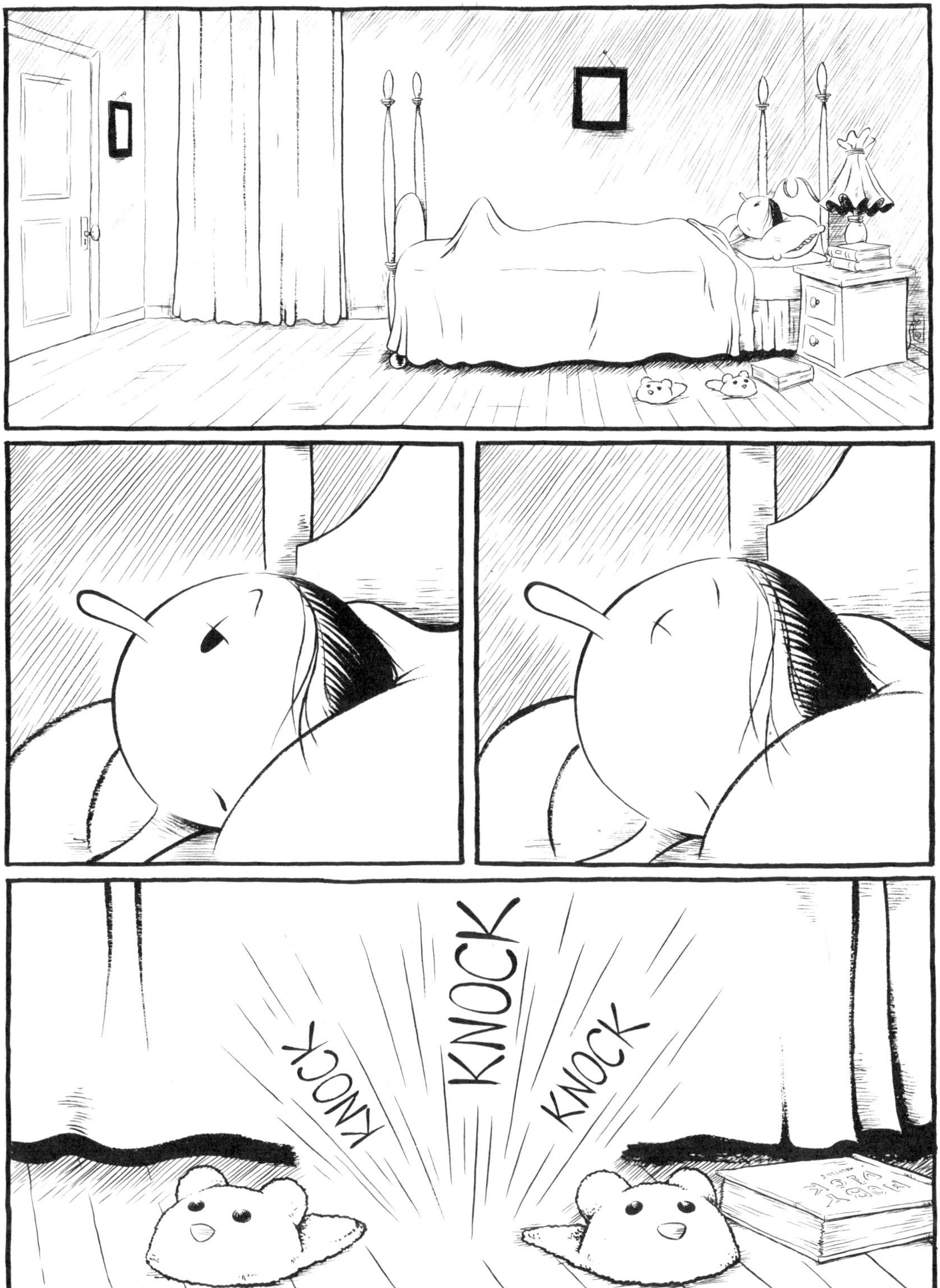
KNOCK
KNOCK
KNOCK

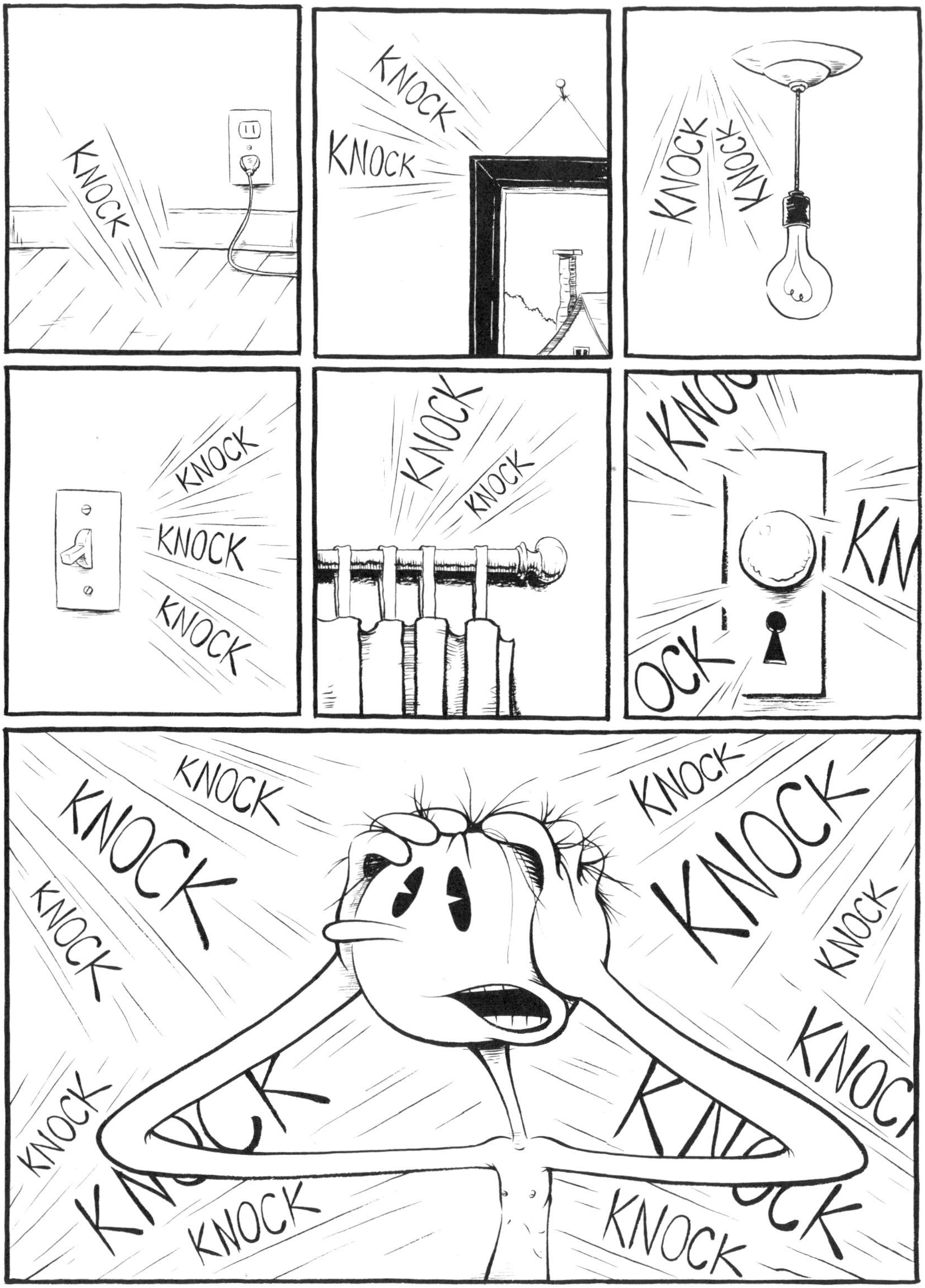
KNOCK
KNOCK
KNOCK
KNOCK
KNOCK
KNOCK
KNOCK
KNOCK
KNOCK
KNOCK
KNOCK
KNOCK
KNOCK
KNOCK
KNOCK
KNOCK
KNOCK
KNOCK
KNOCK
KNOCK

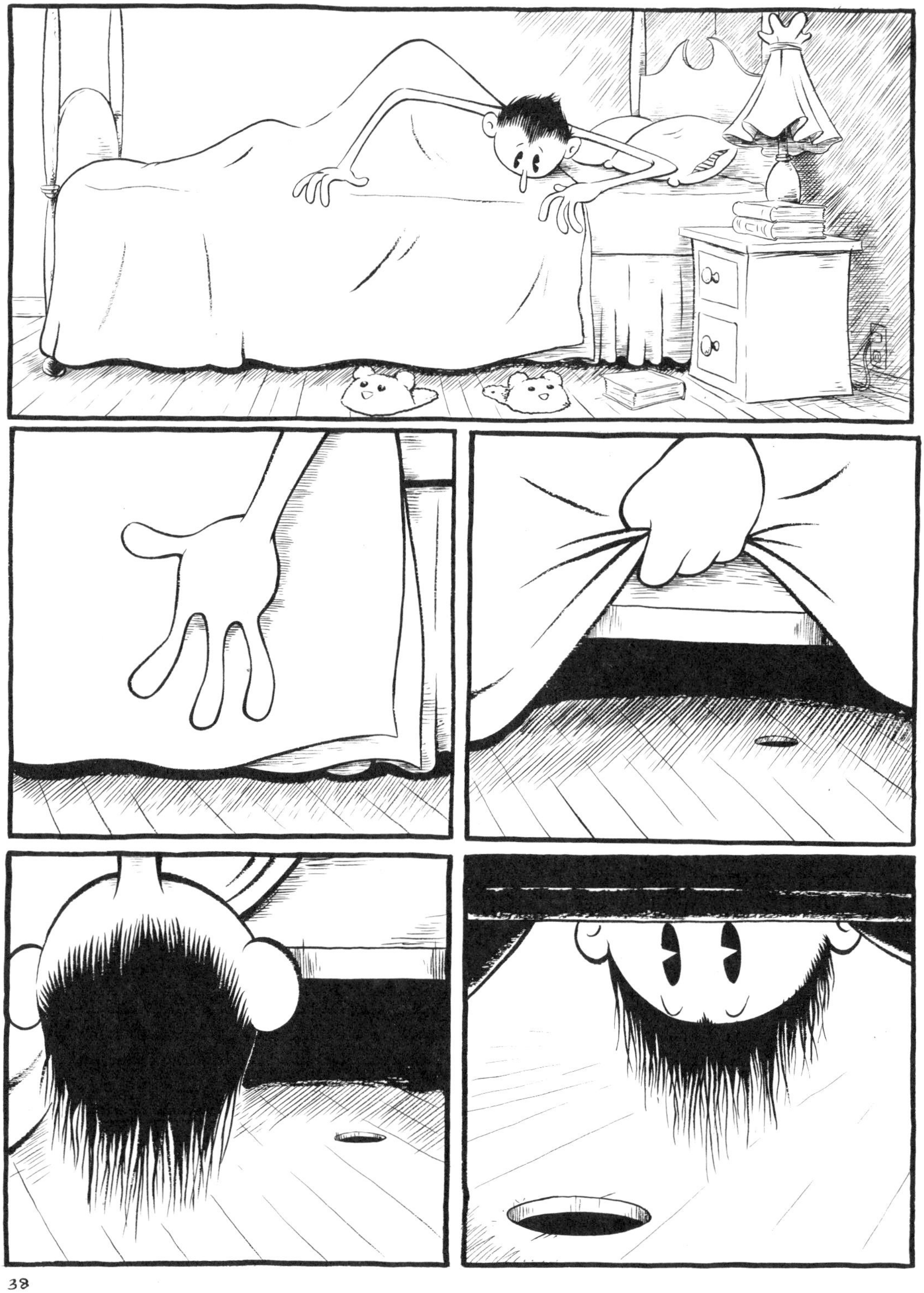

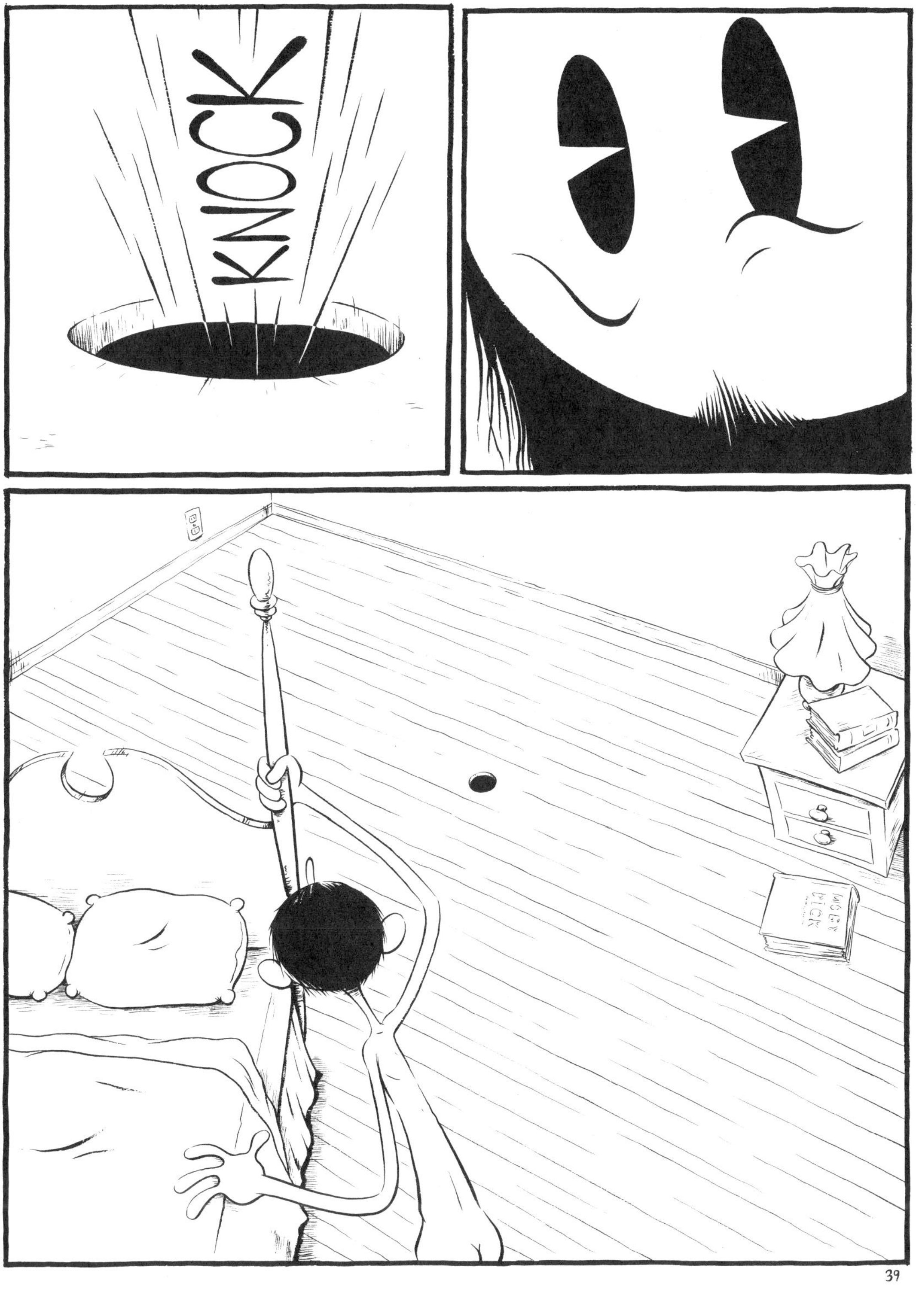
KNOCK
MOBY DICK

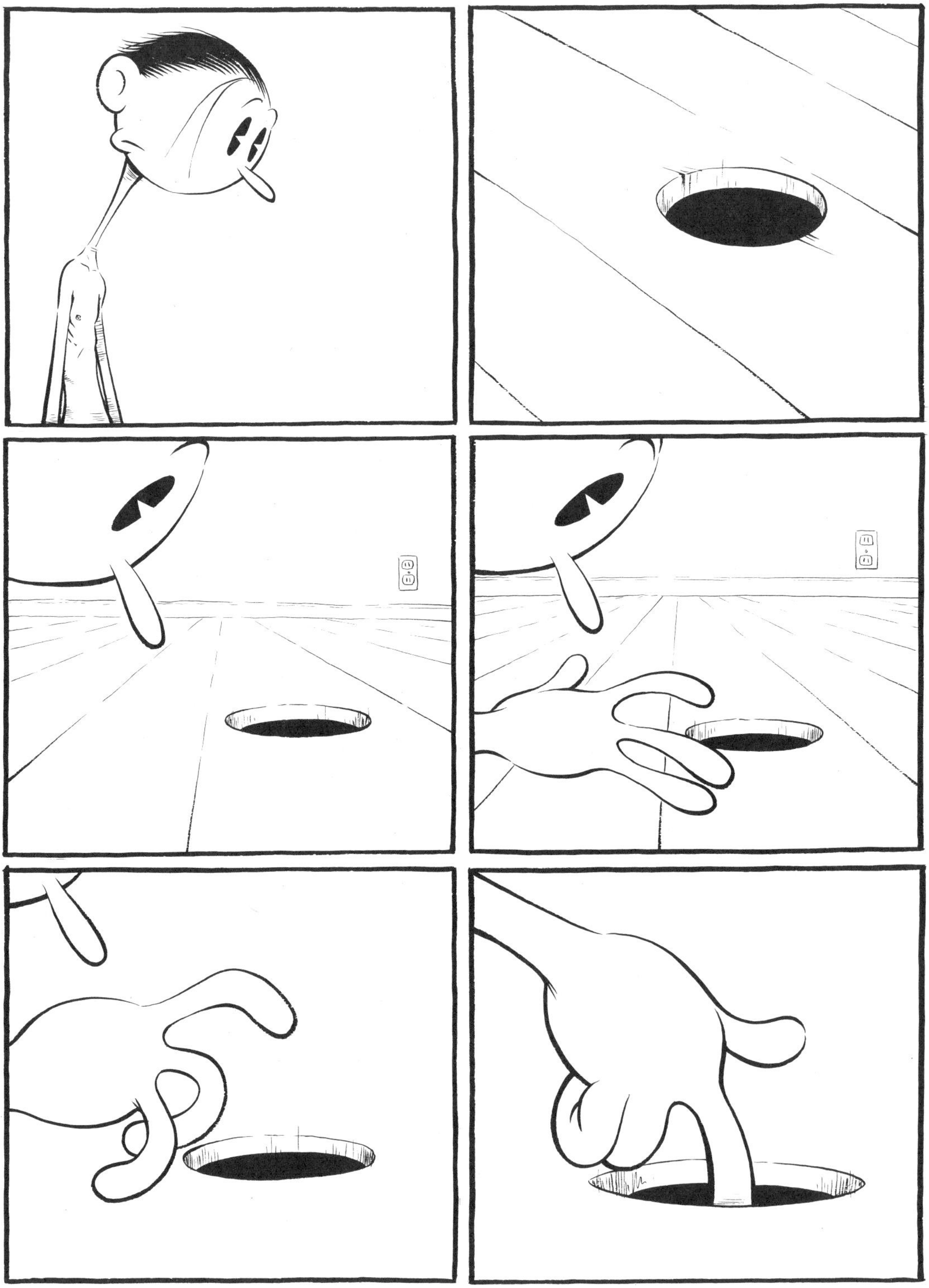

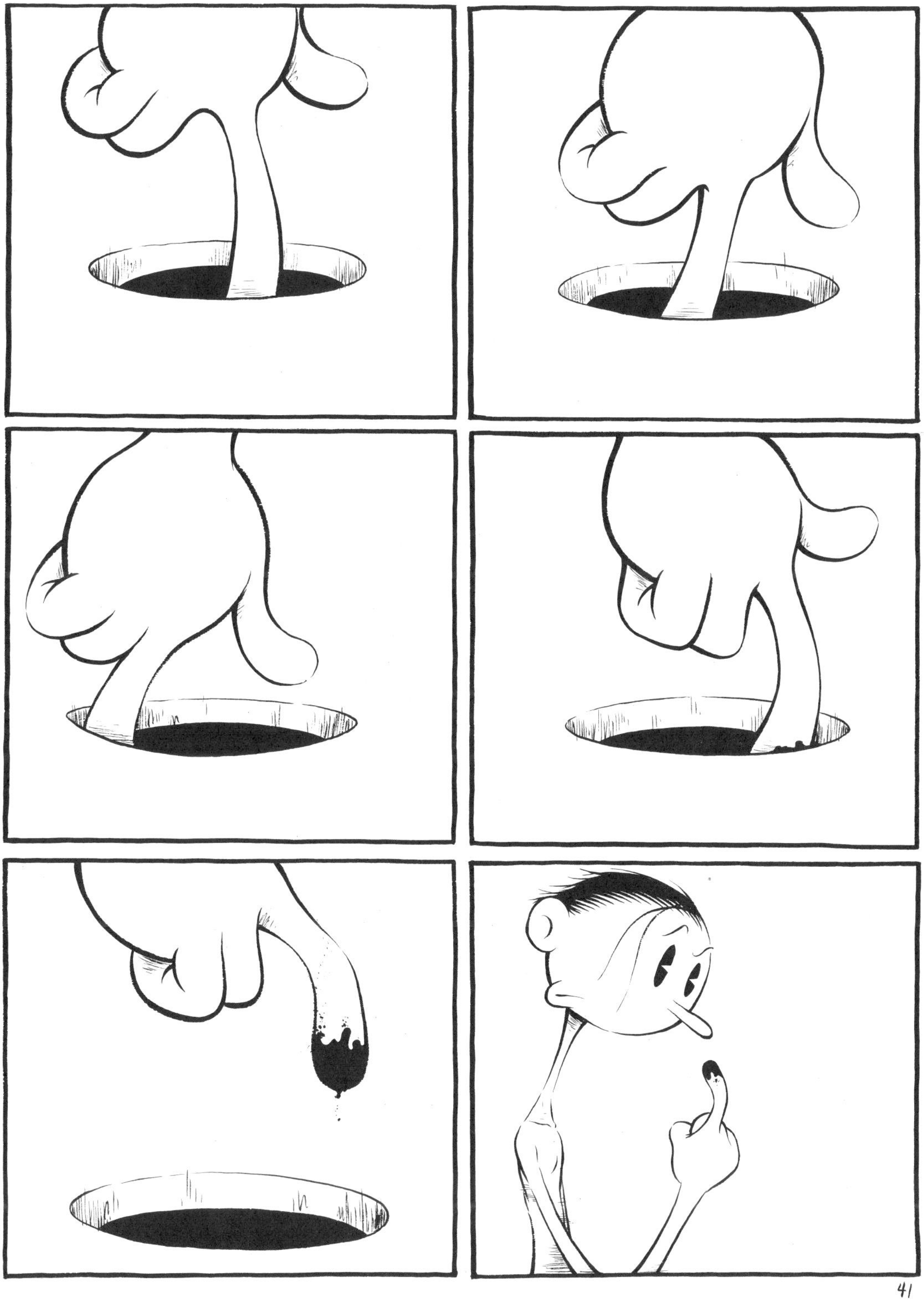

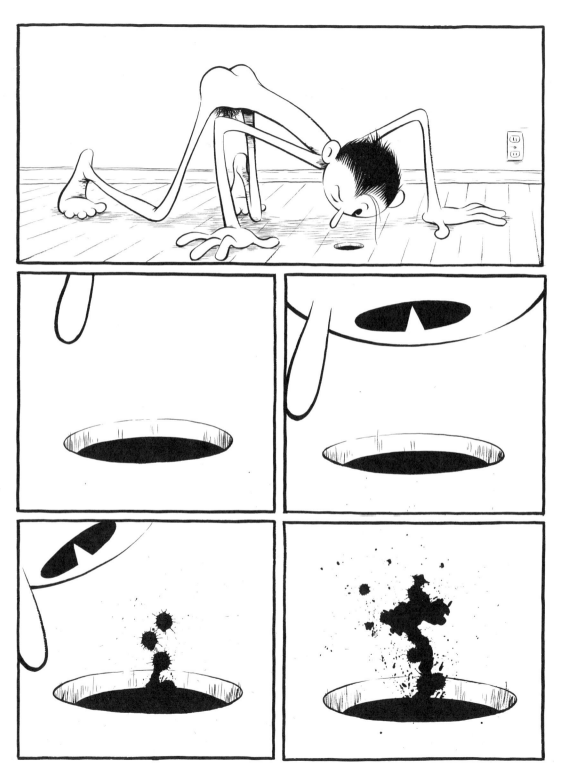

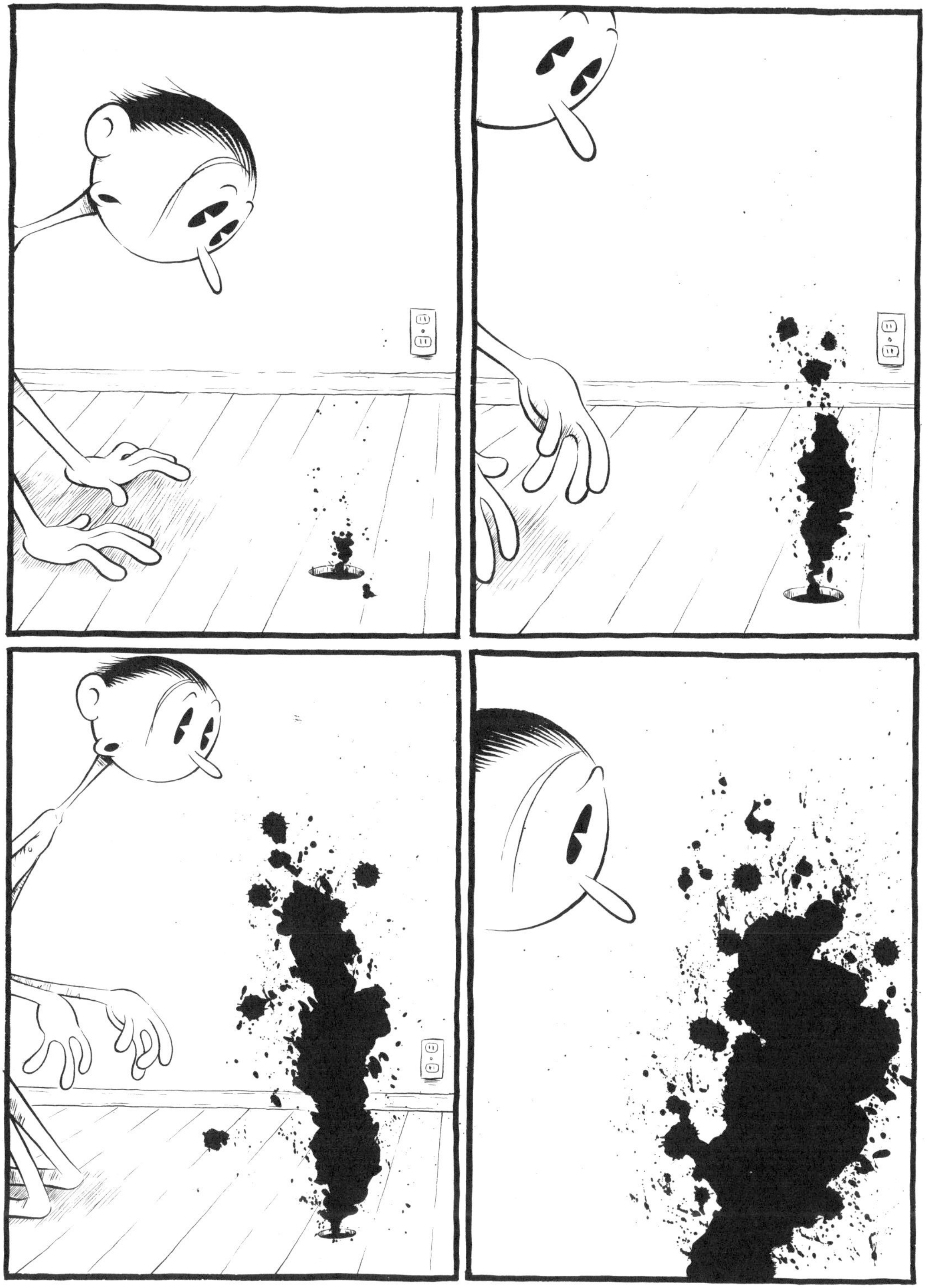

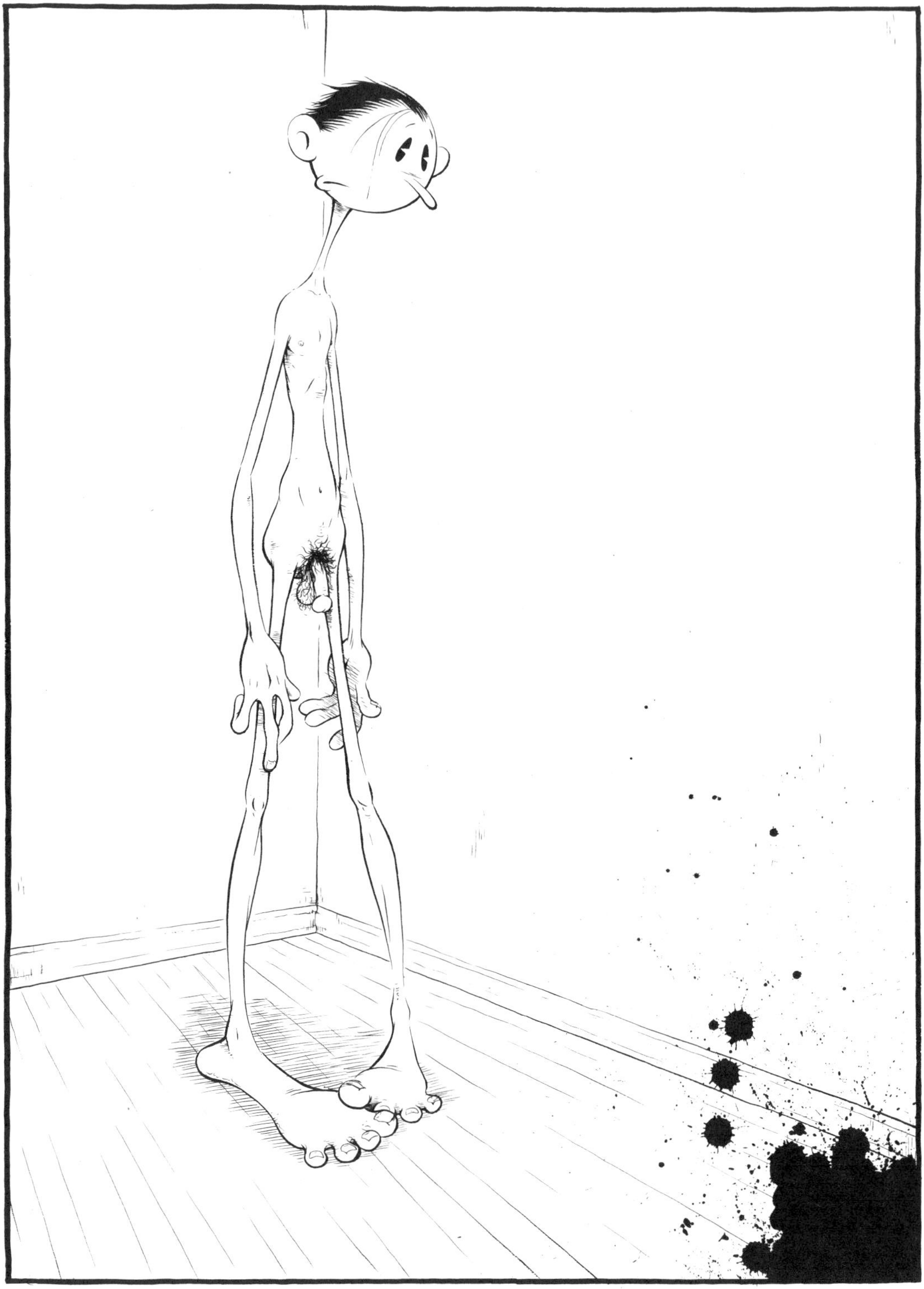

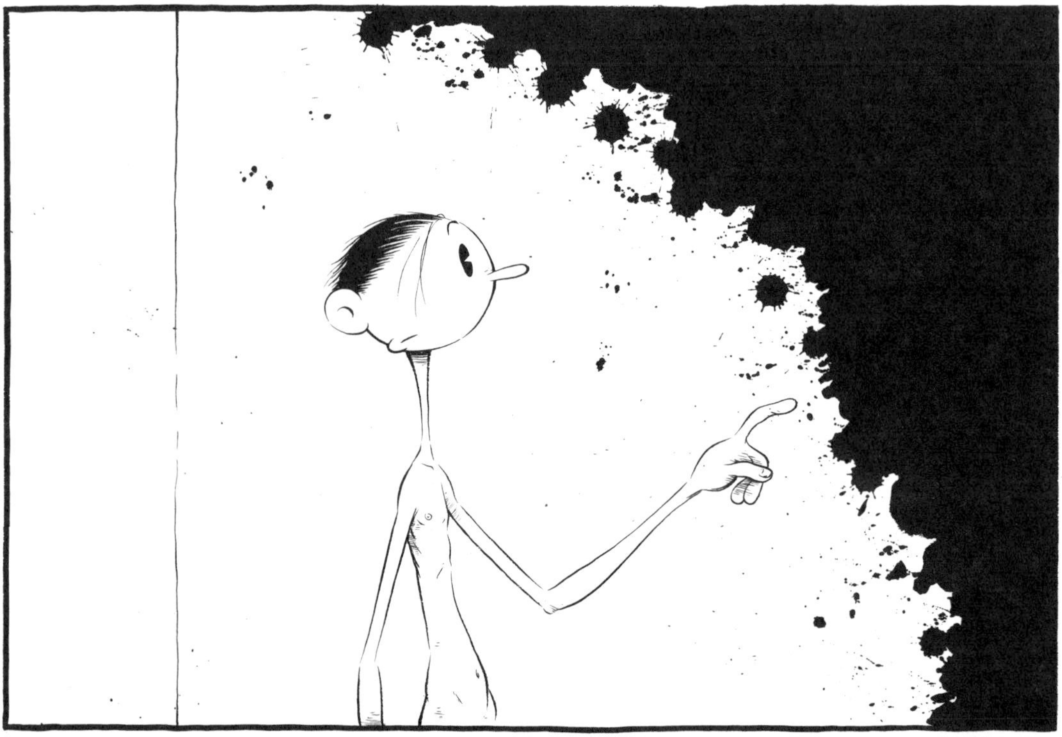

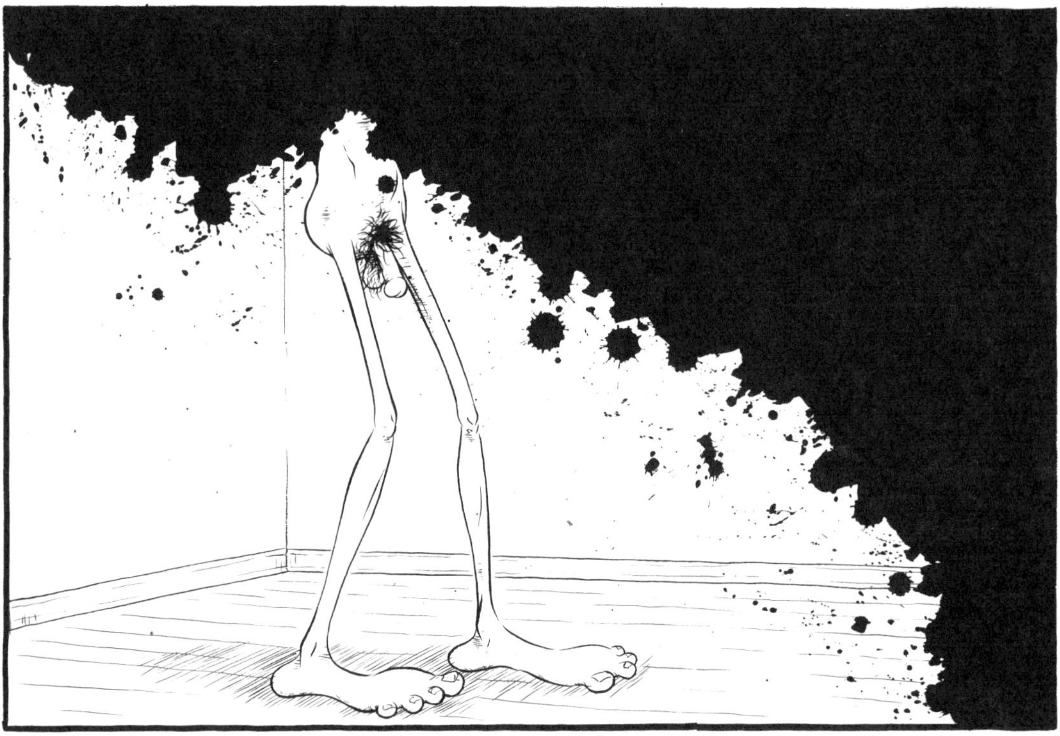

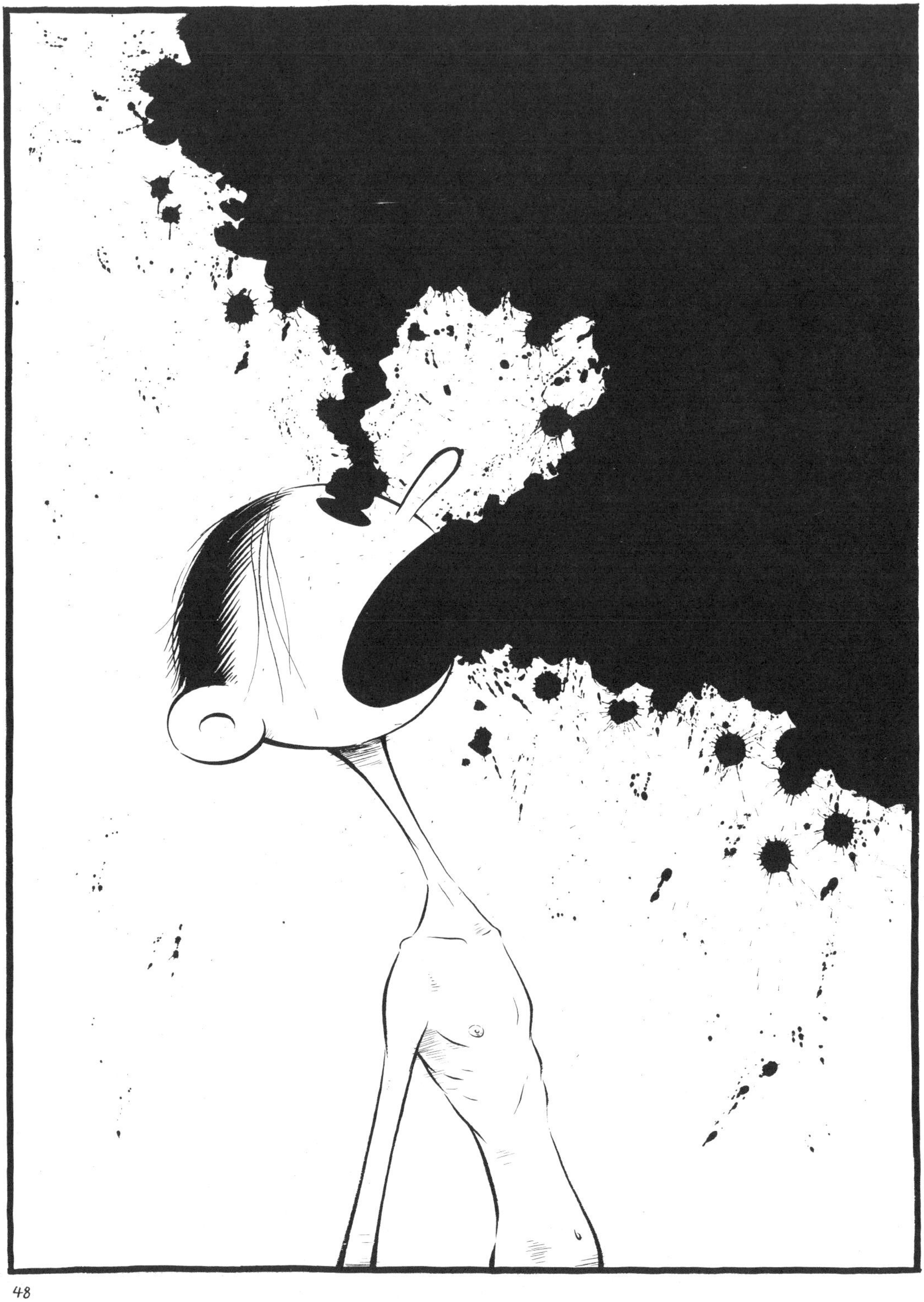

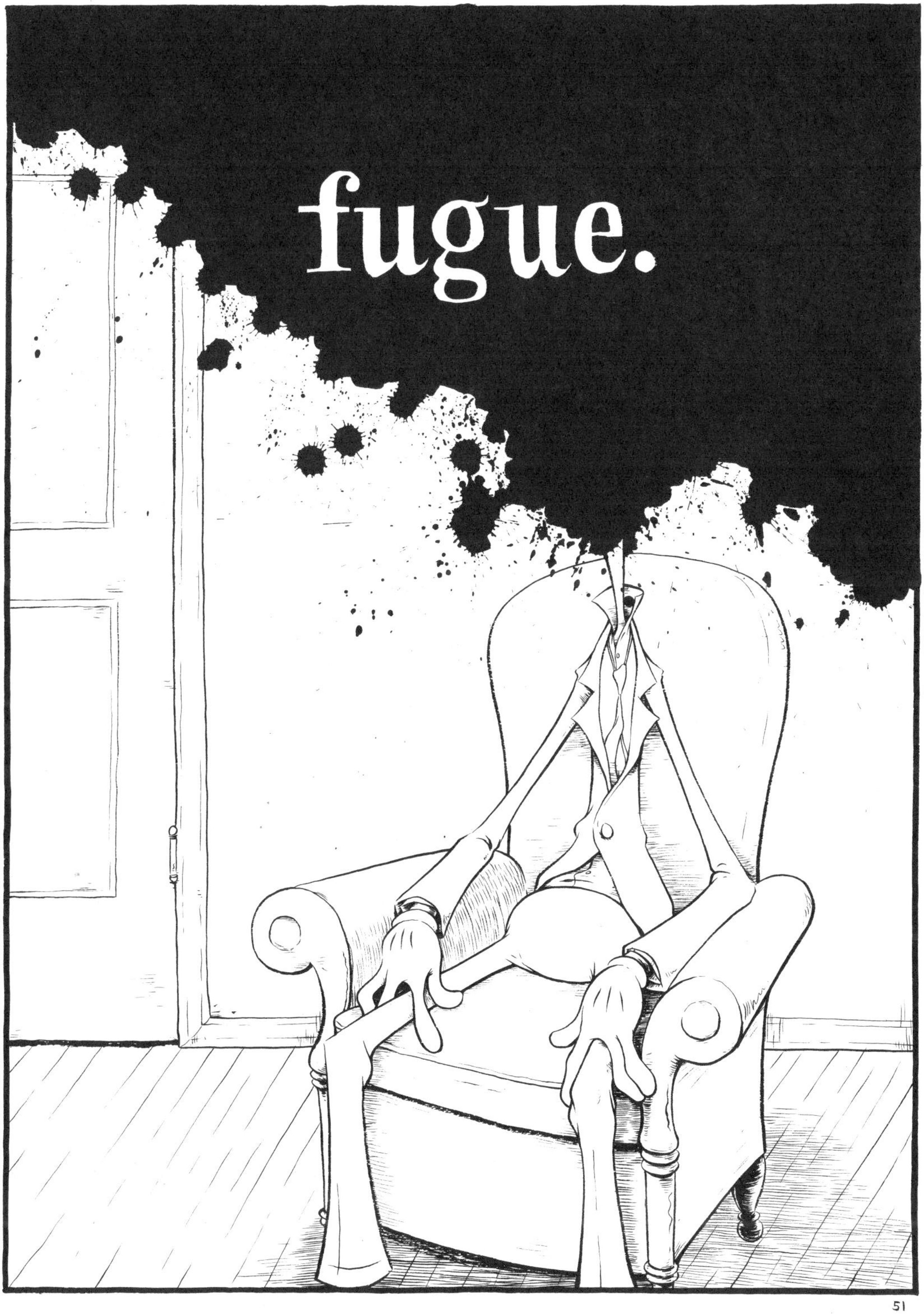
fugue.

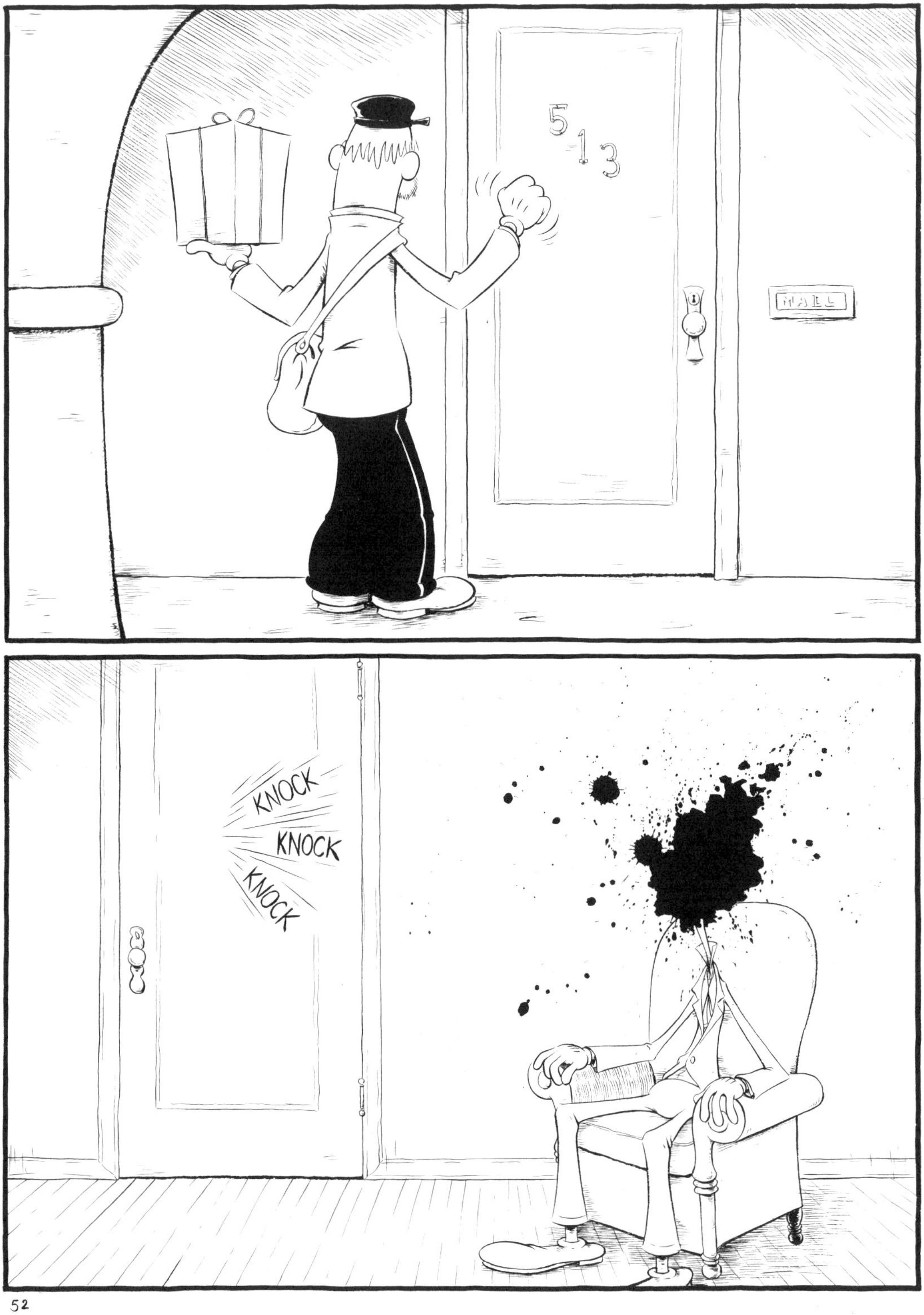
513
MAIL
KNOCK
KNOCK
KNOCK

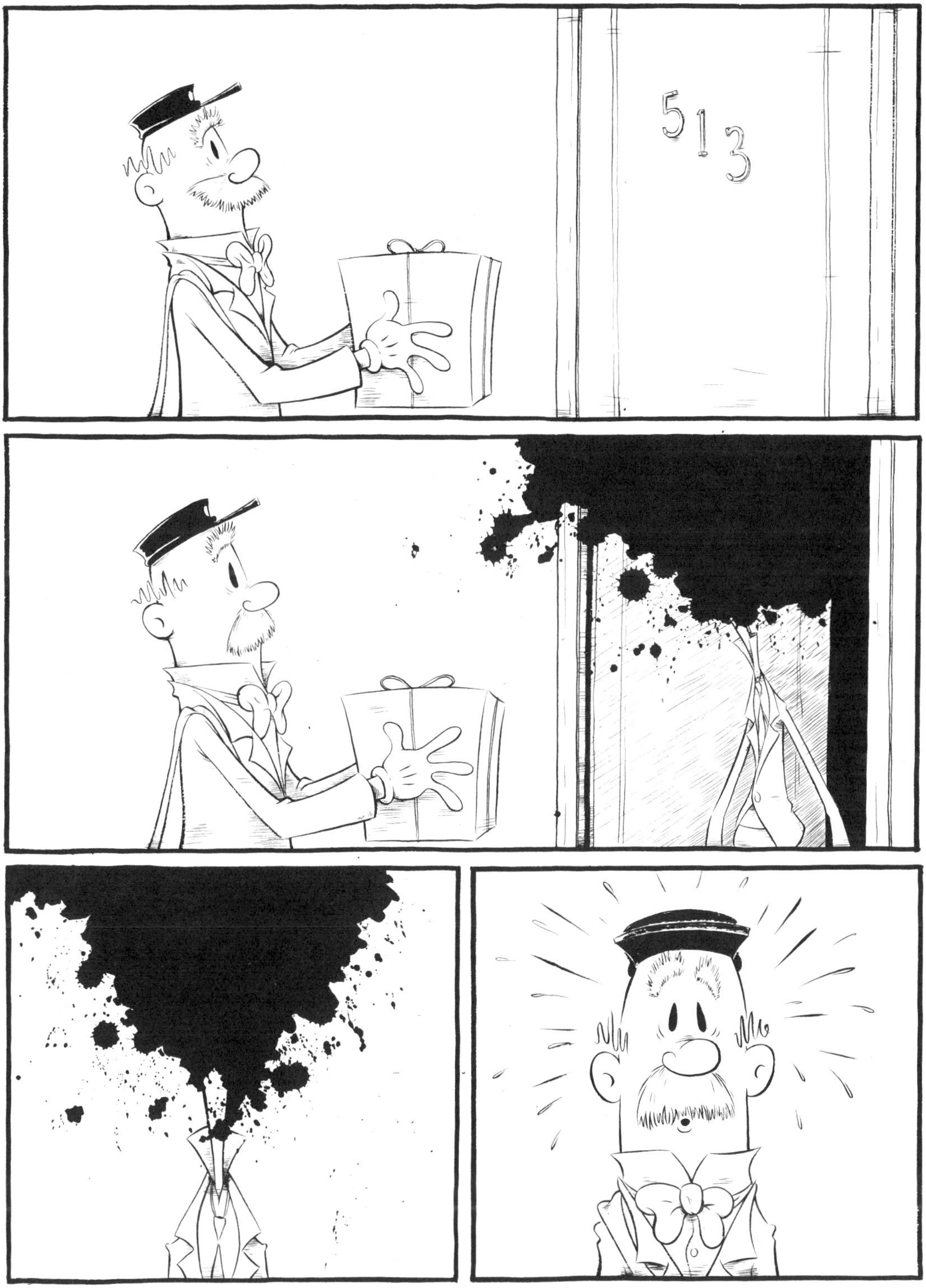
513

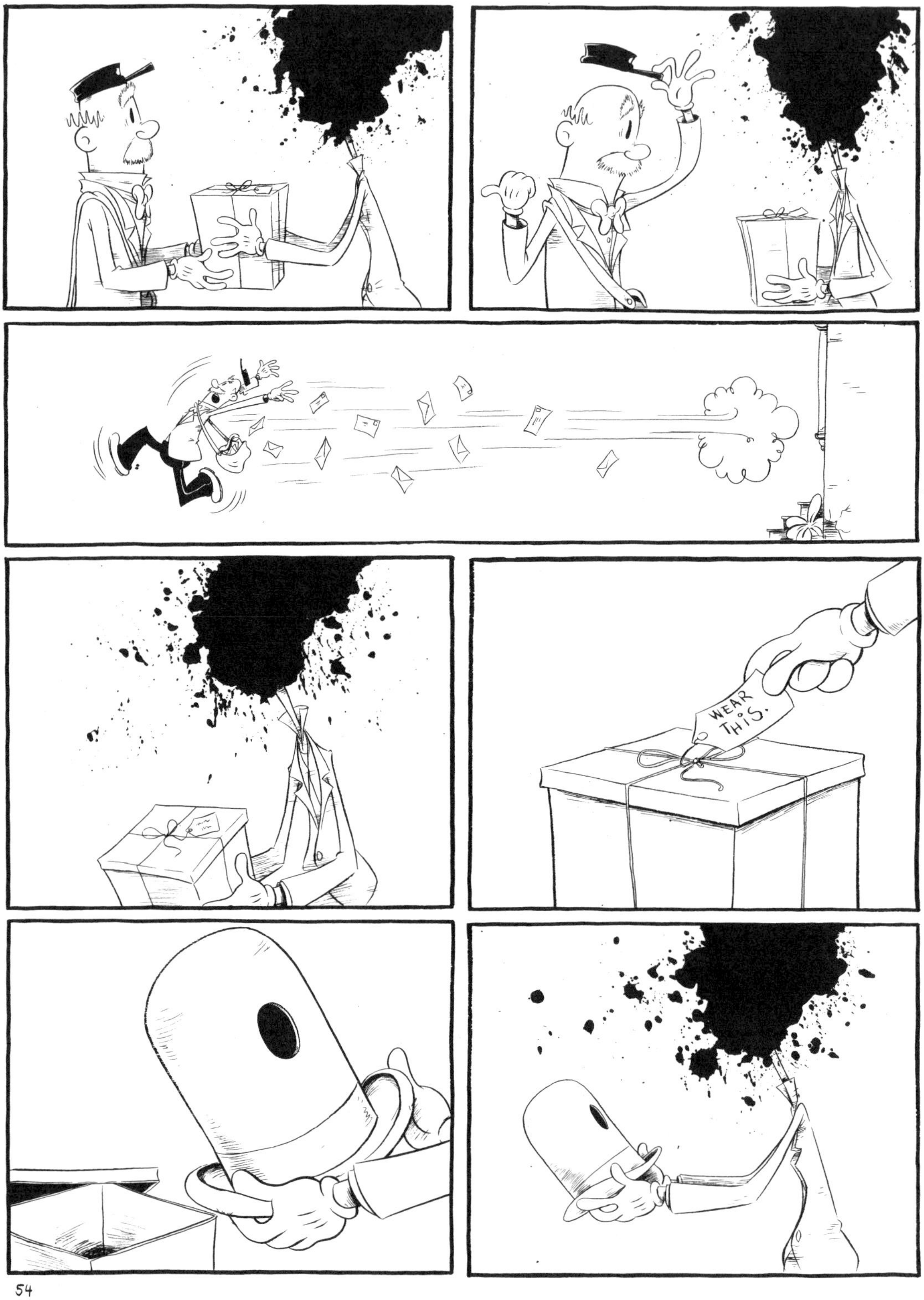
WEAR THIS.

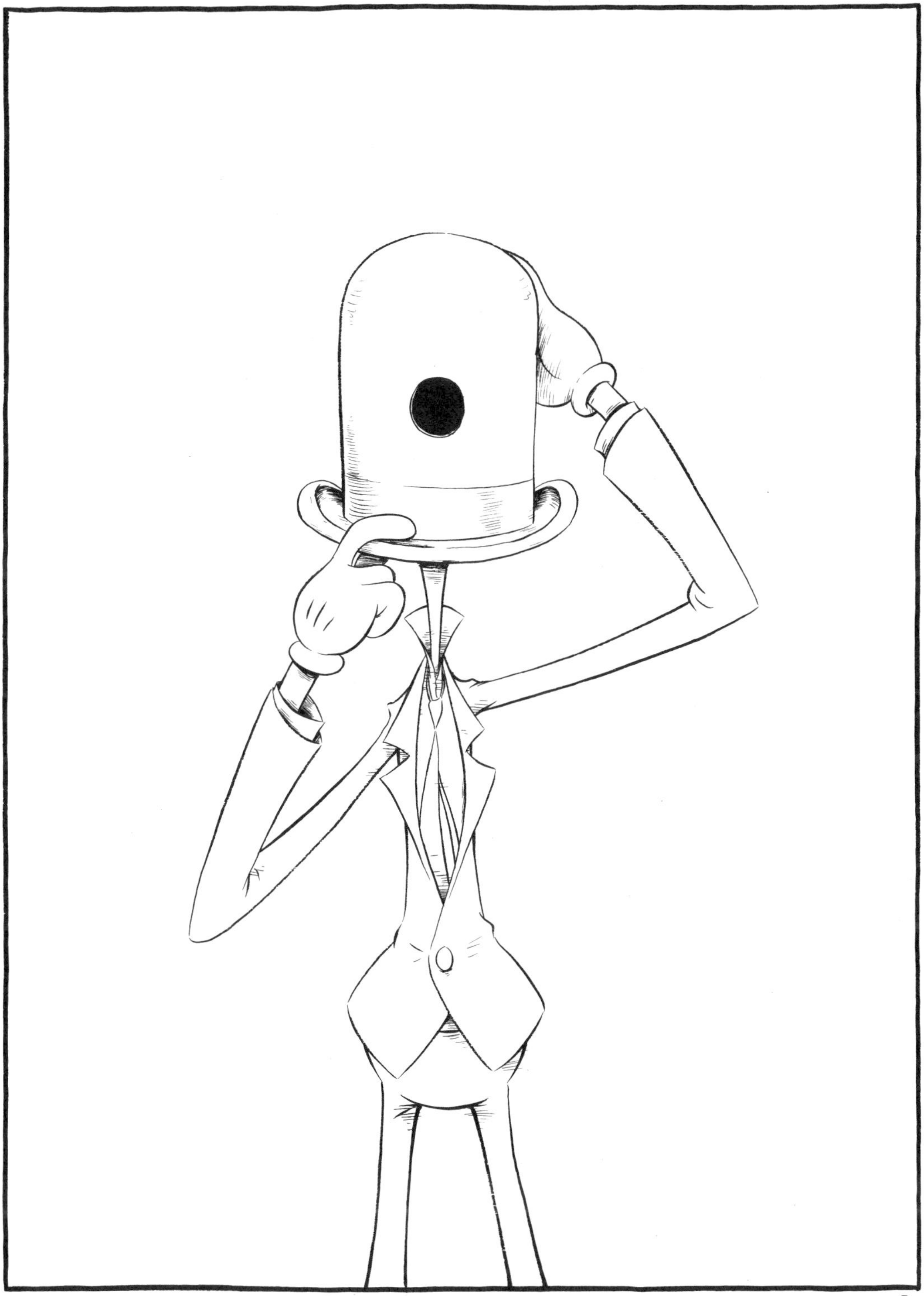

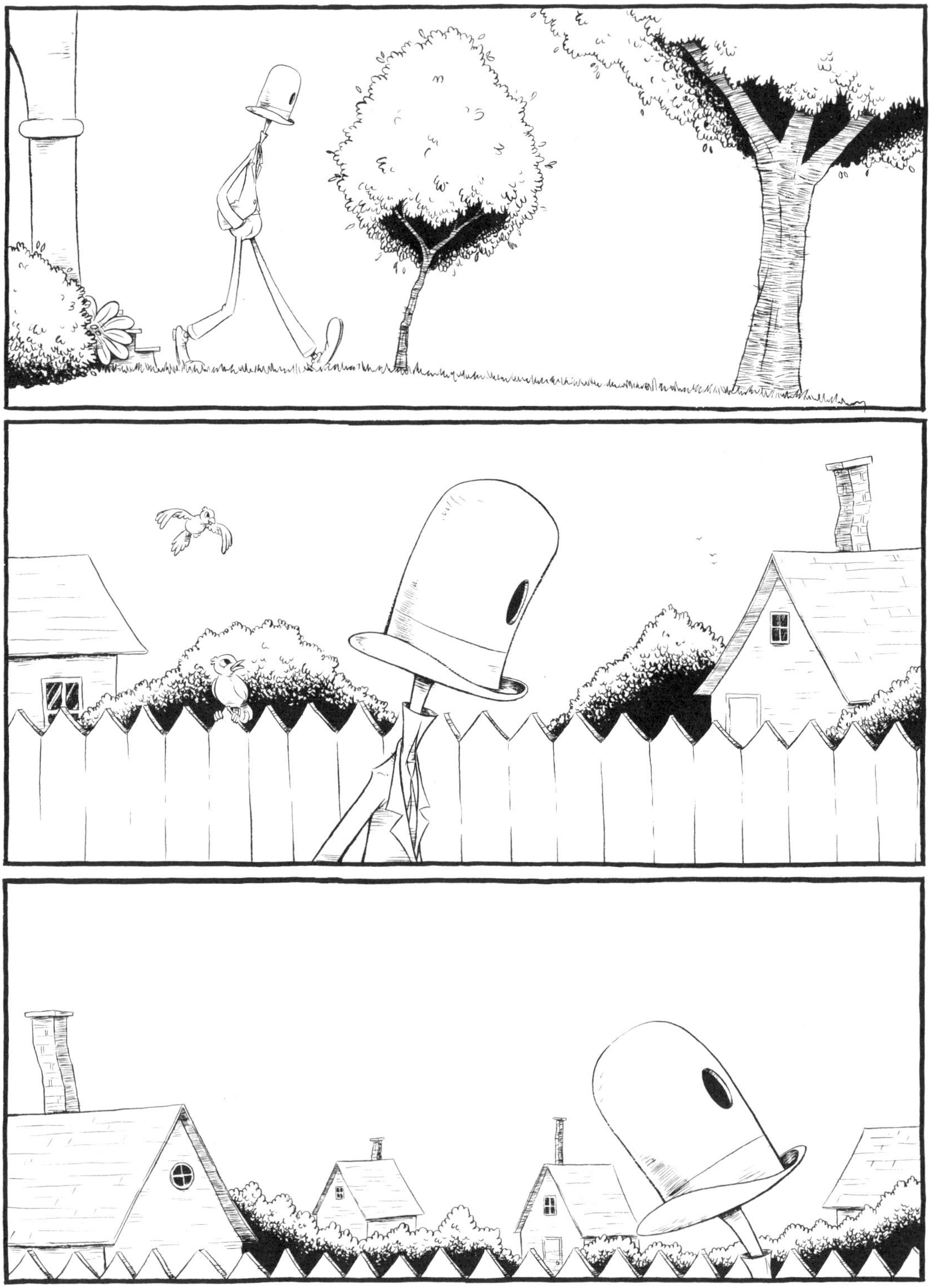

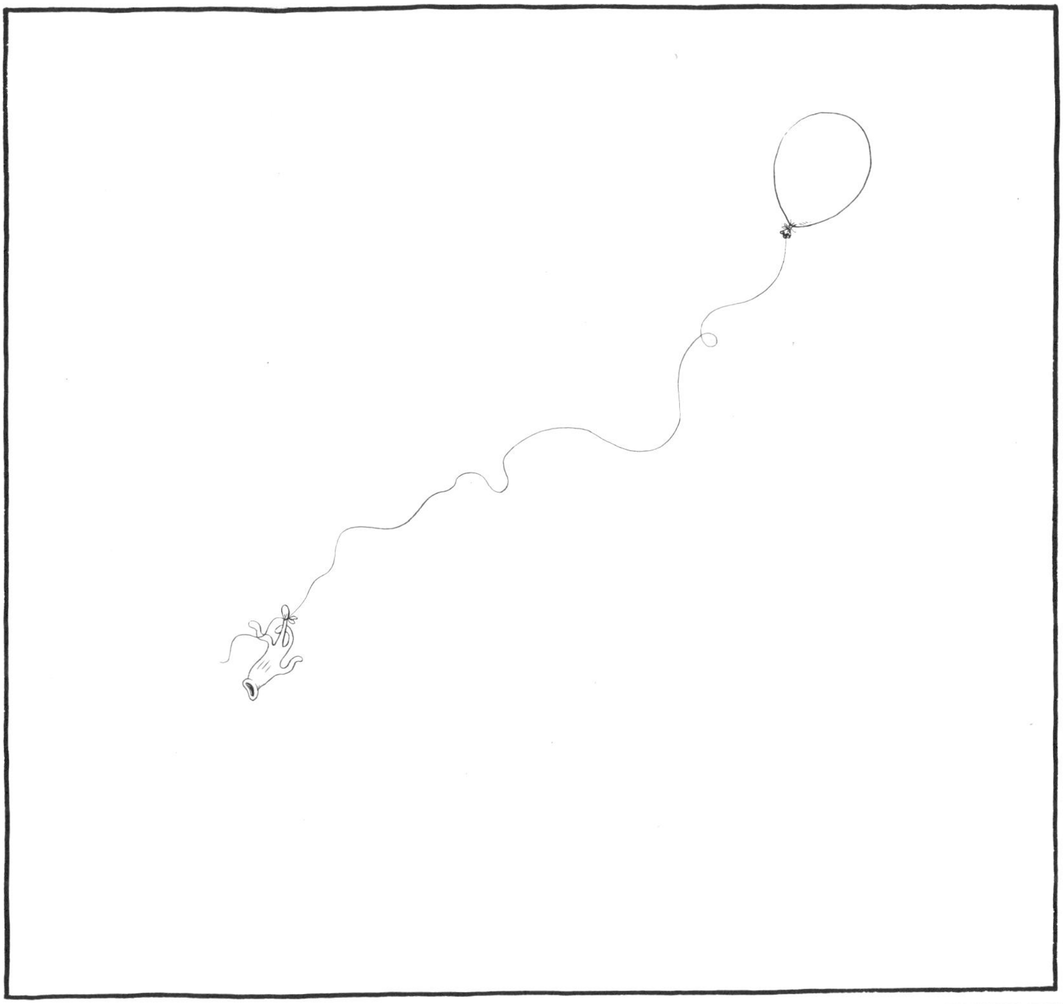

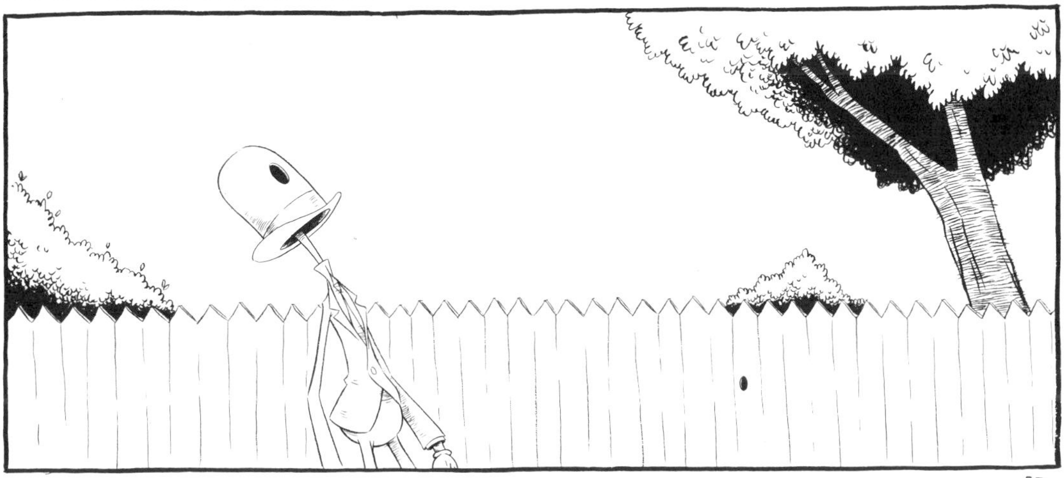

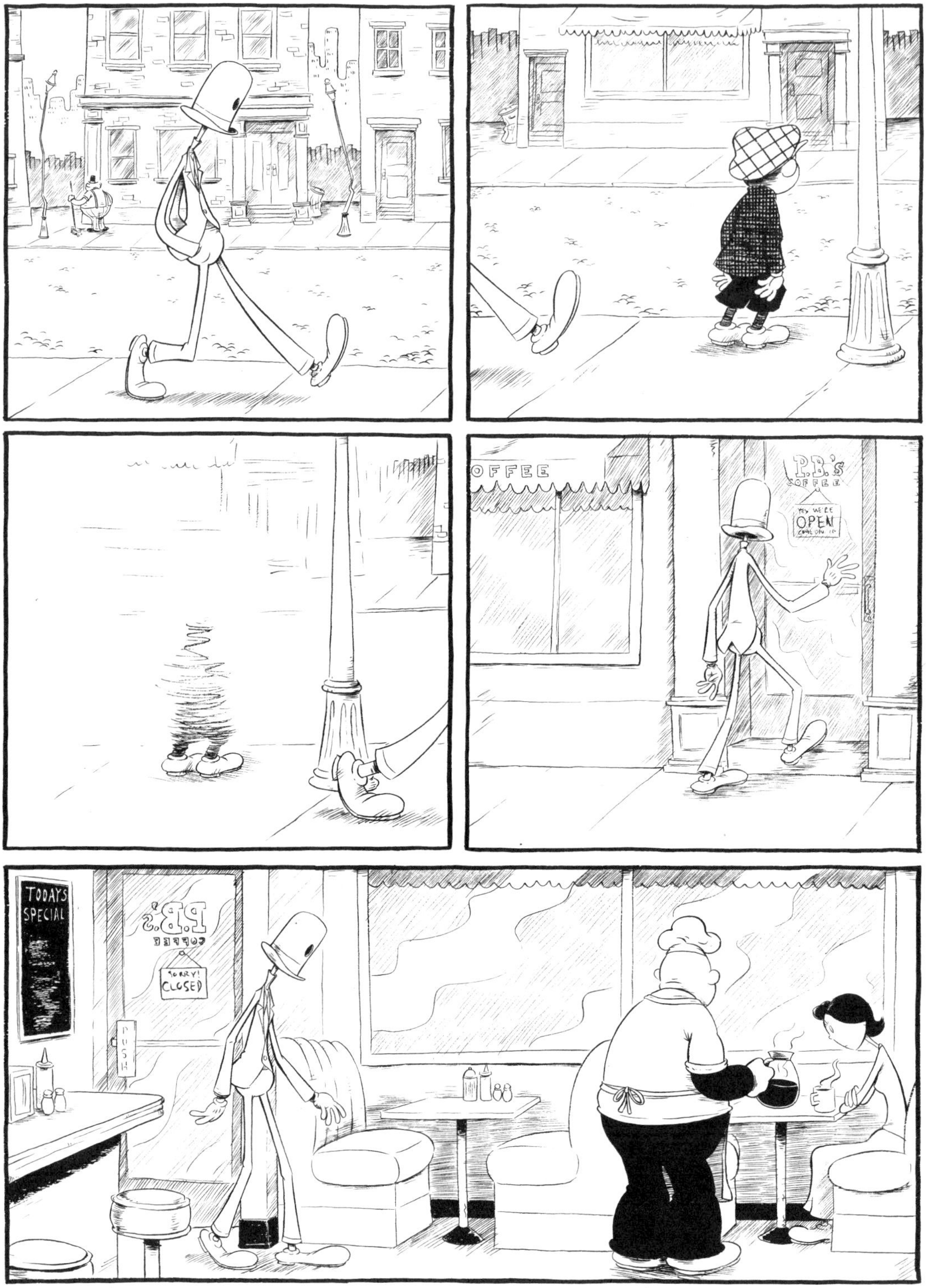
OFFEE
P.B.'s
COFFEE
YES WE'RE
OPEN
TODAYS
SPECIAL
P.B.'s
COFFEE
SORRY!
CLOSED
PUSH

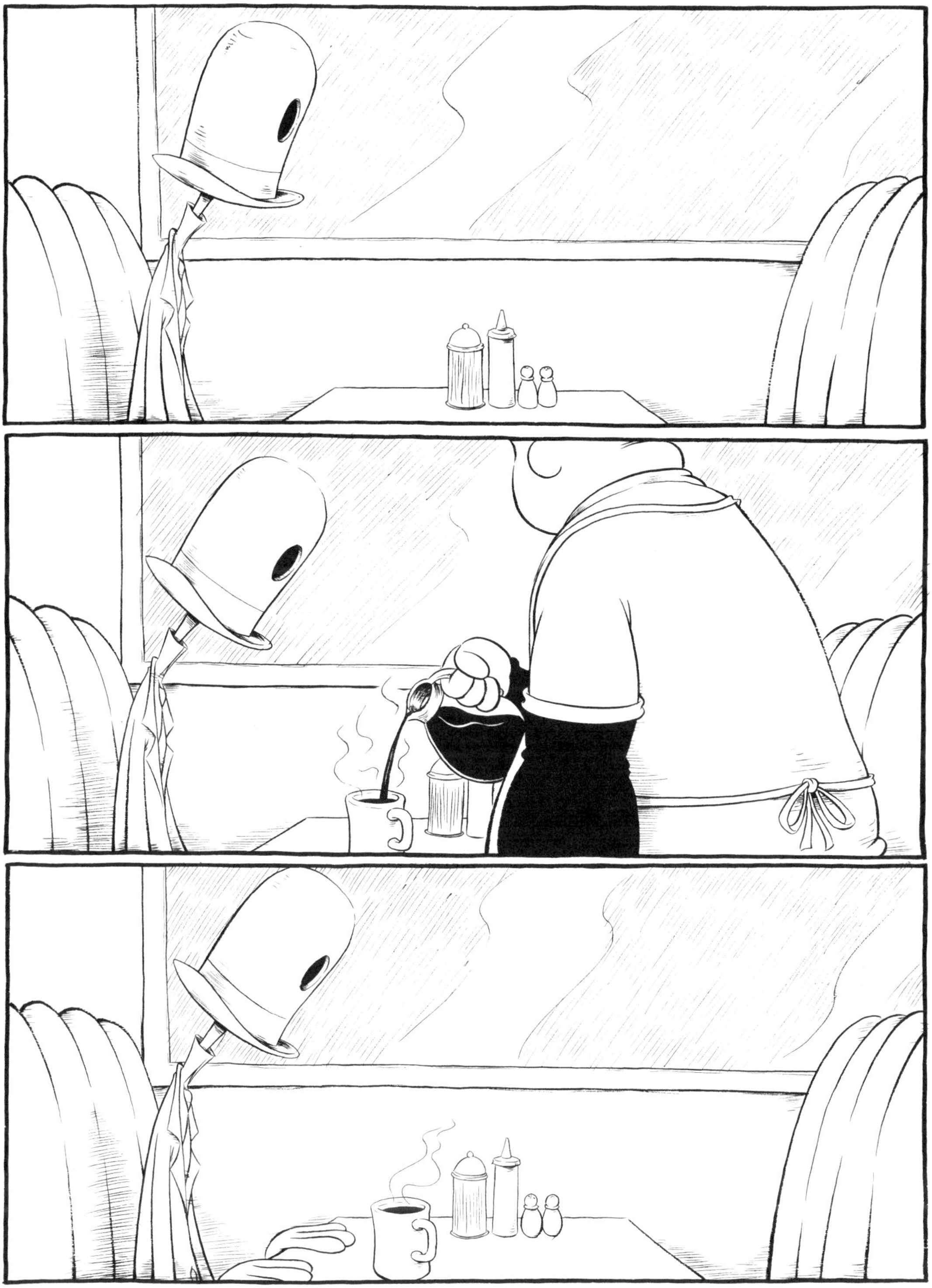

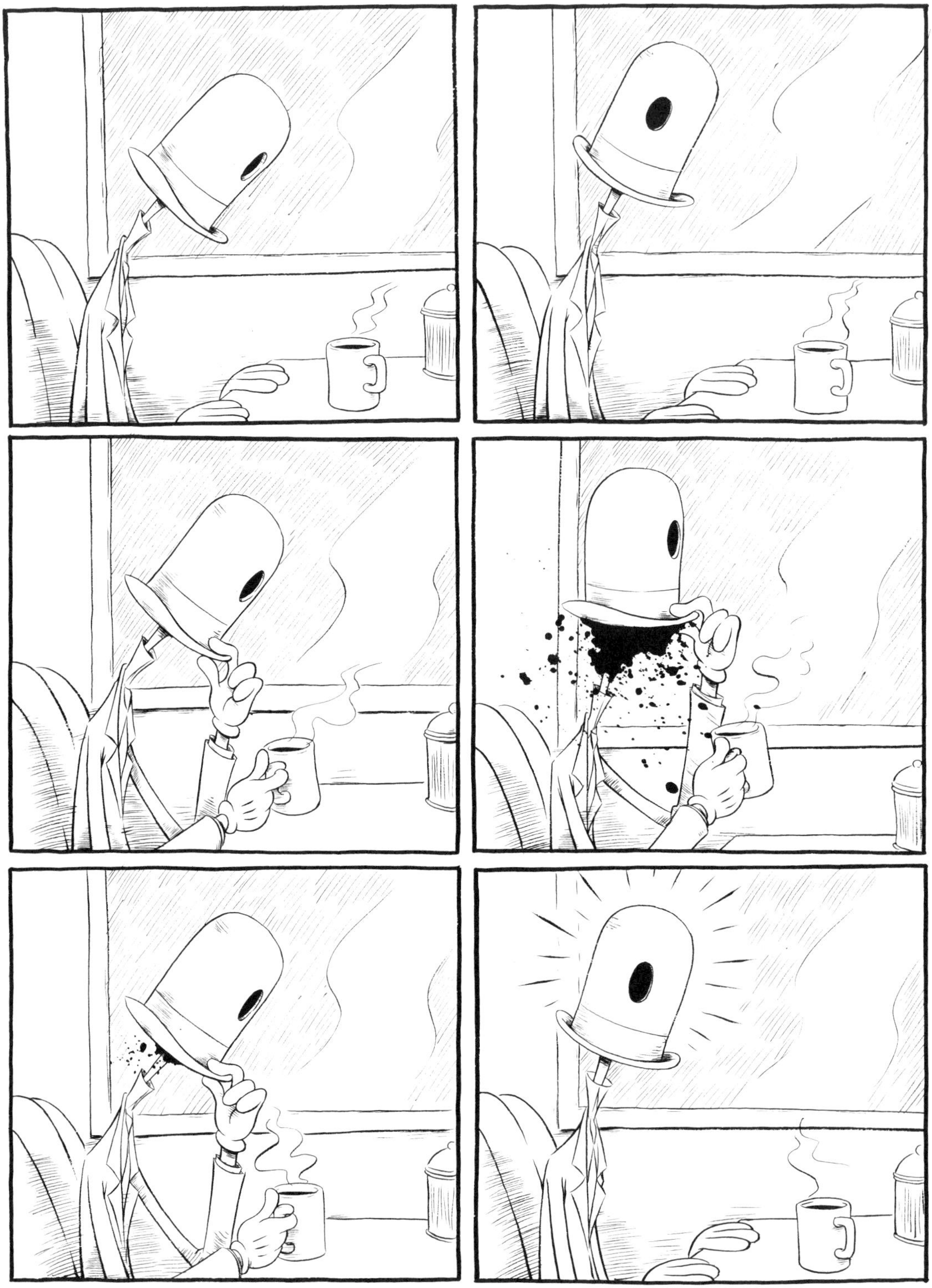

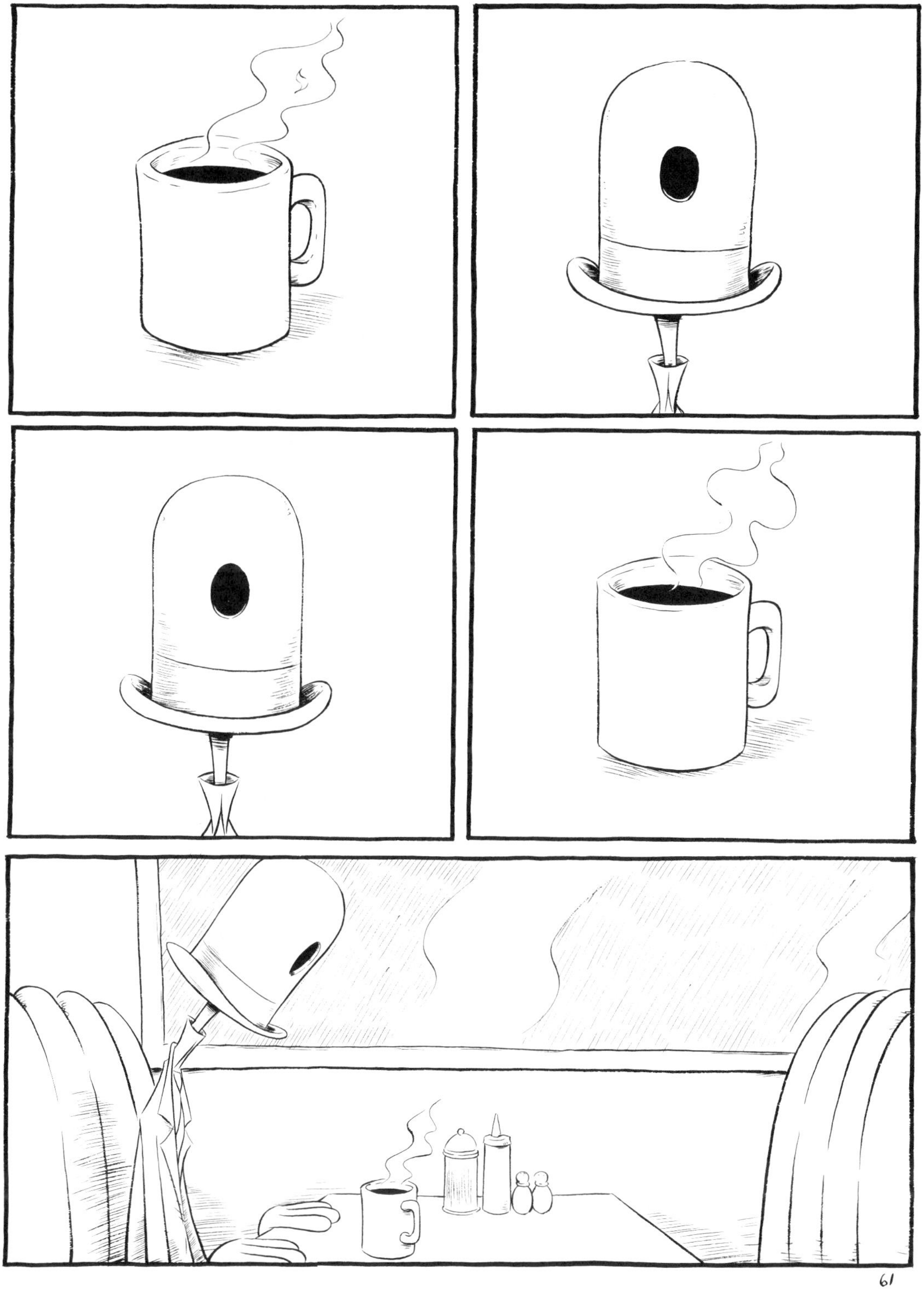

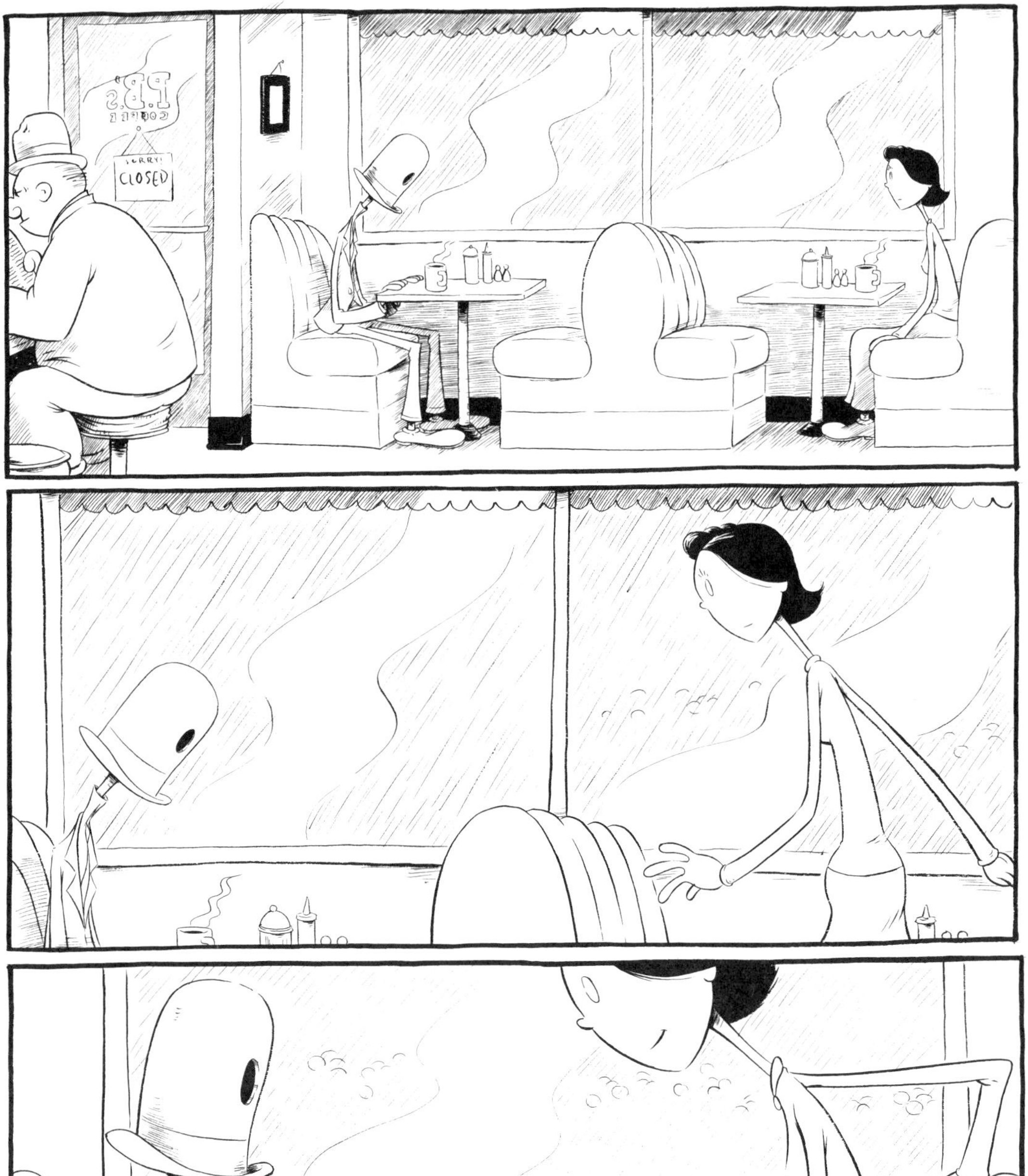
P.B.'S
COFFEE
SORRY!
CLOSED

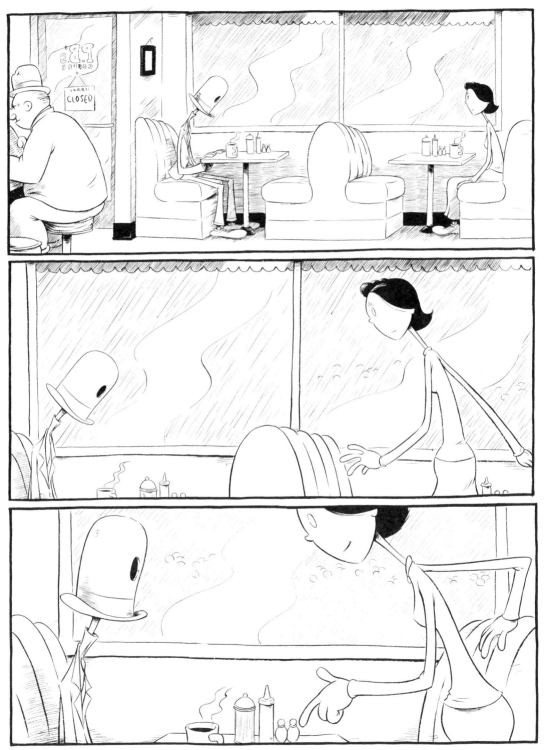

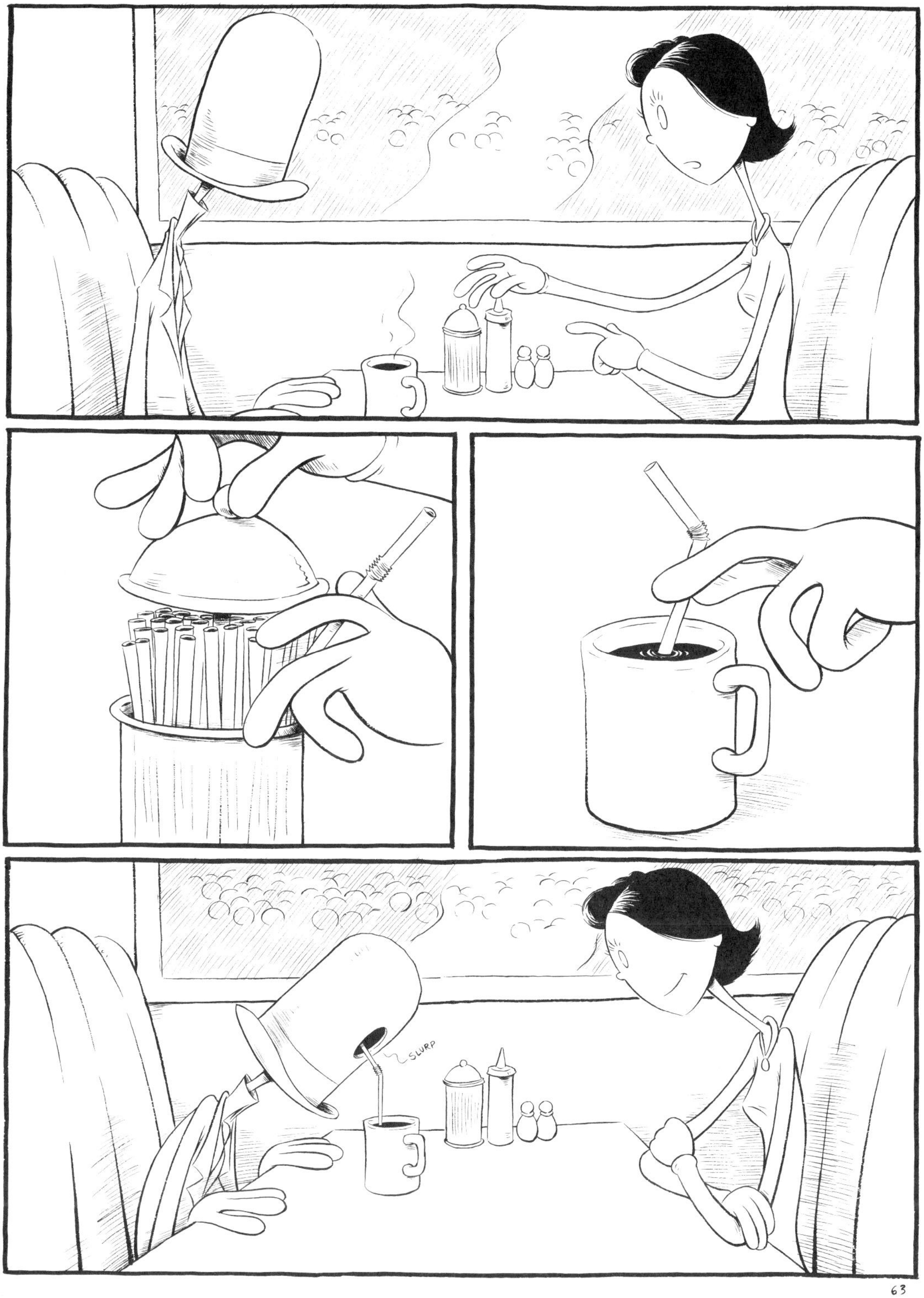
SLURP

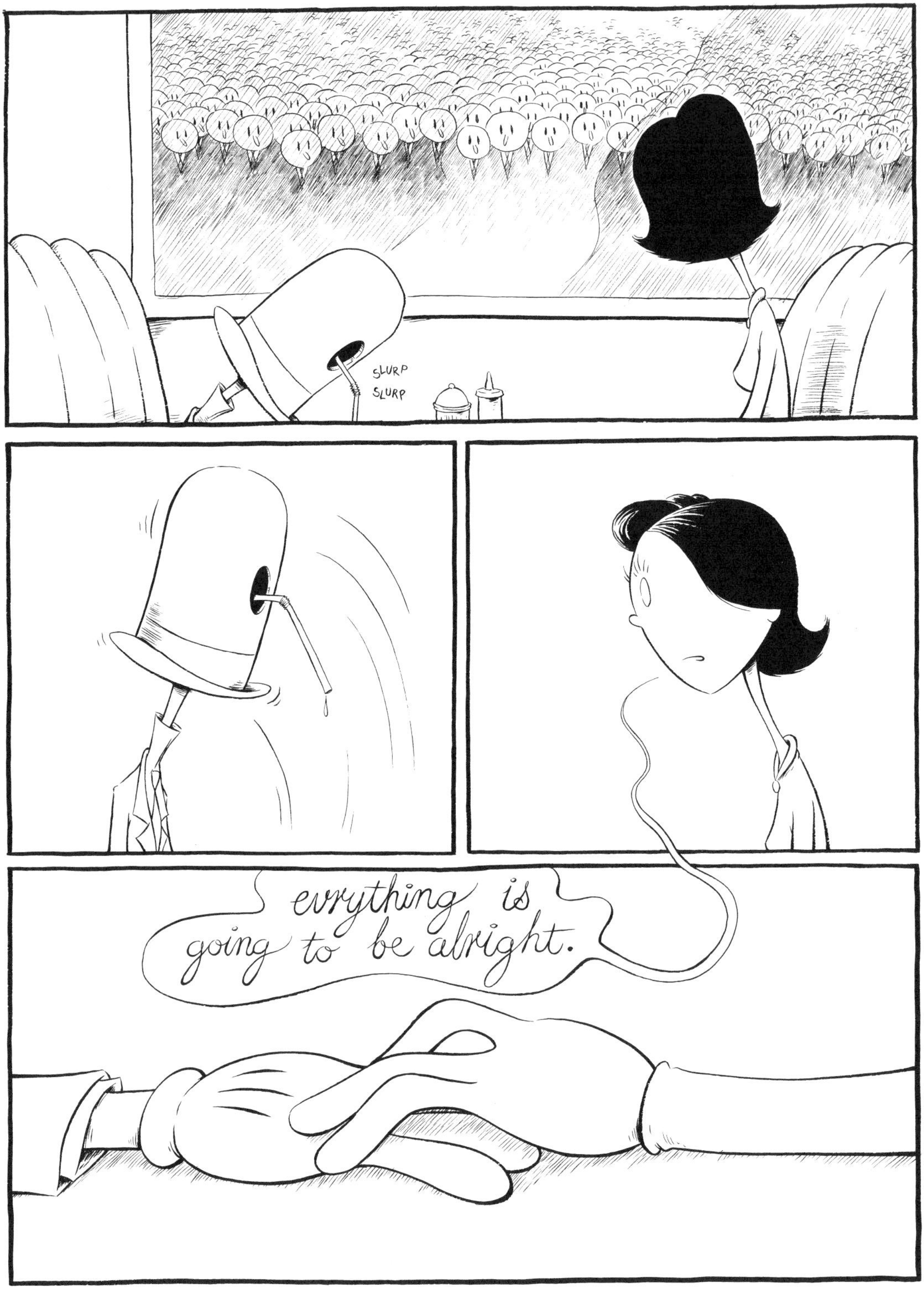
SLURP
SLURP
evrything is going to be alright.

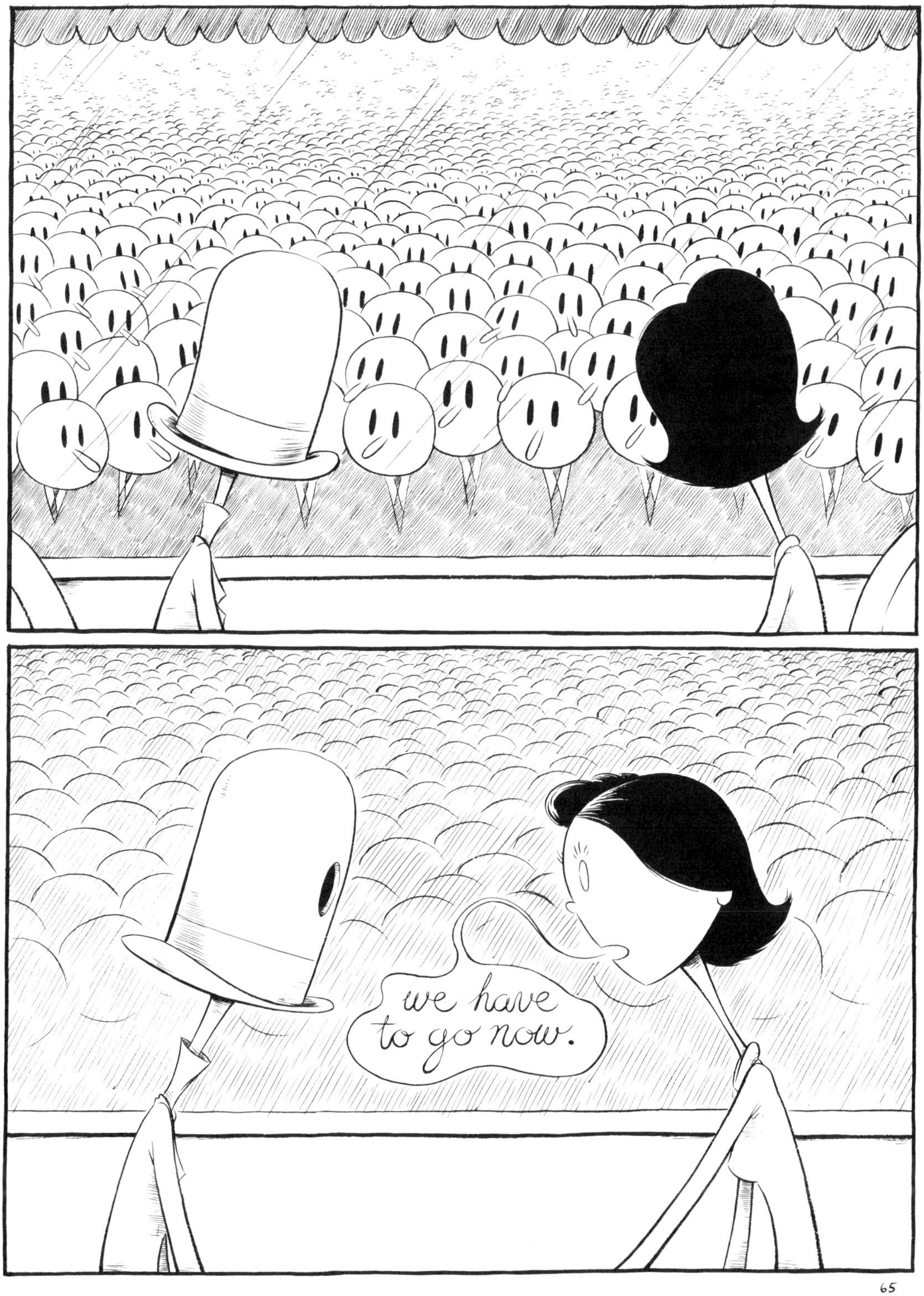
we have to go now.

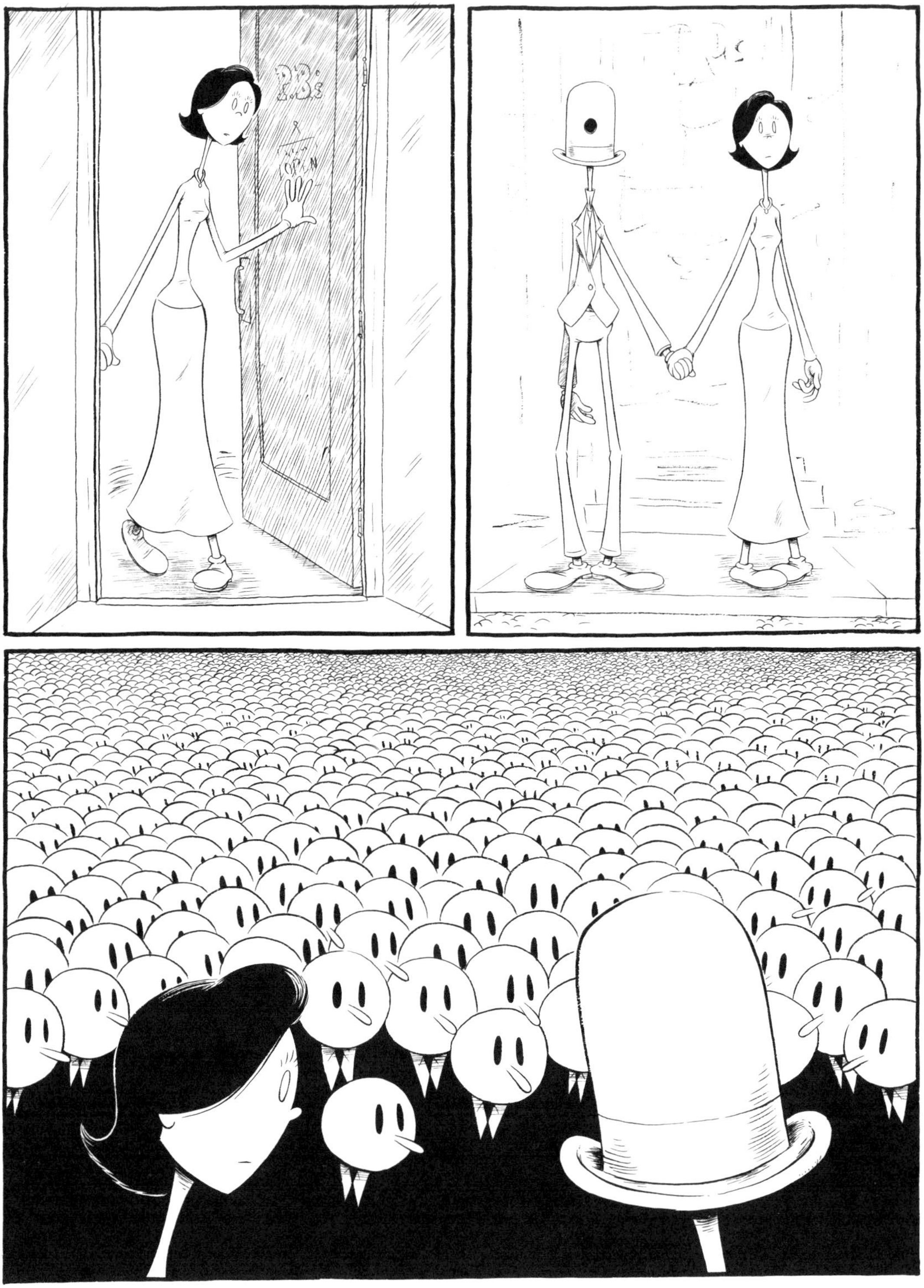

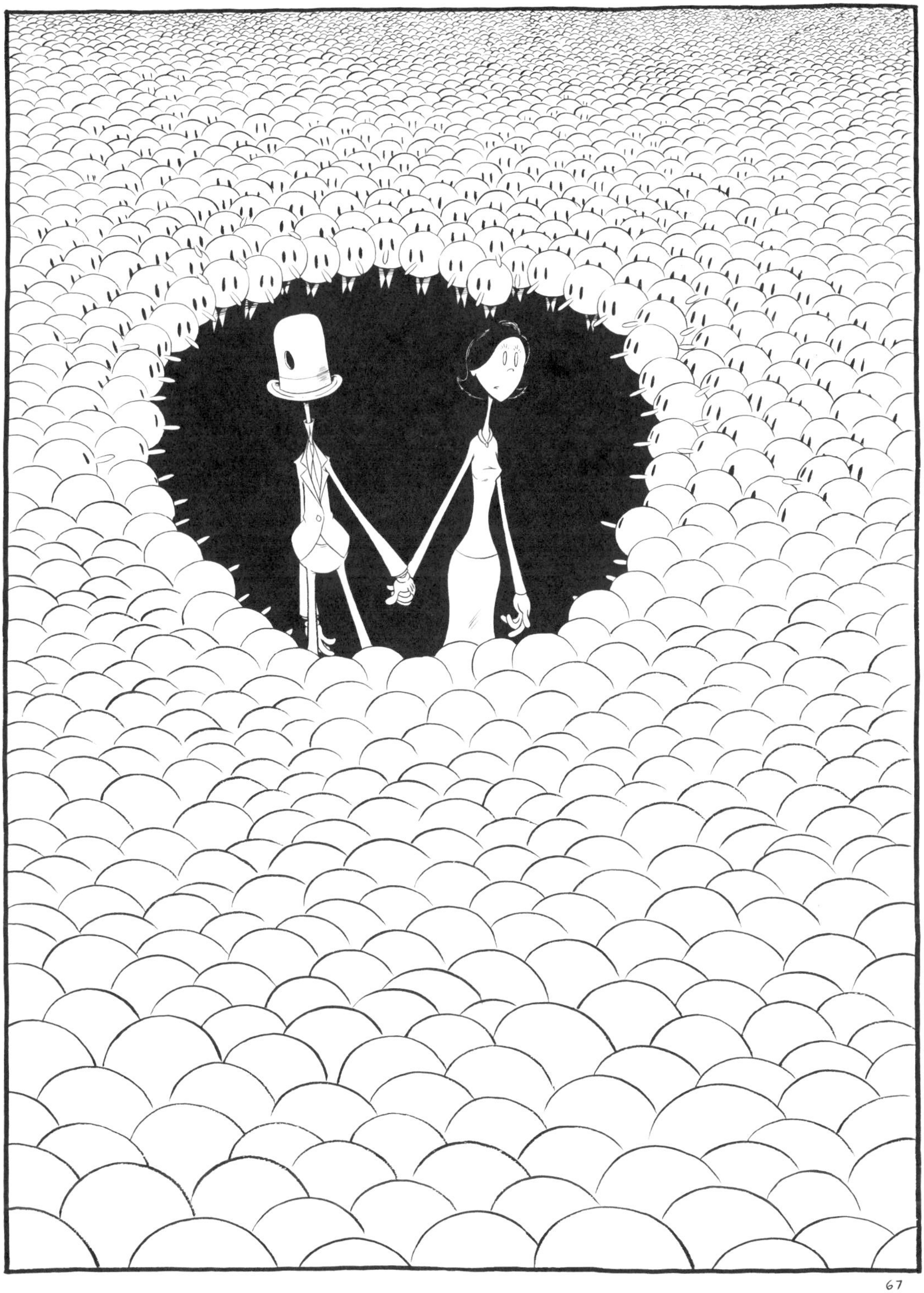

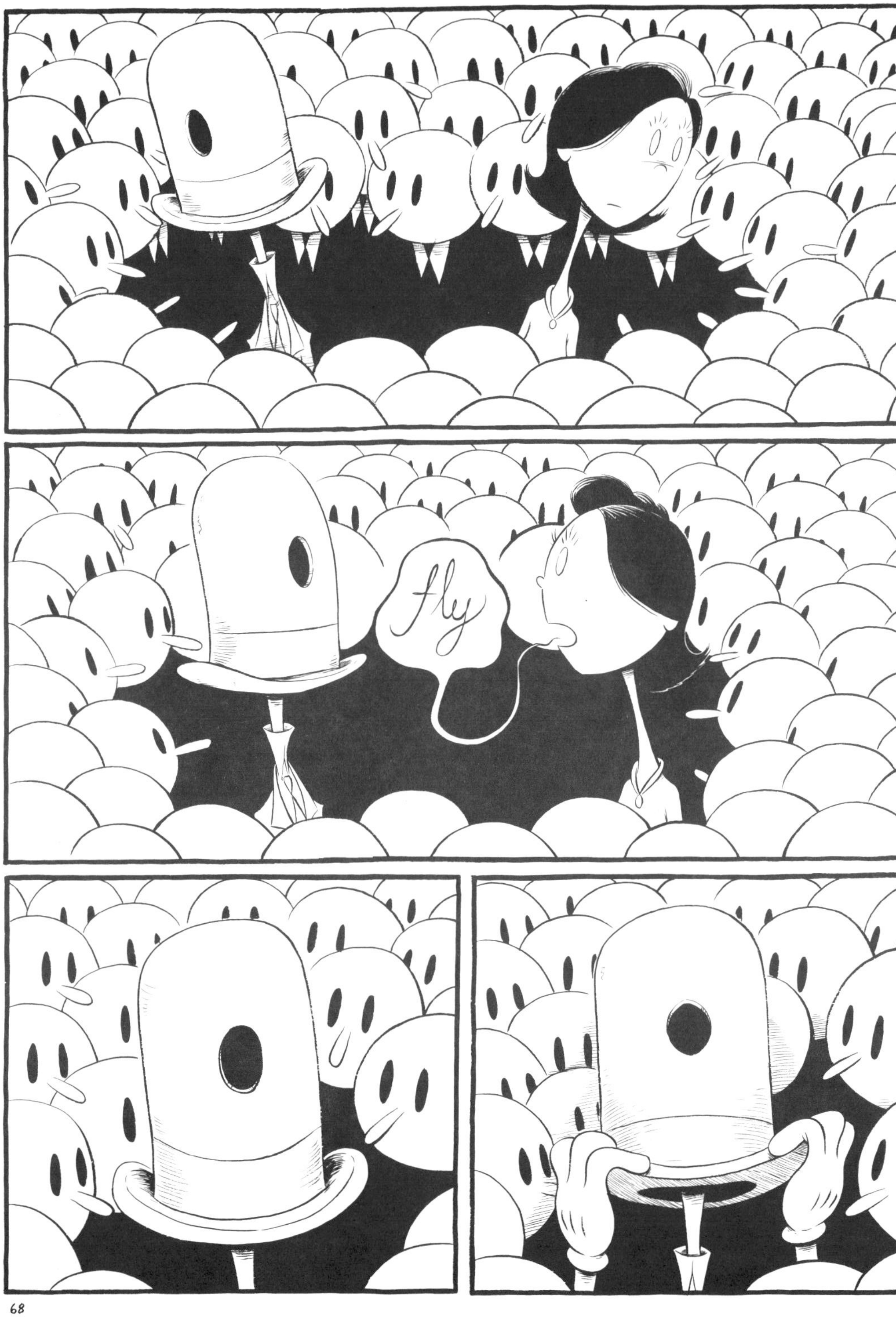
fly

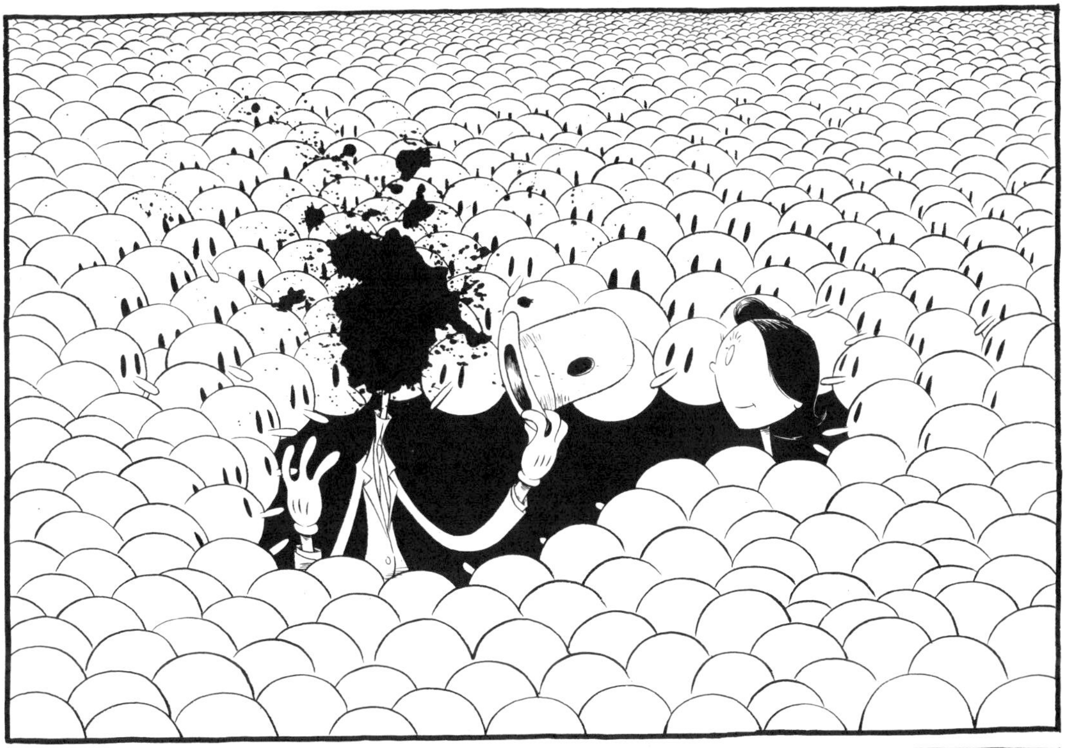

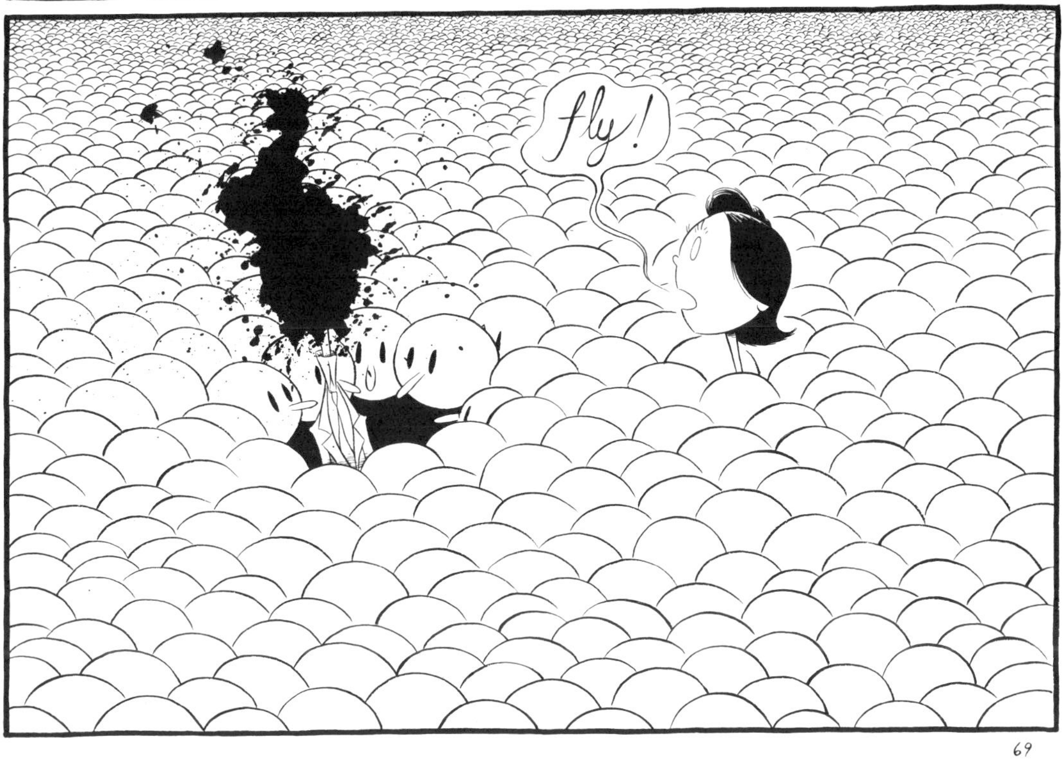
fly!

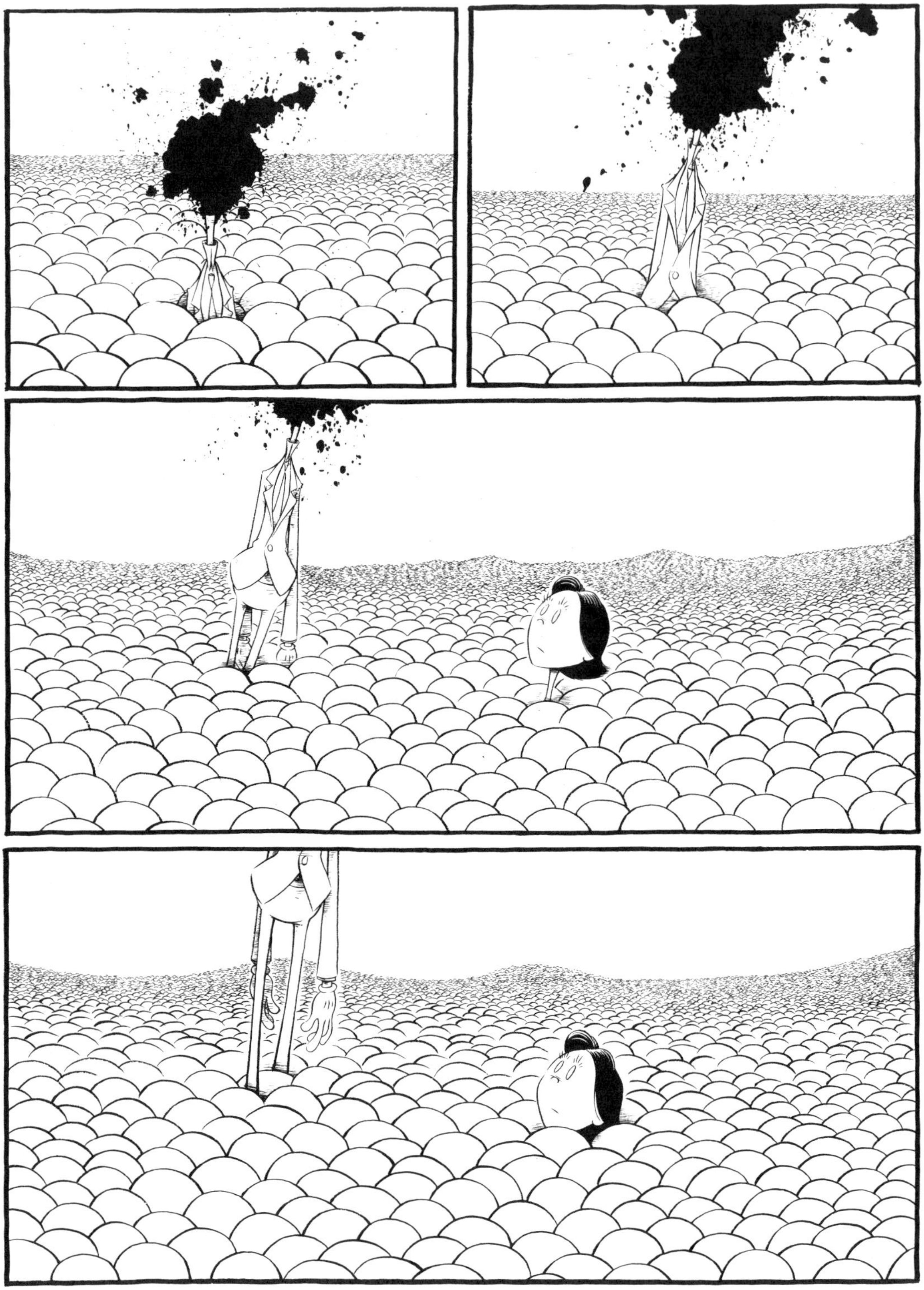

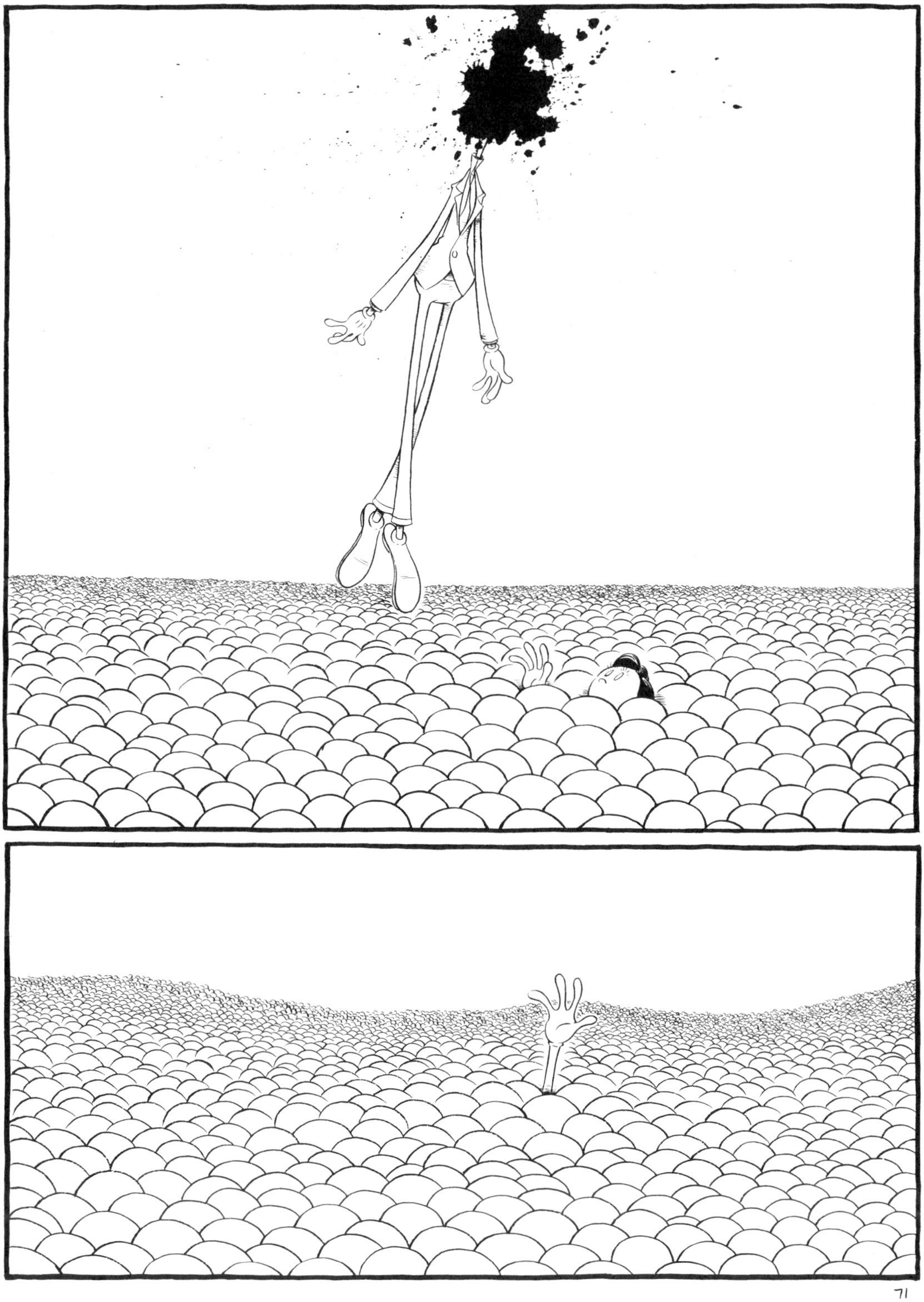

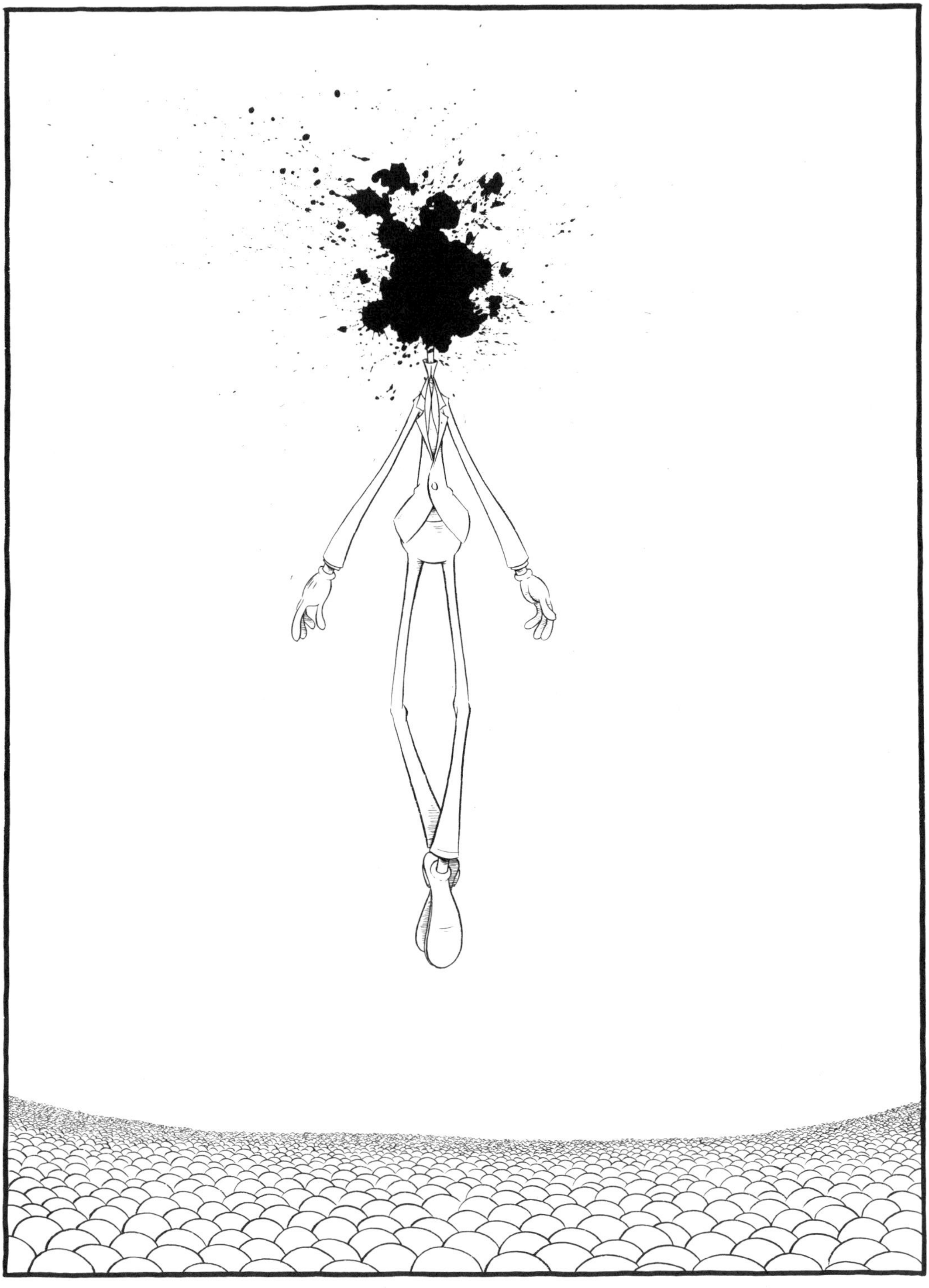

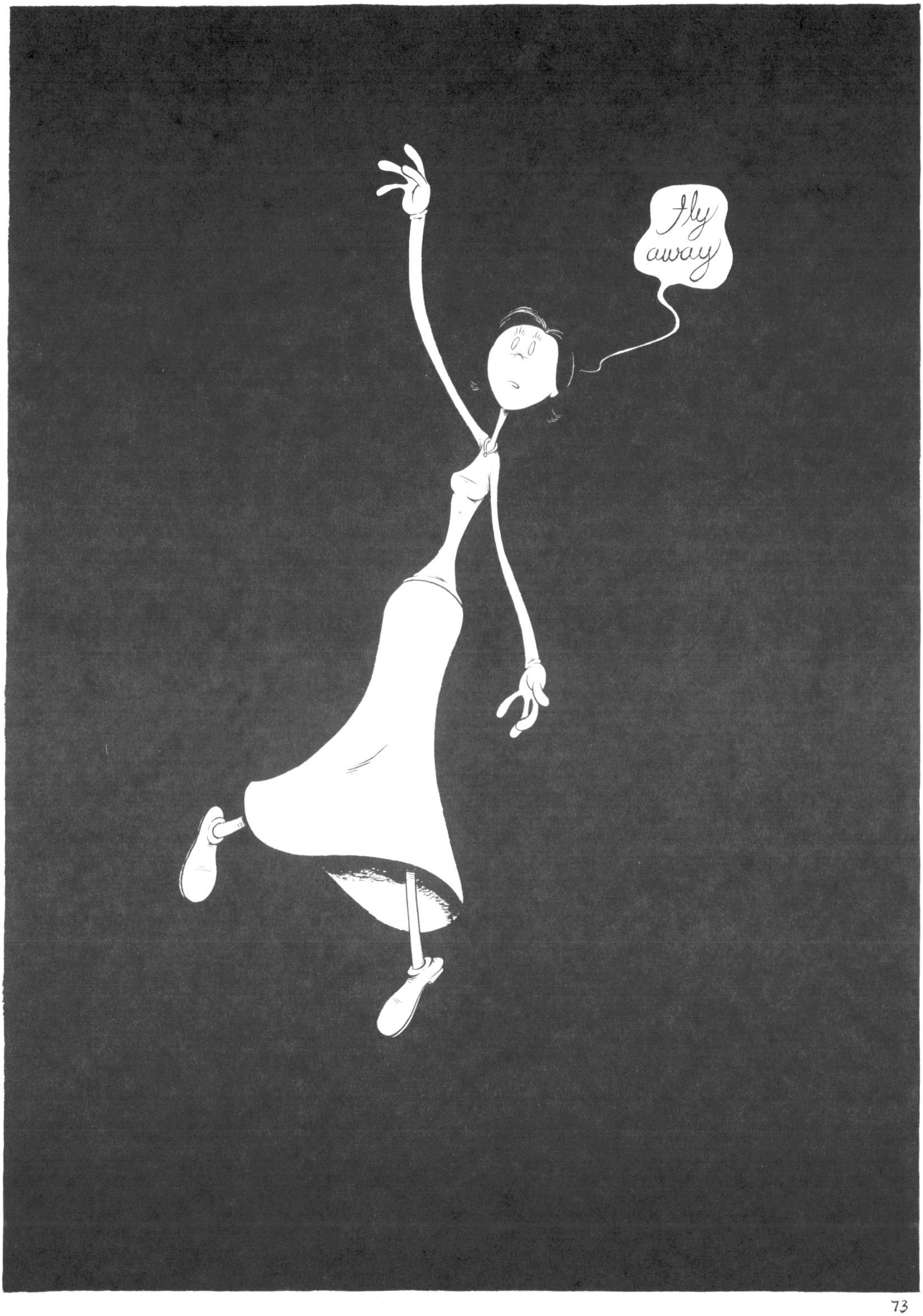
fly away

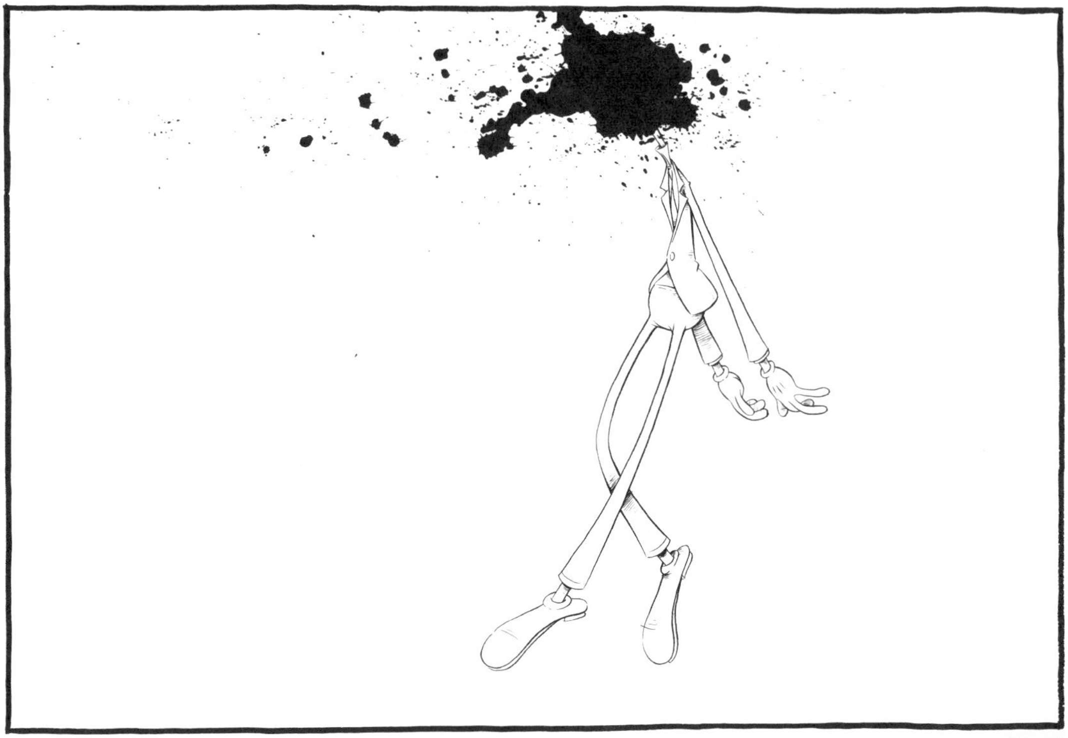

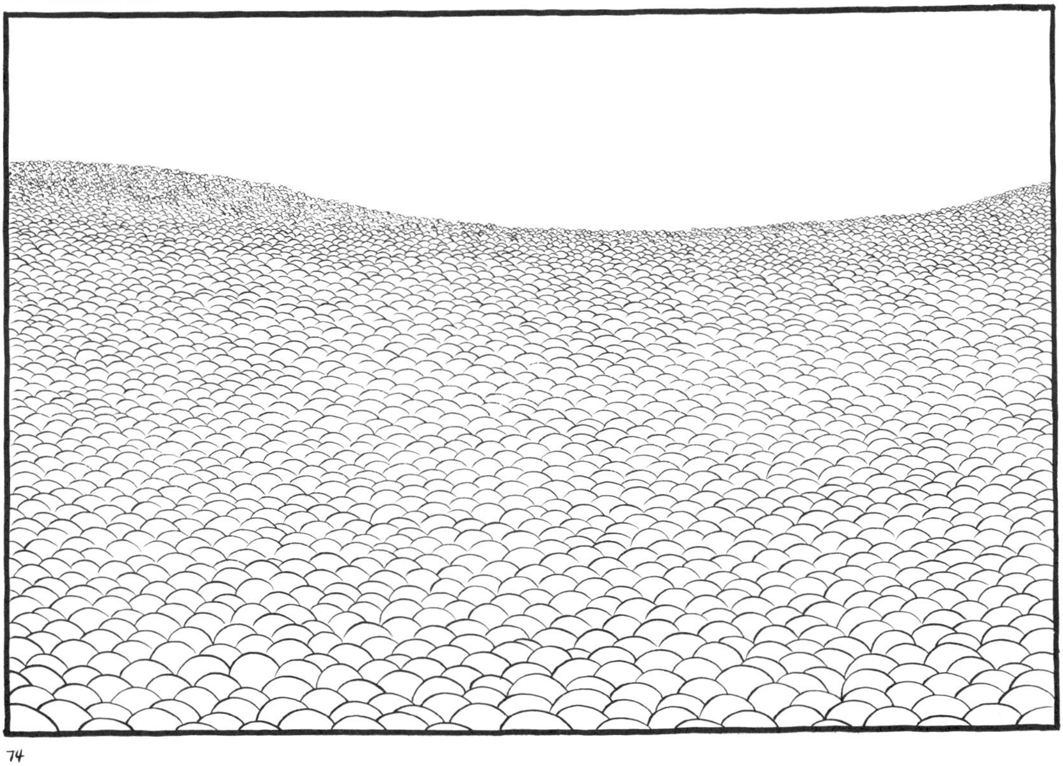

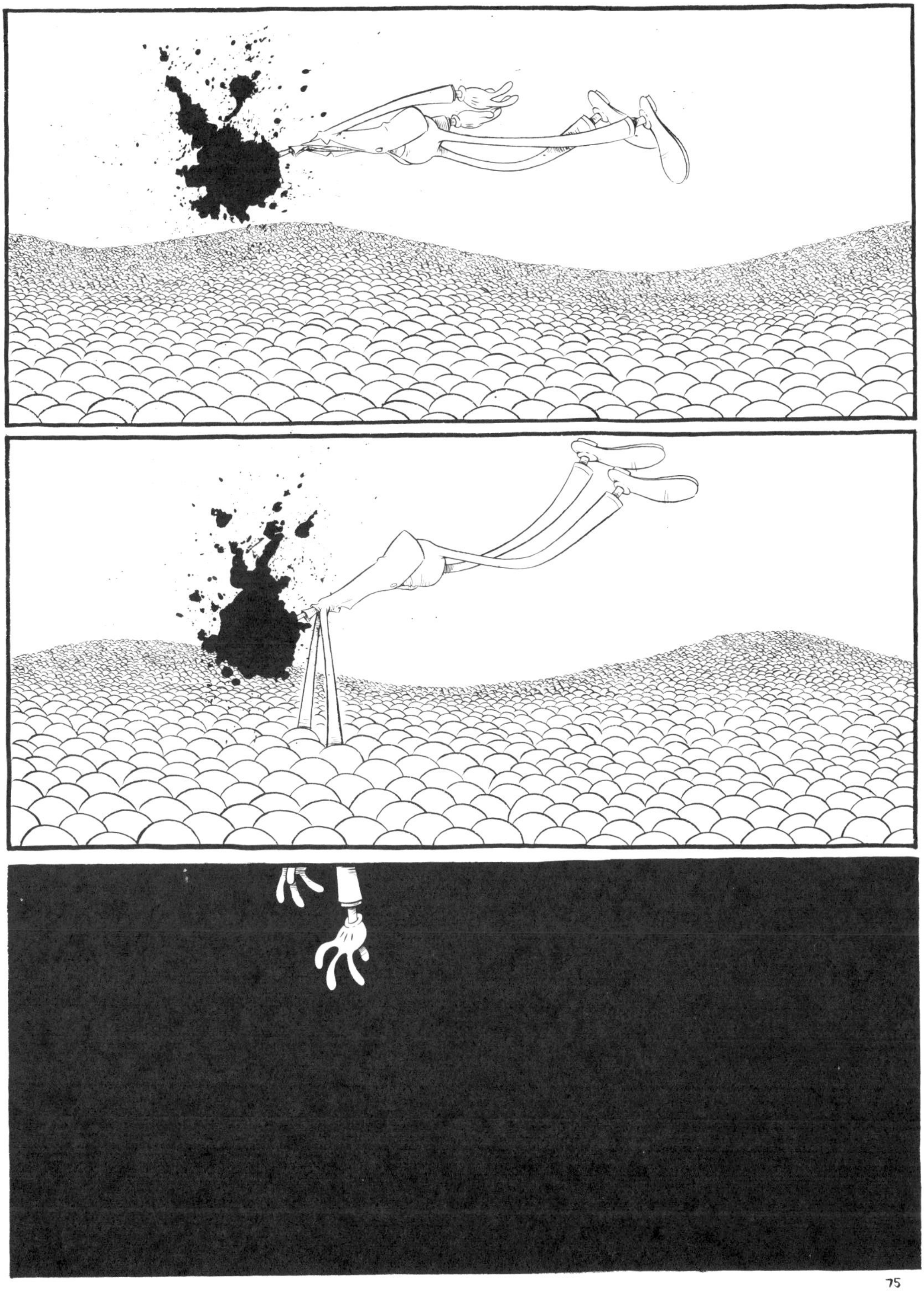

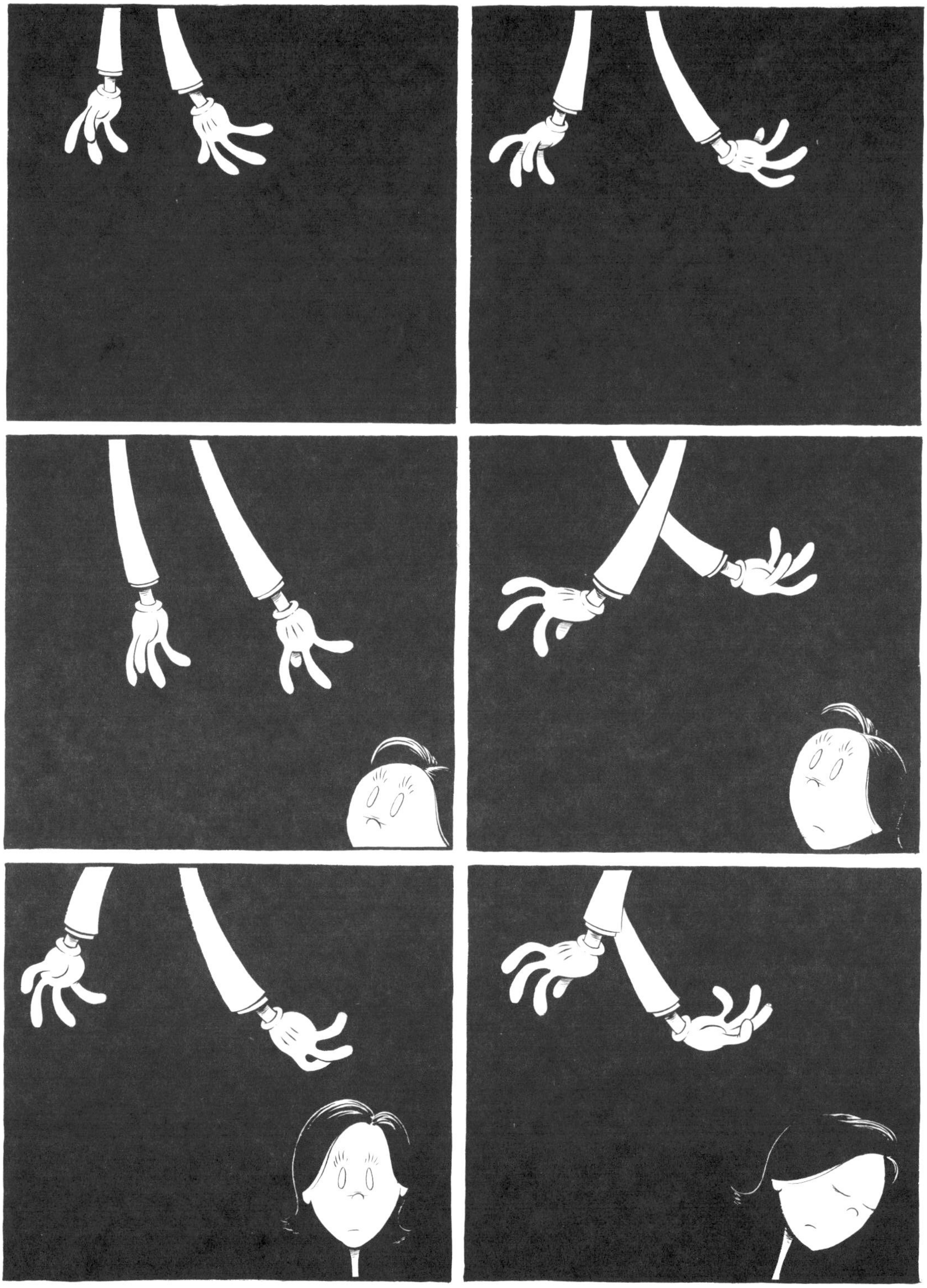

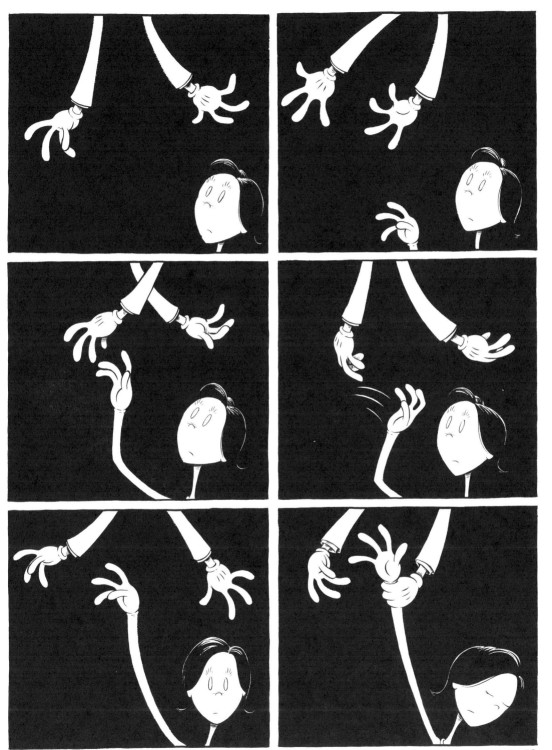

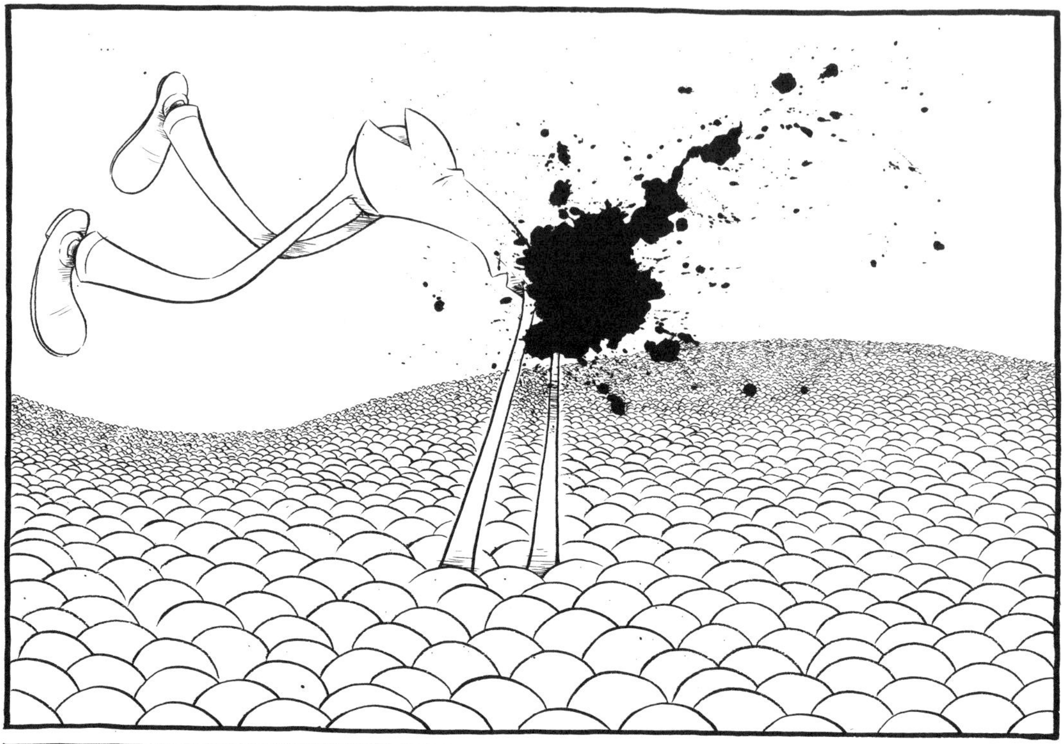

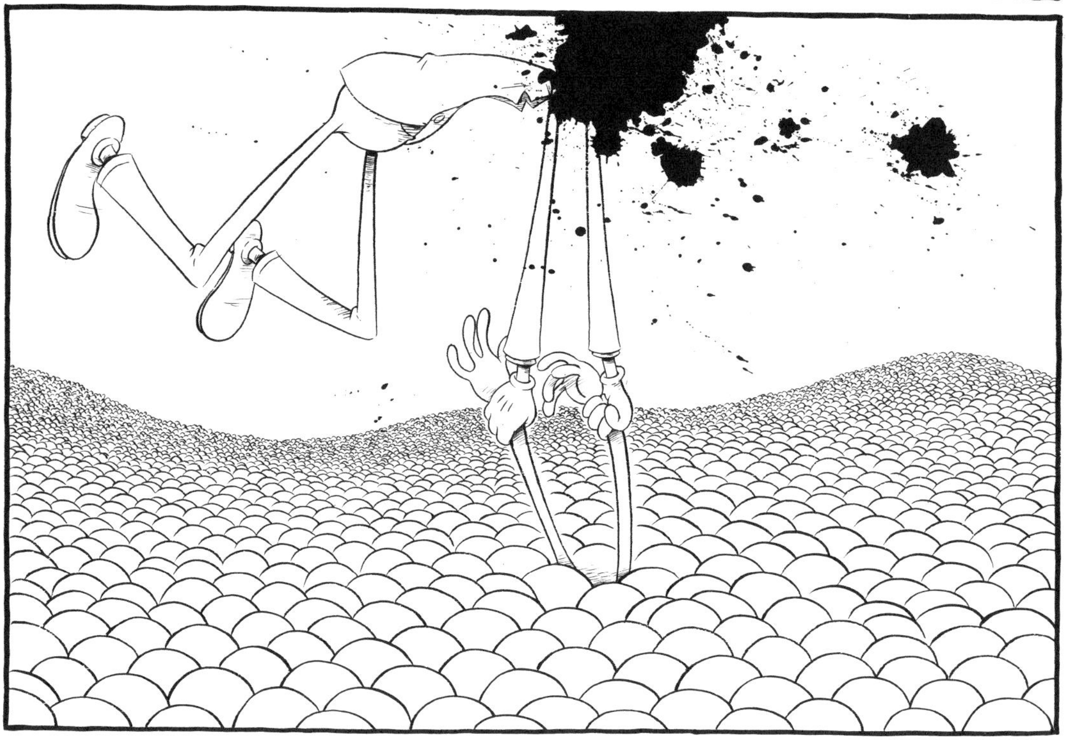

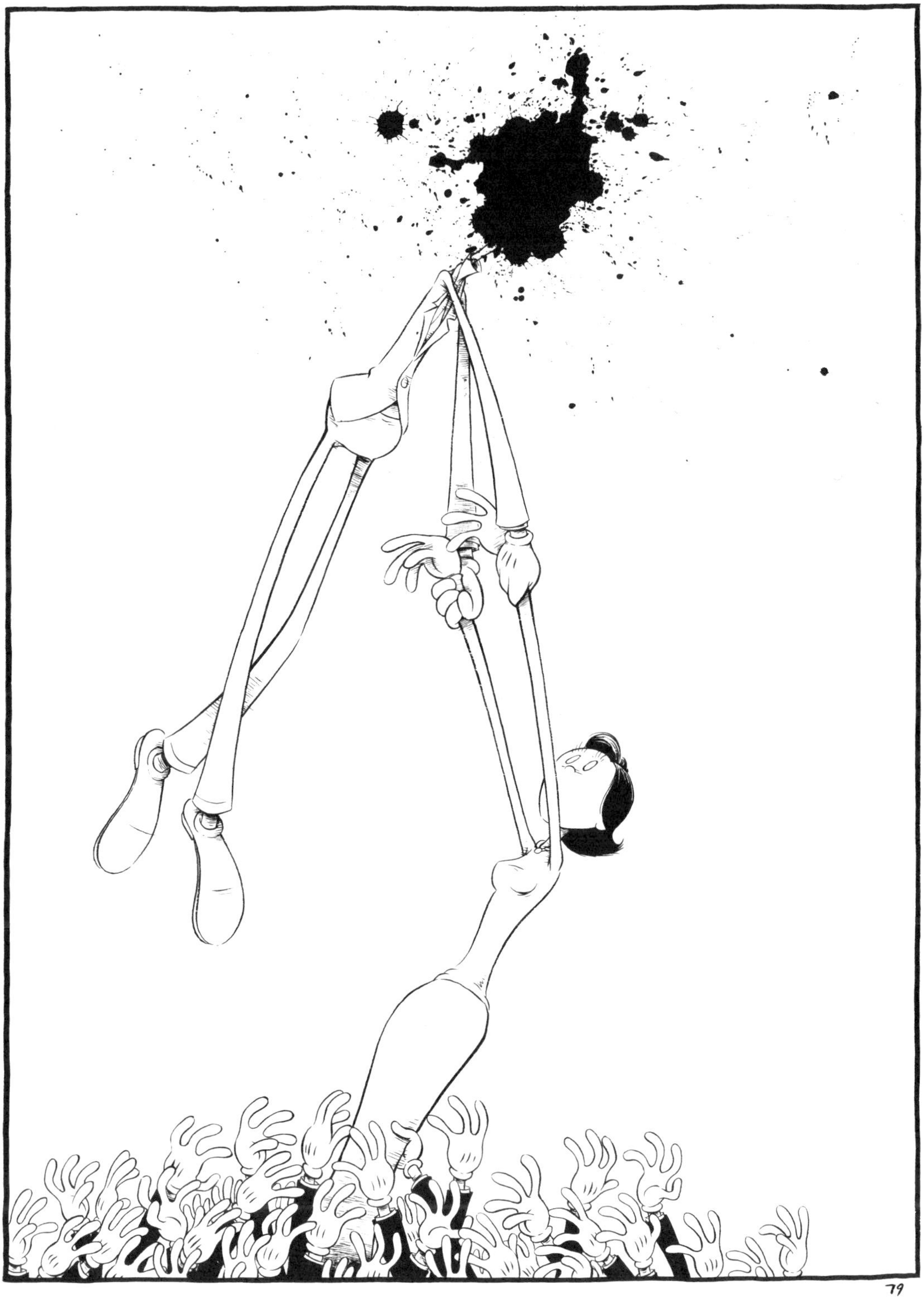

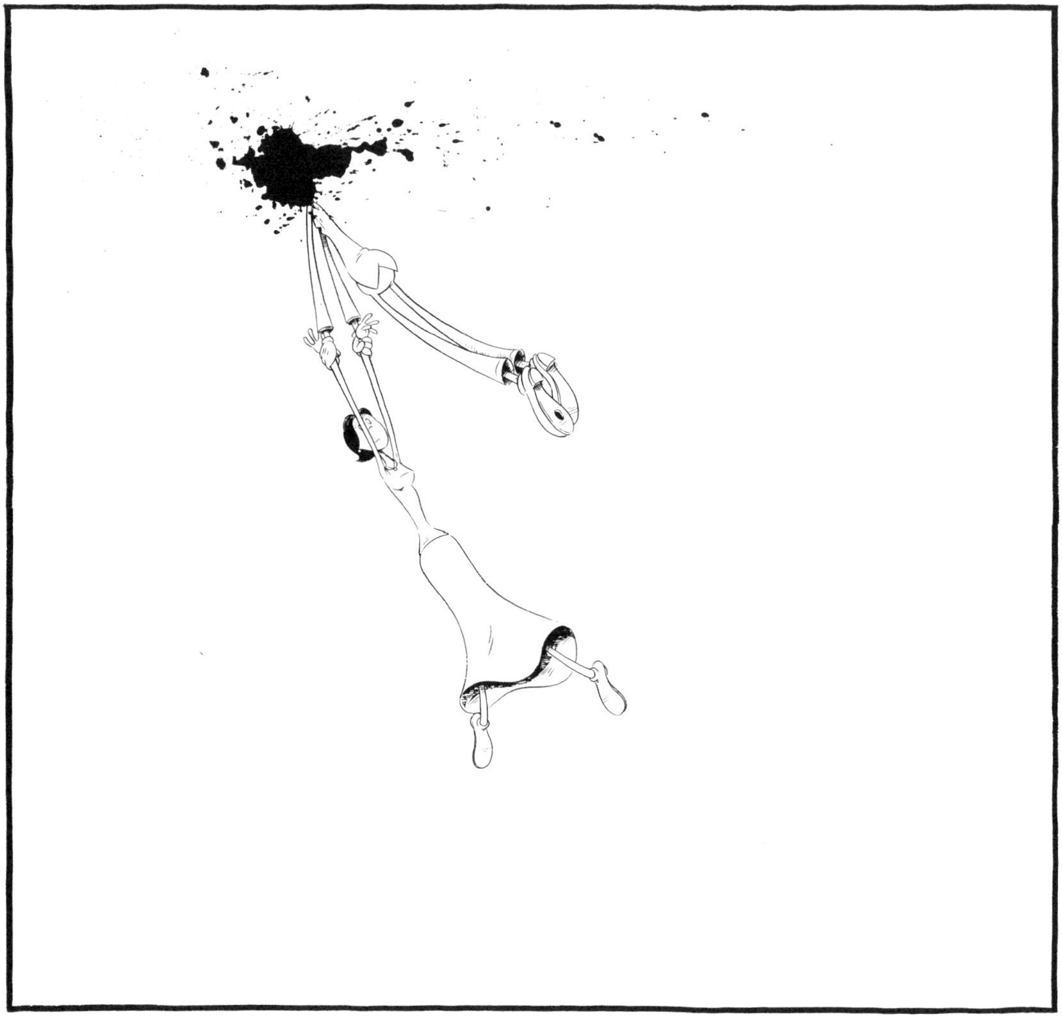

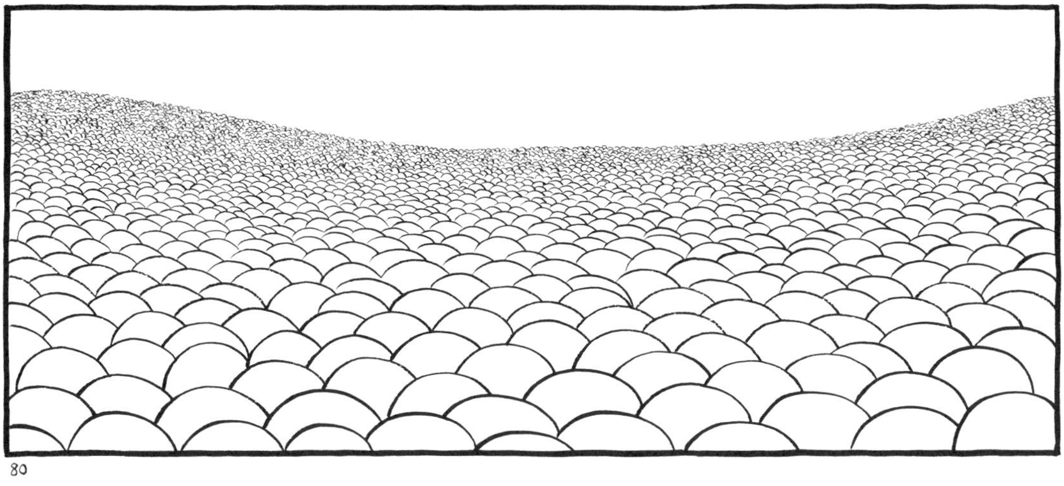

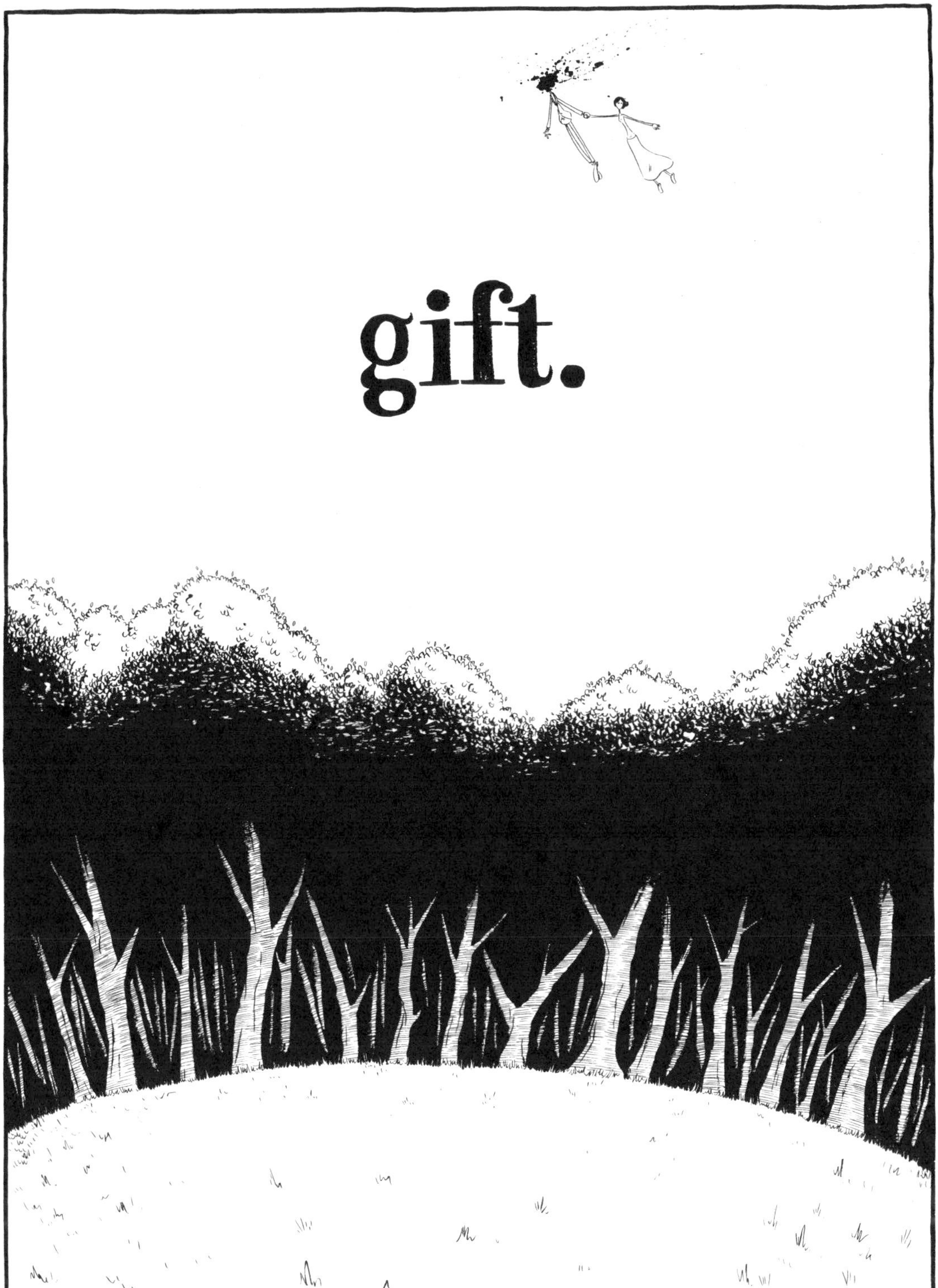
gift.

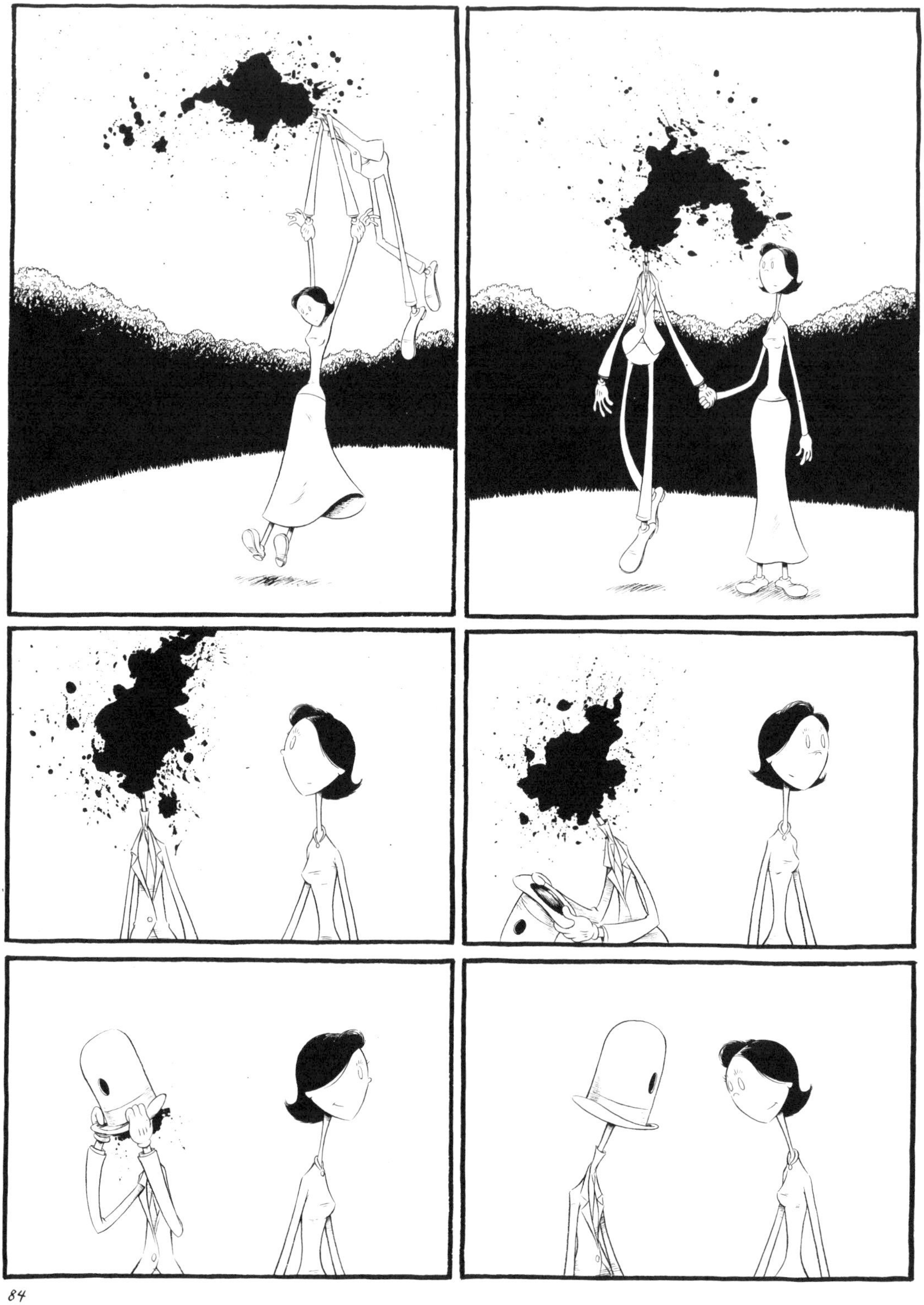

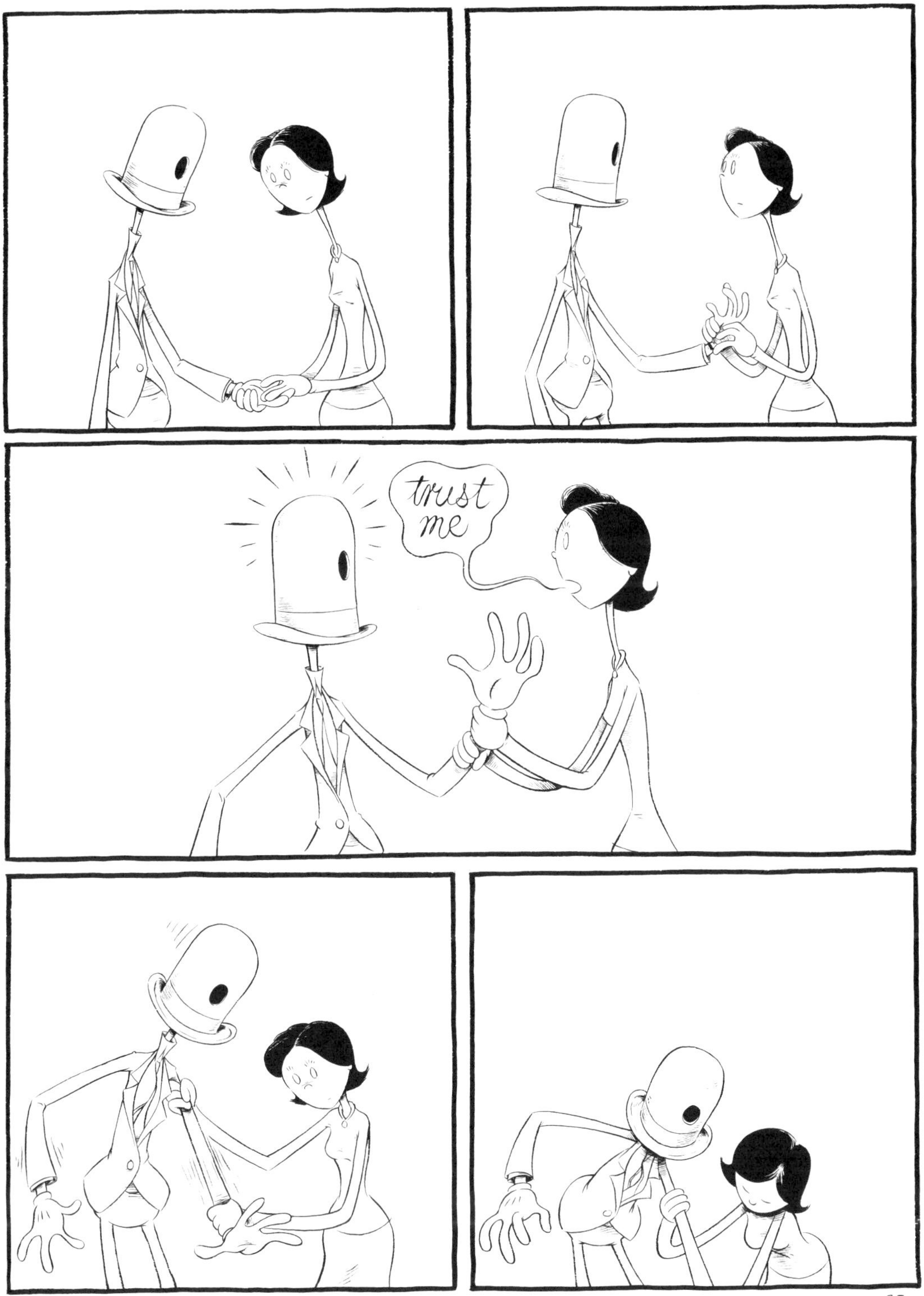
trust me

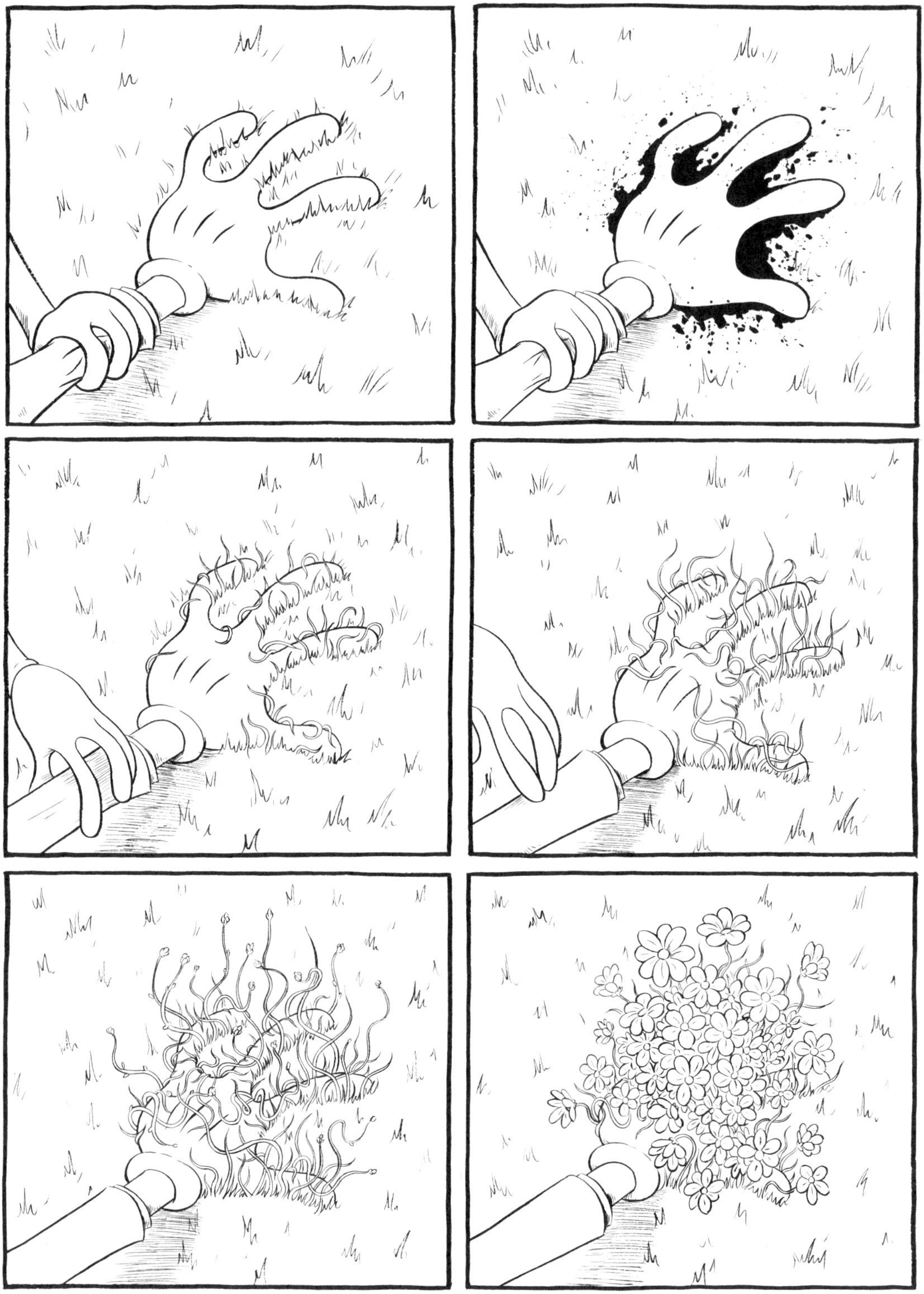

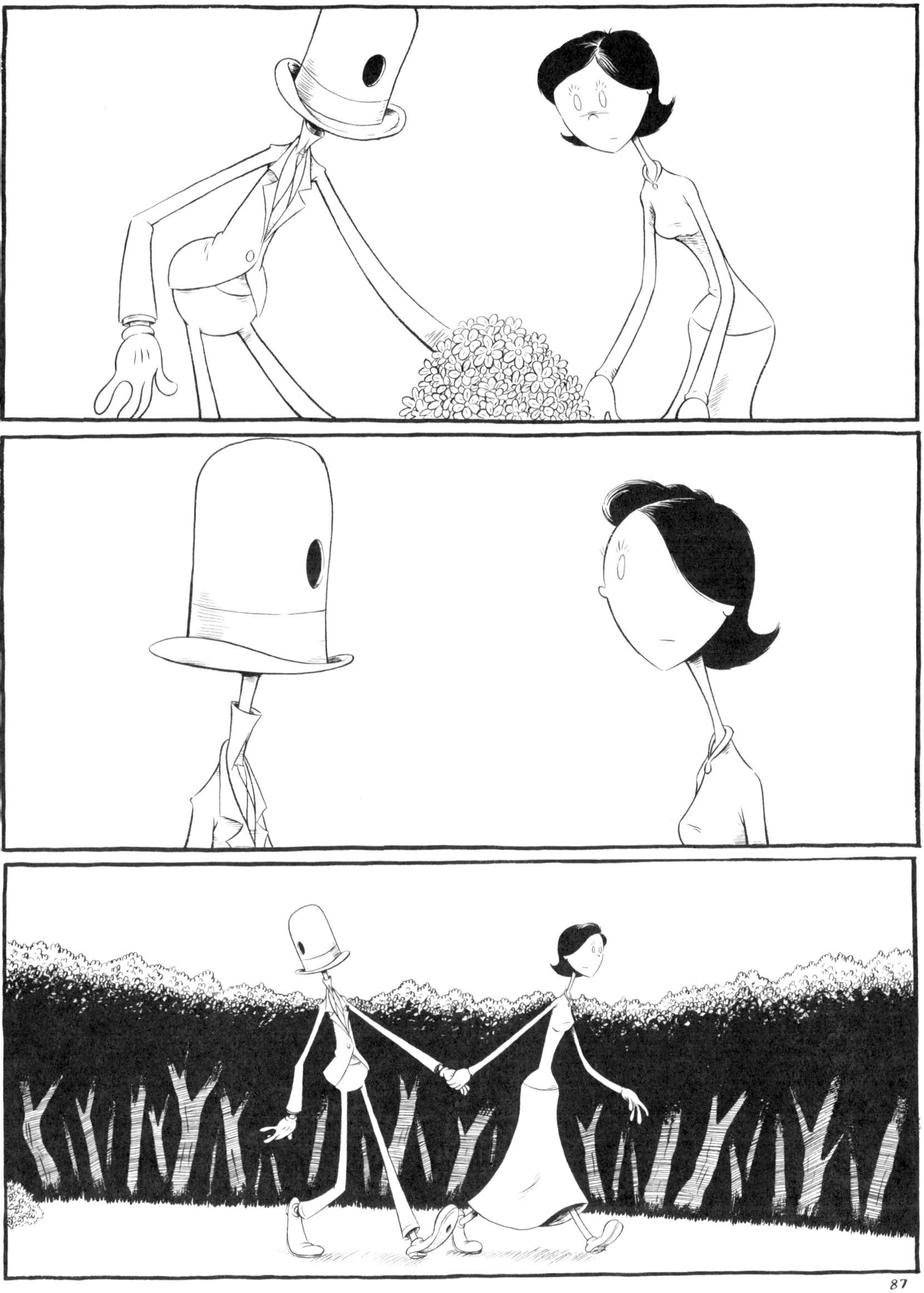

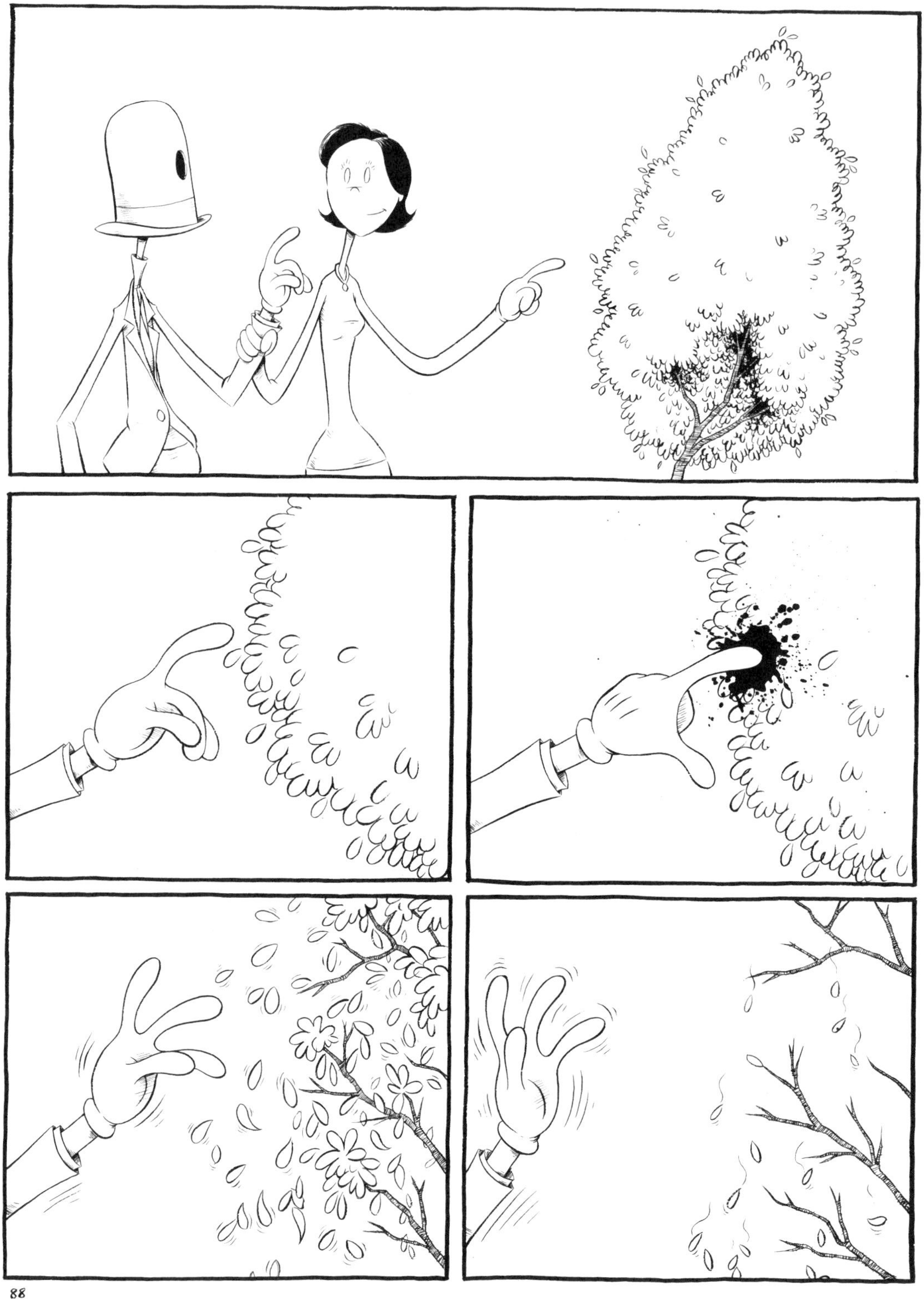

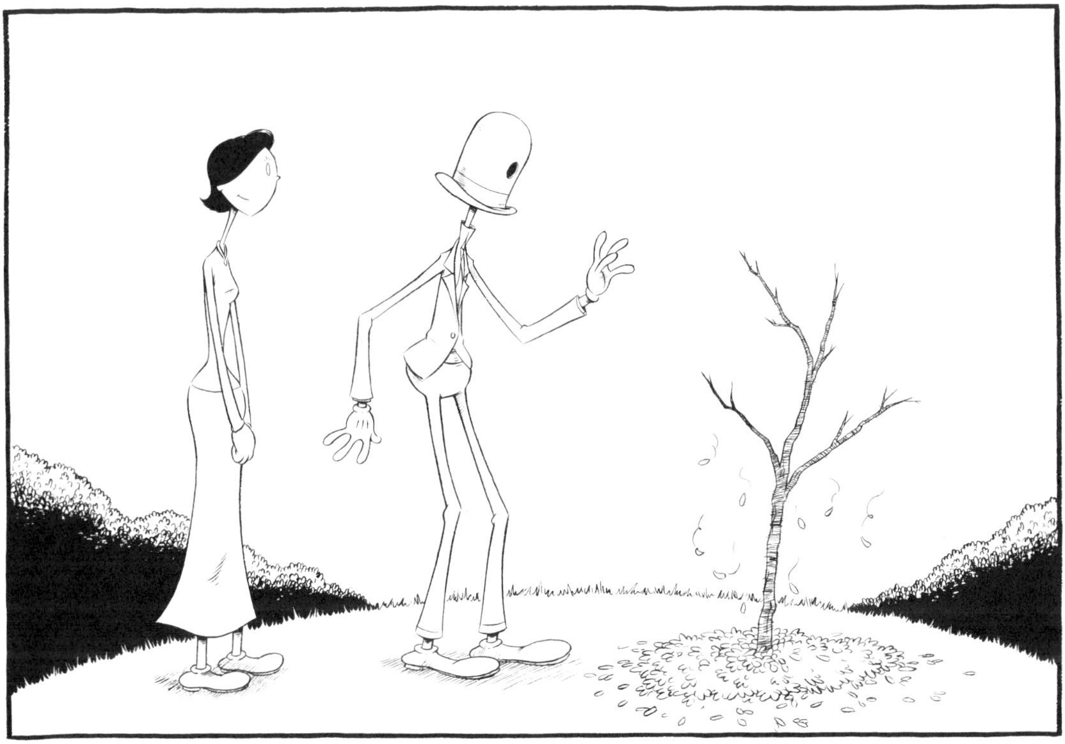

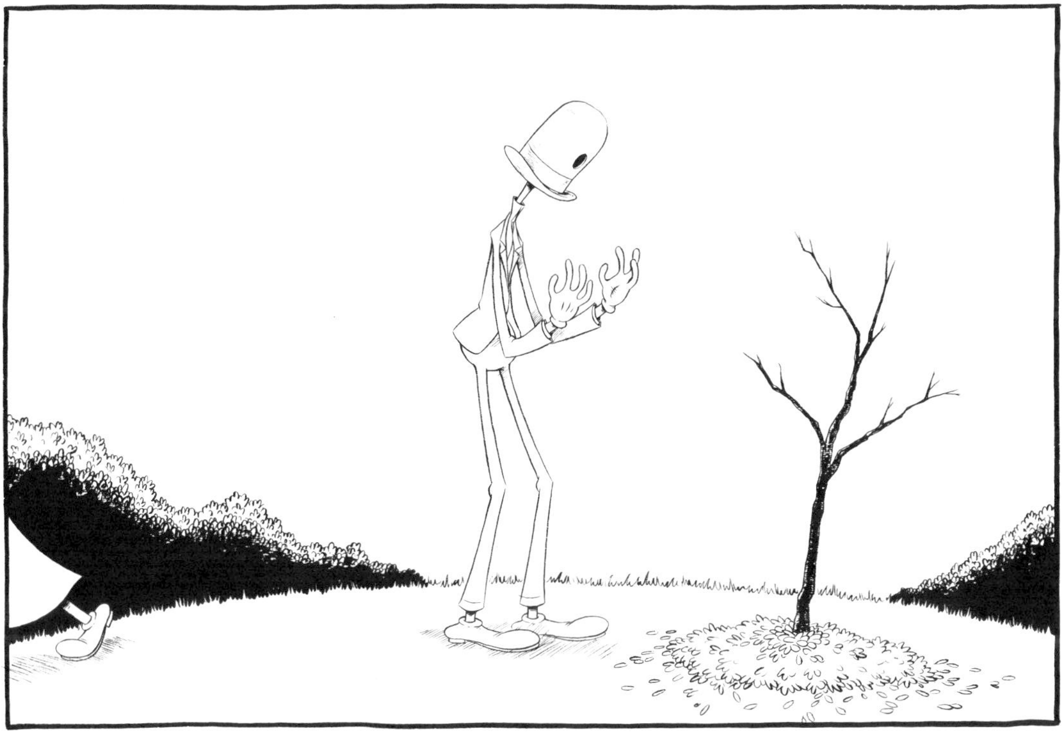

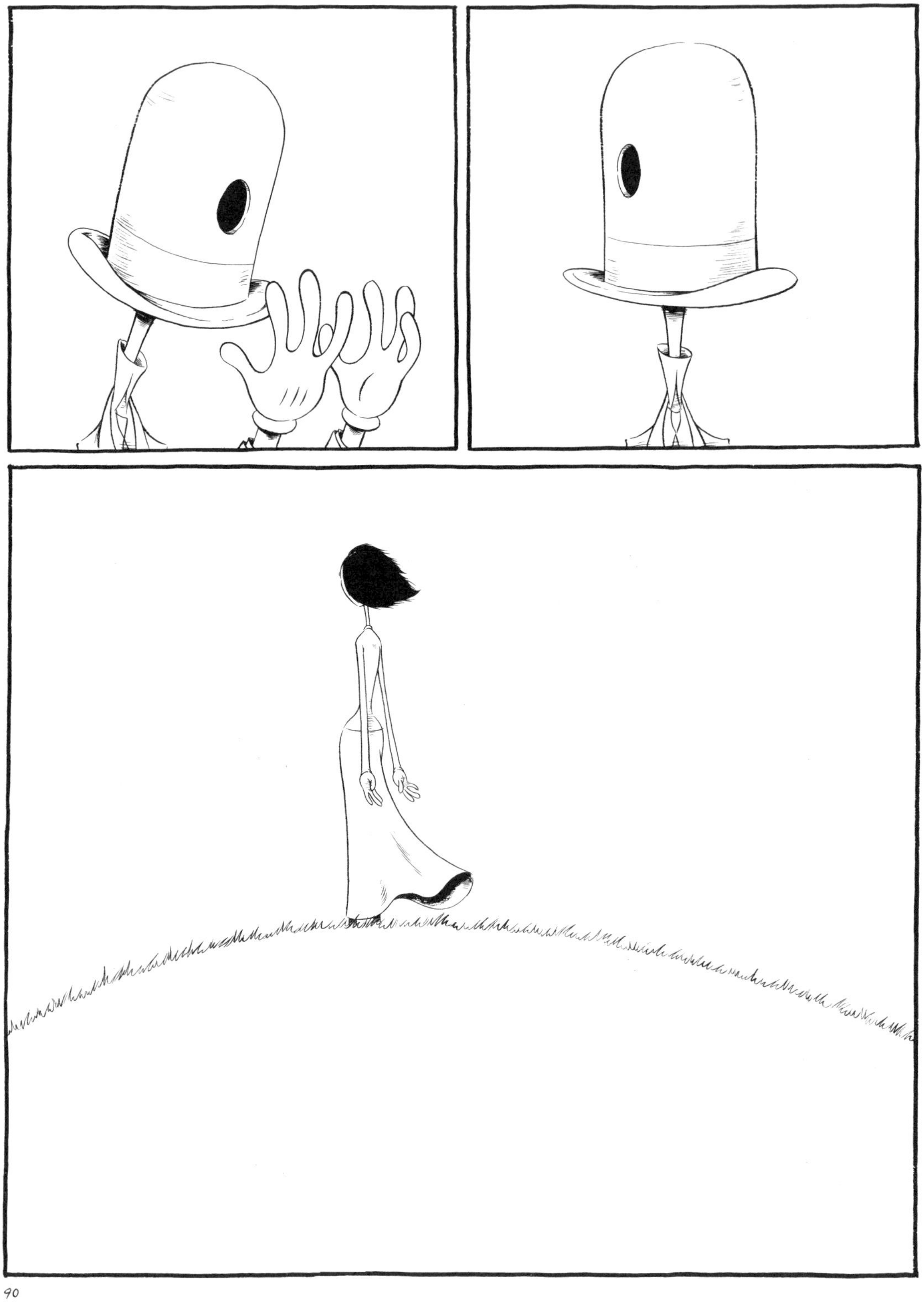

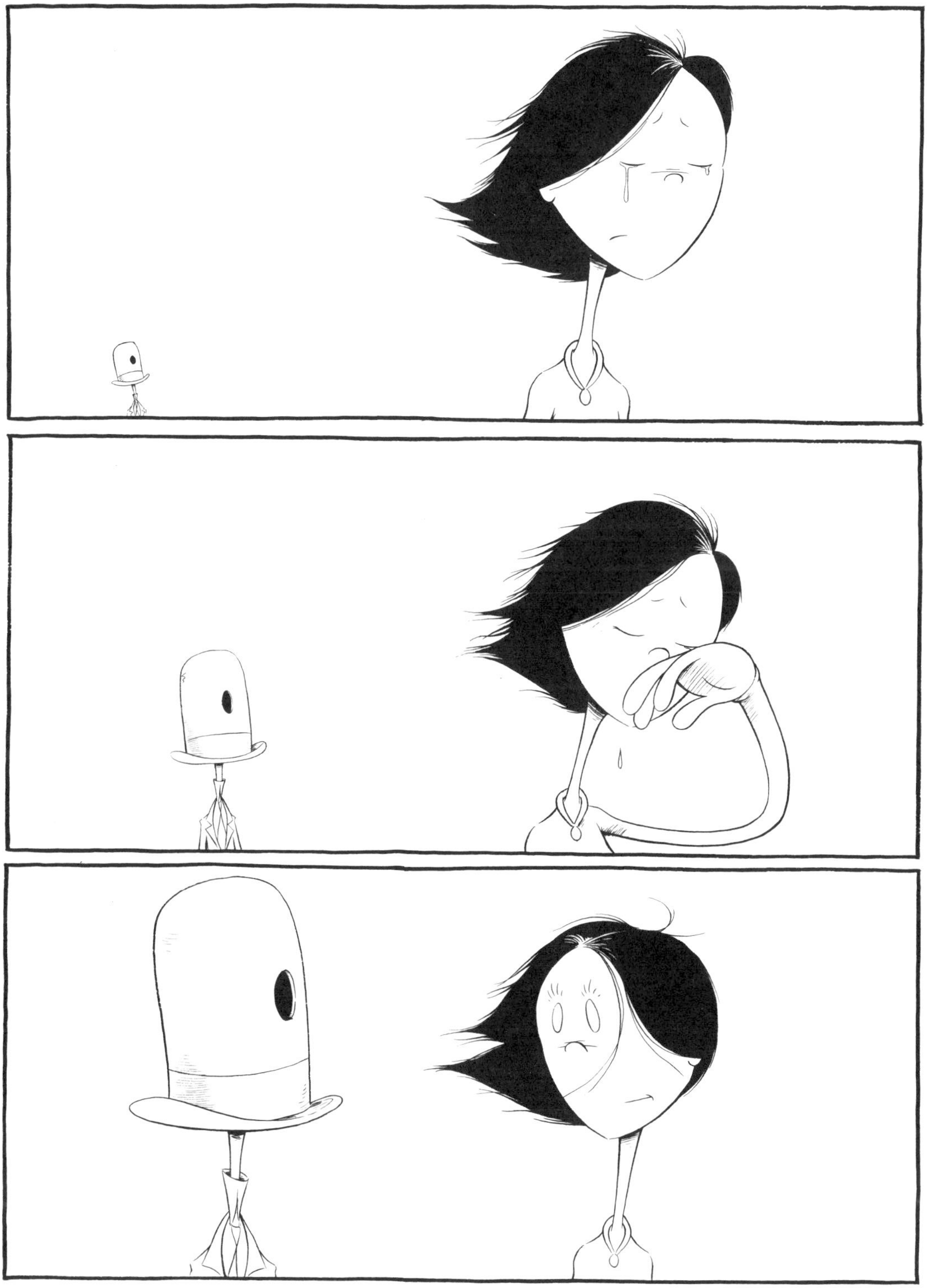

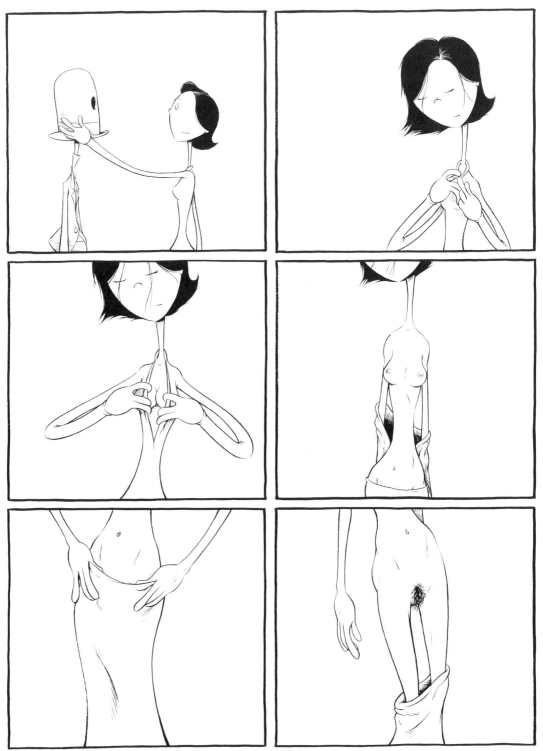

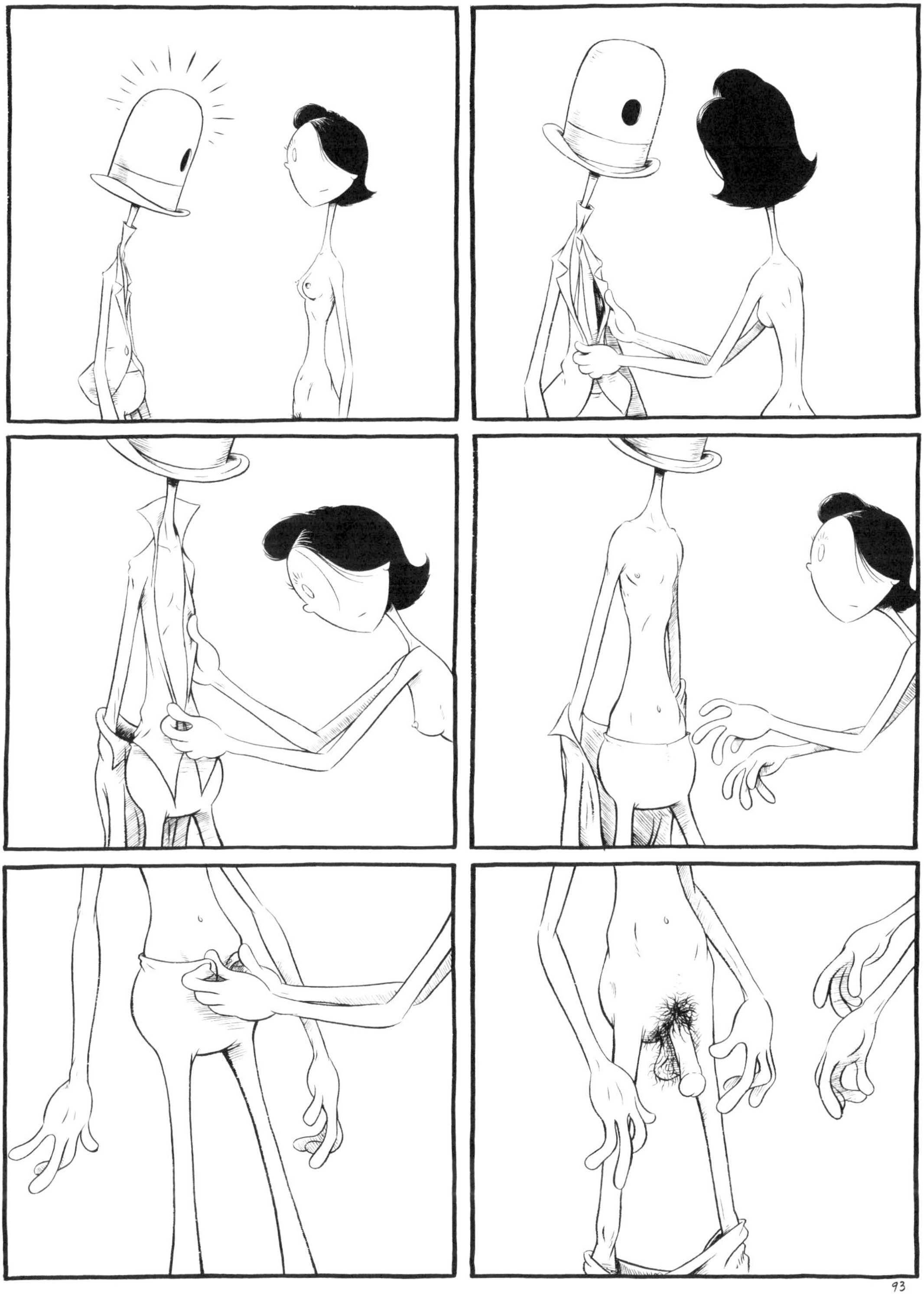

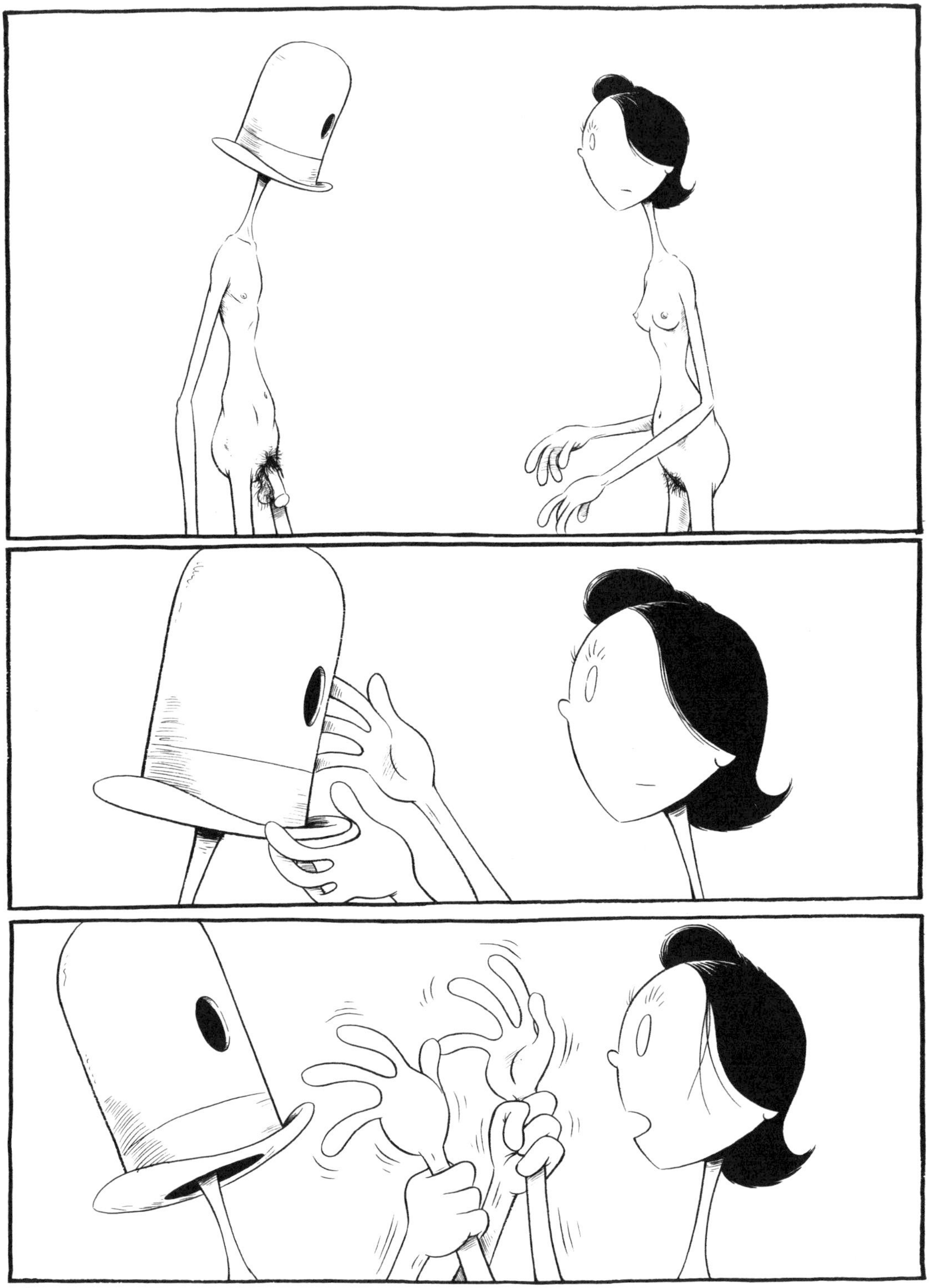

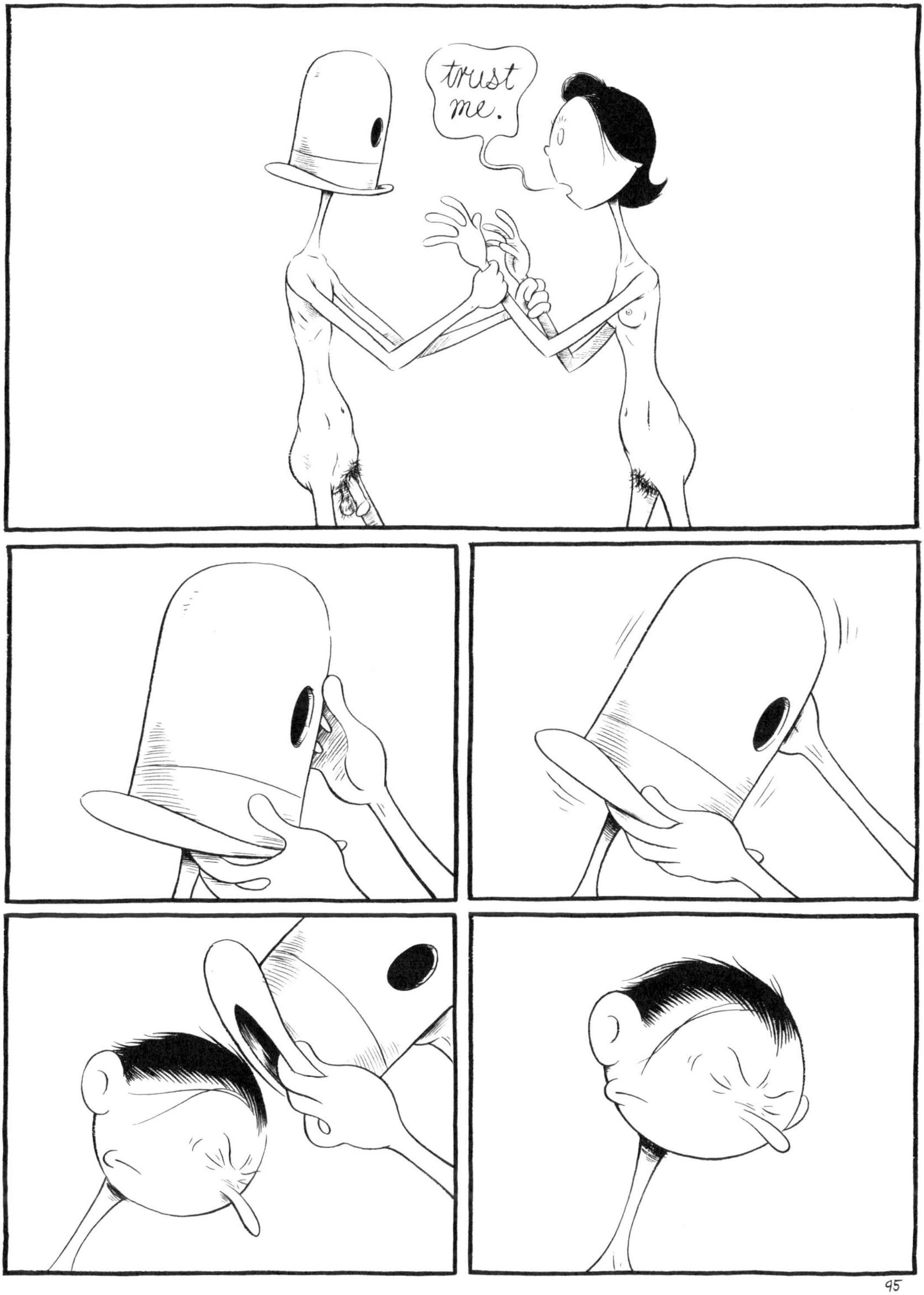
trust me.

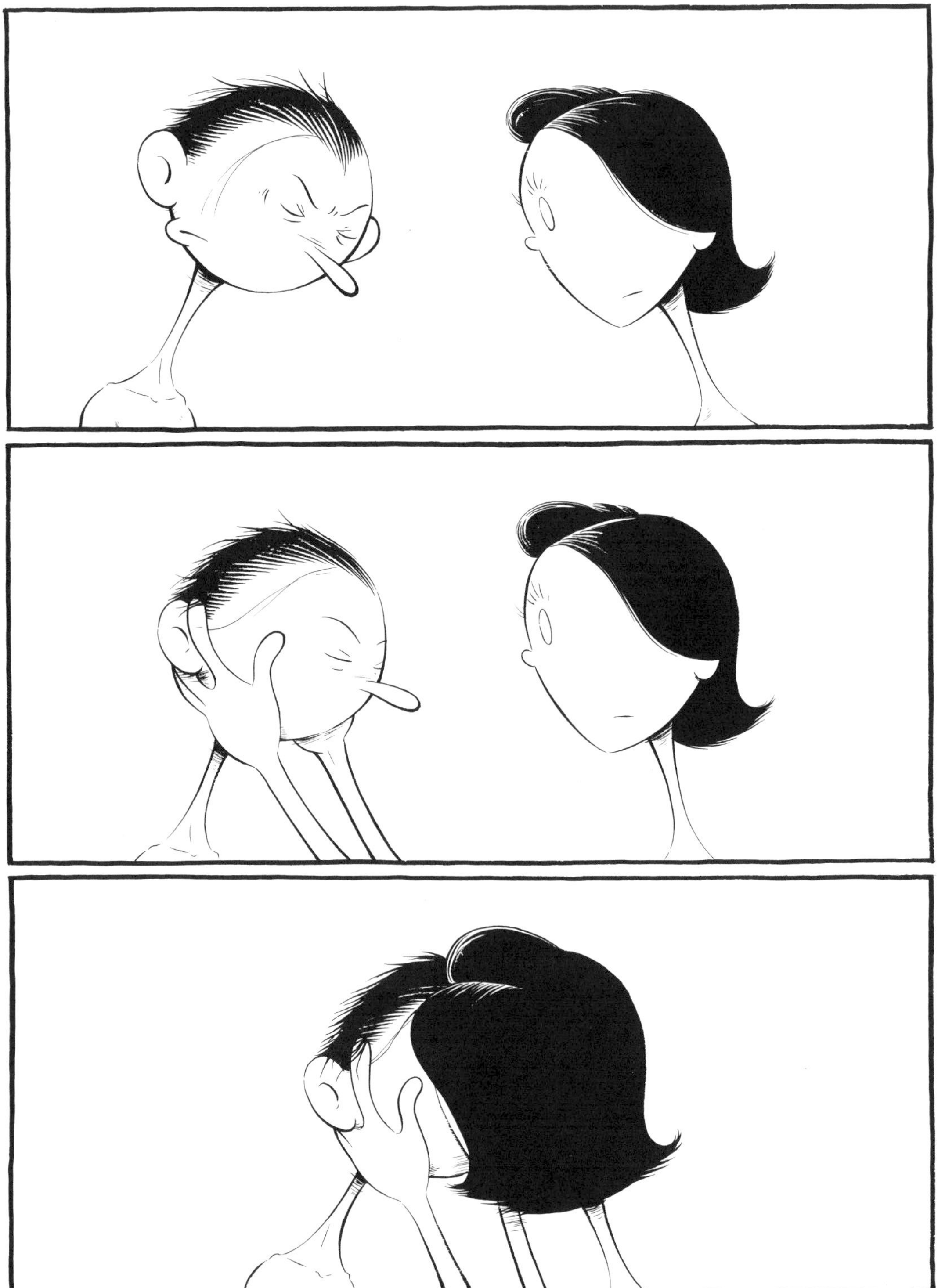

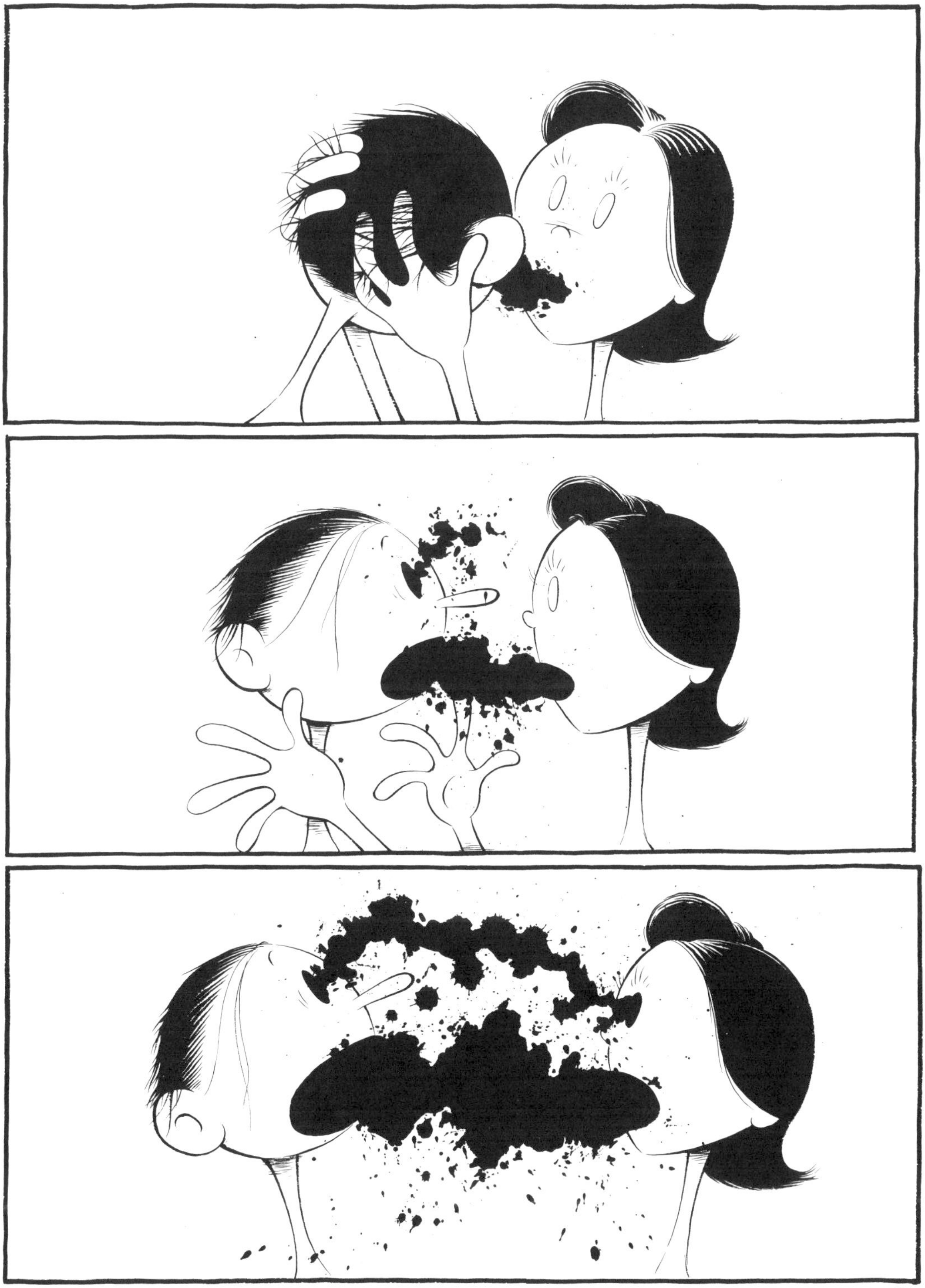

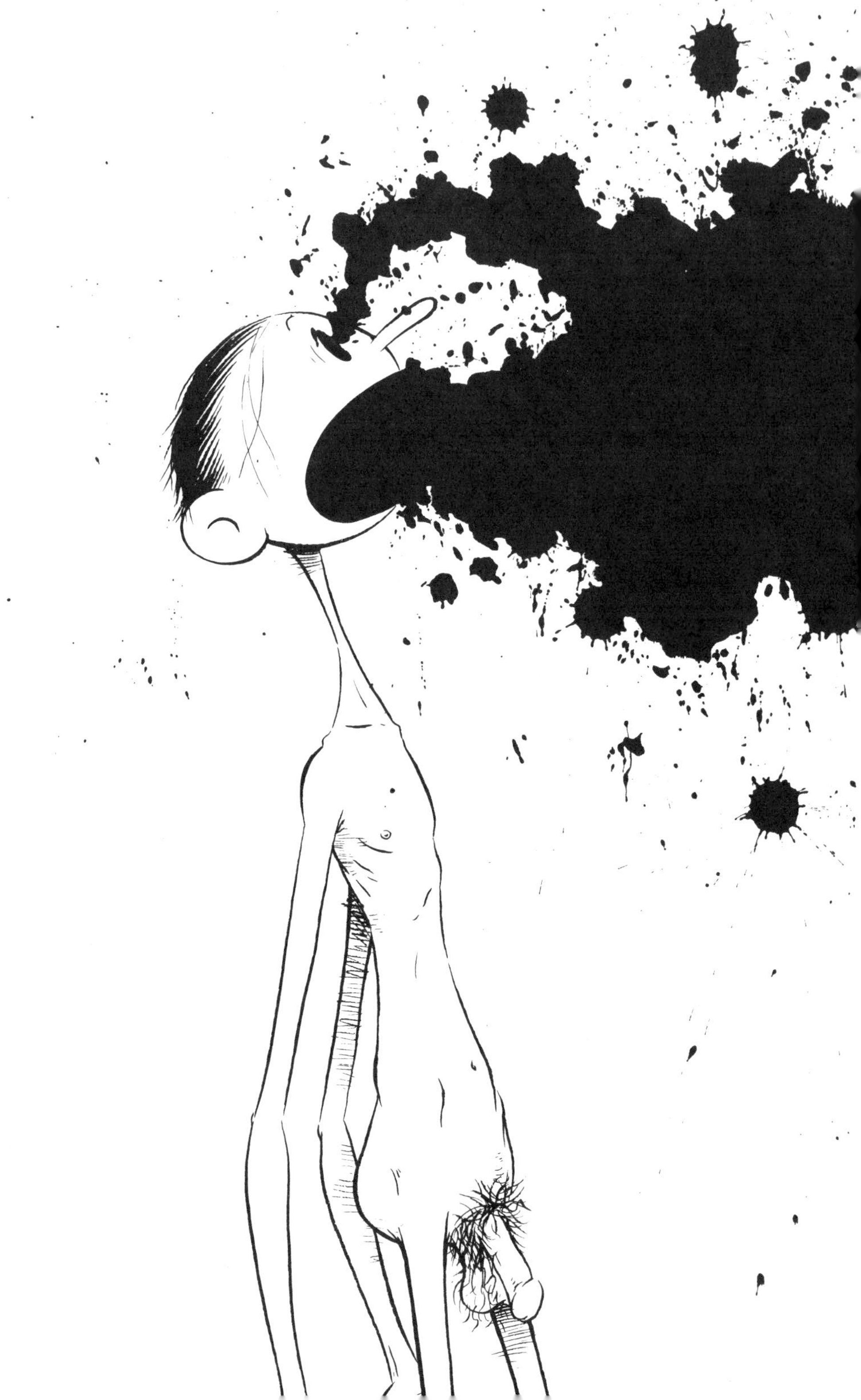

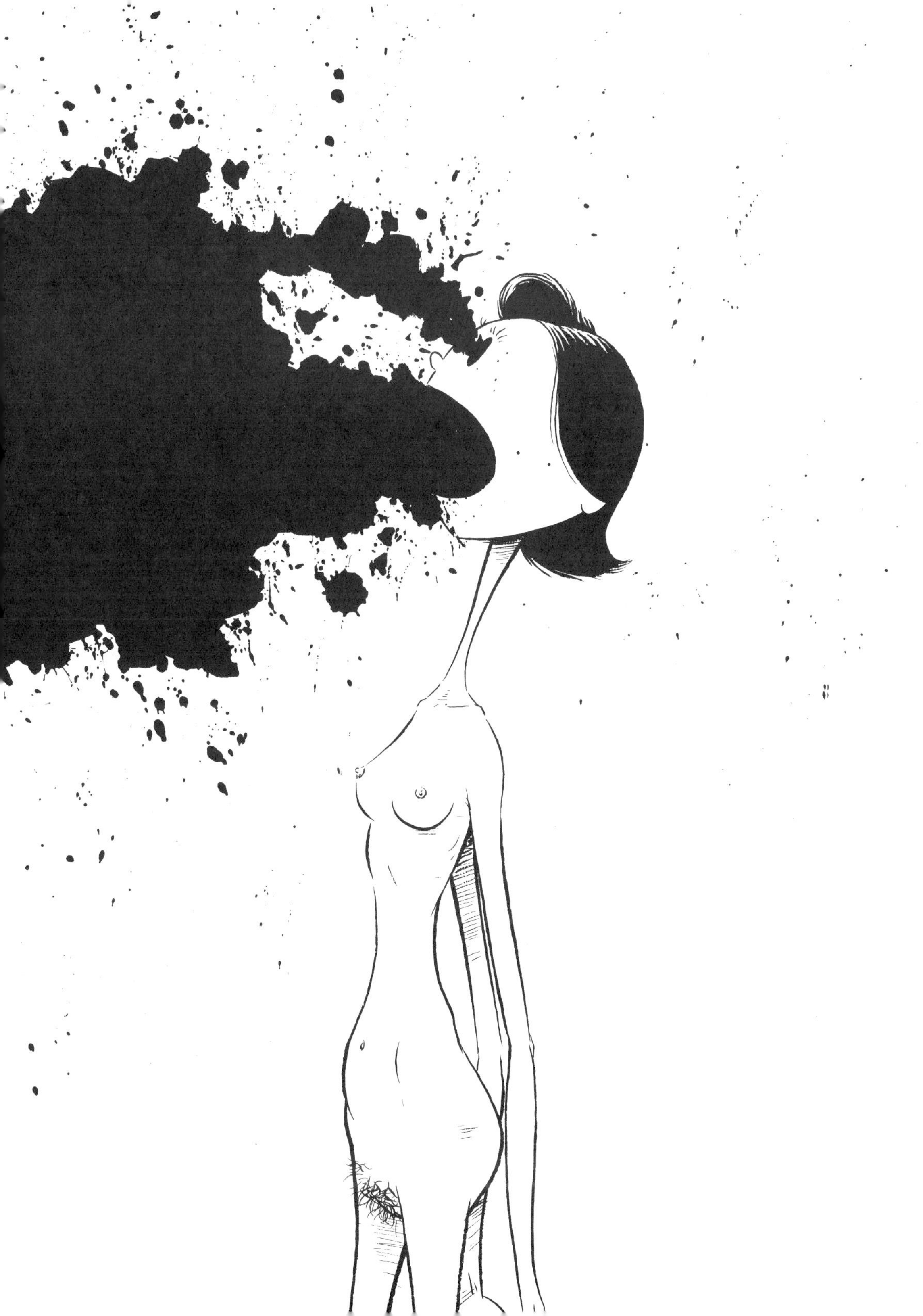

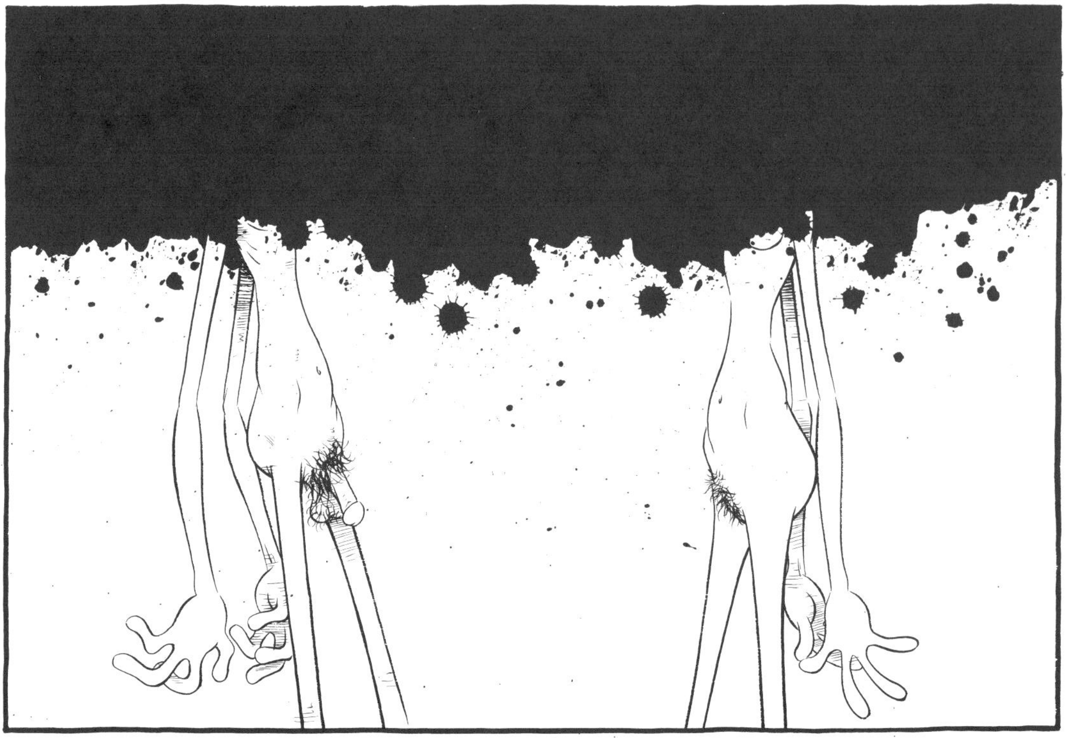

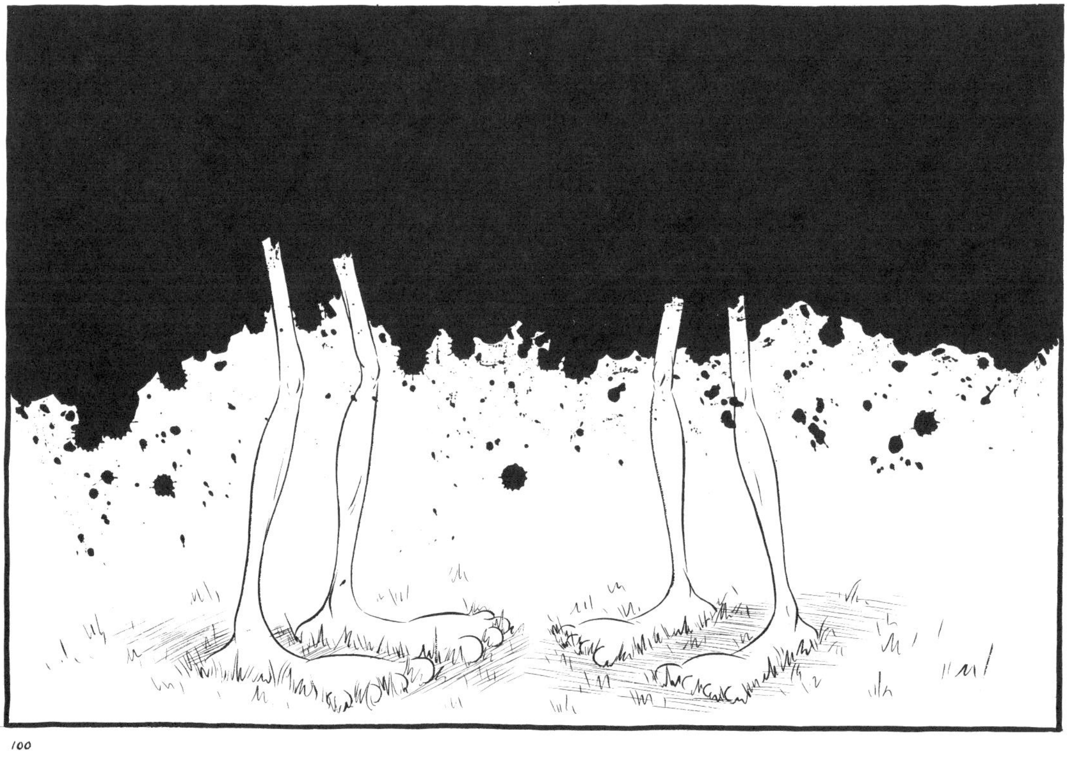

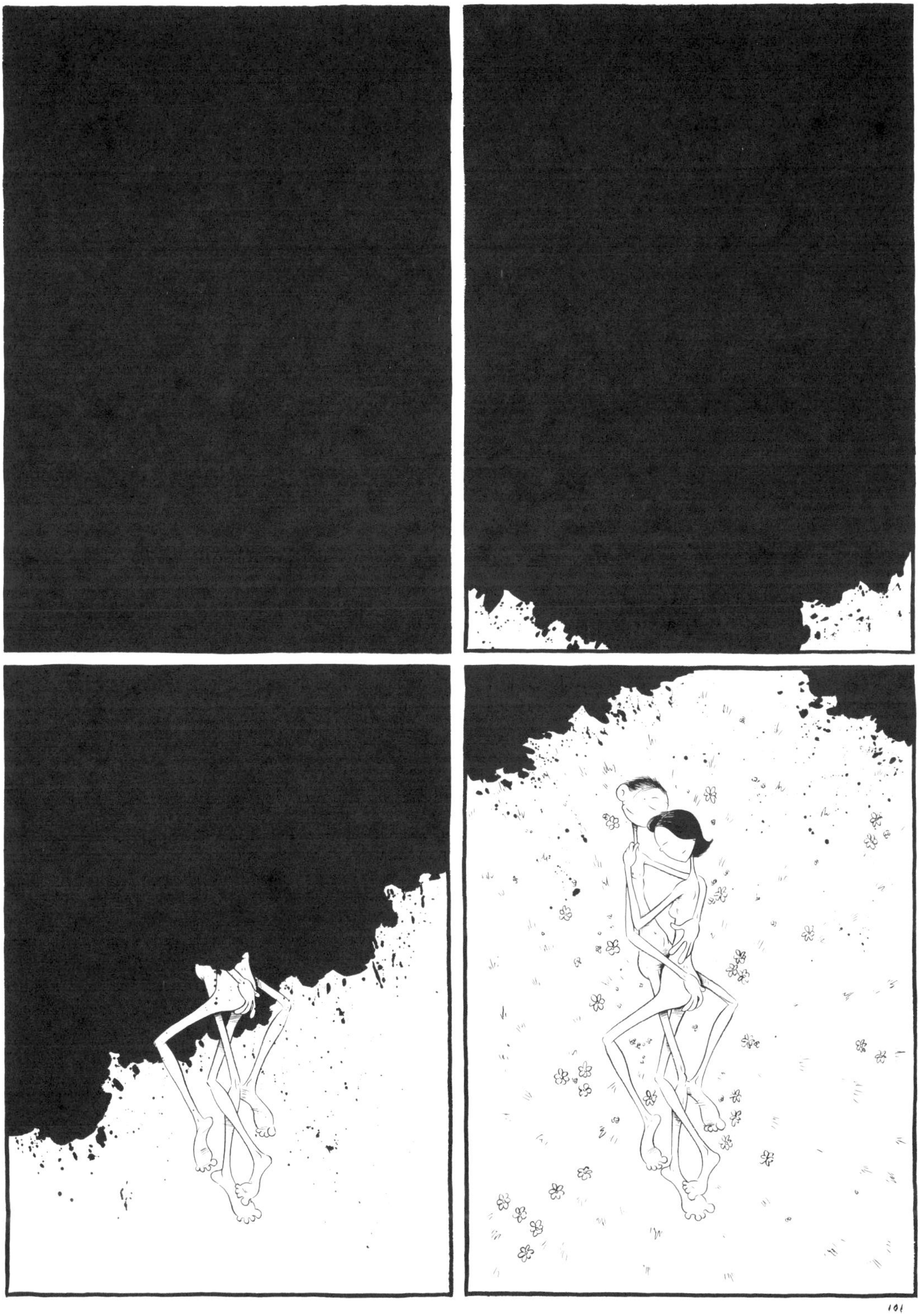

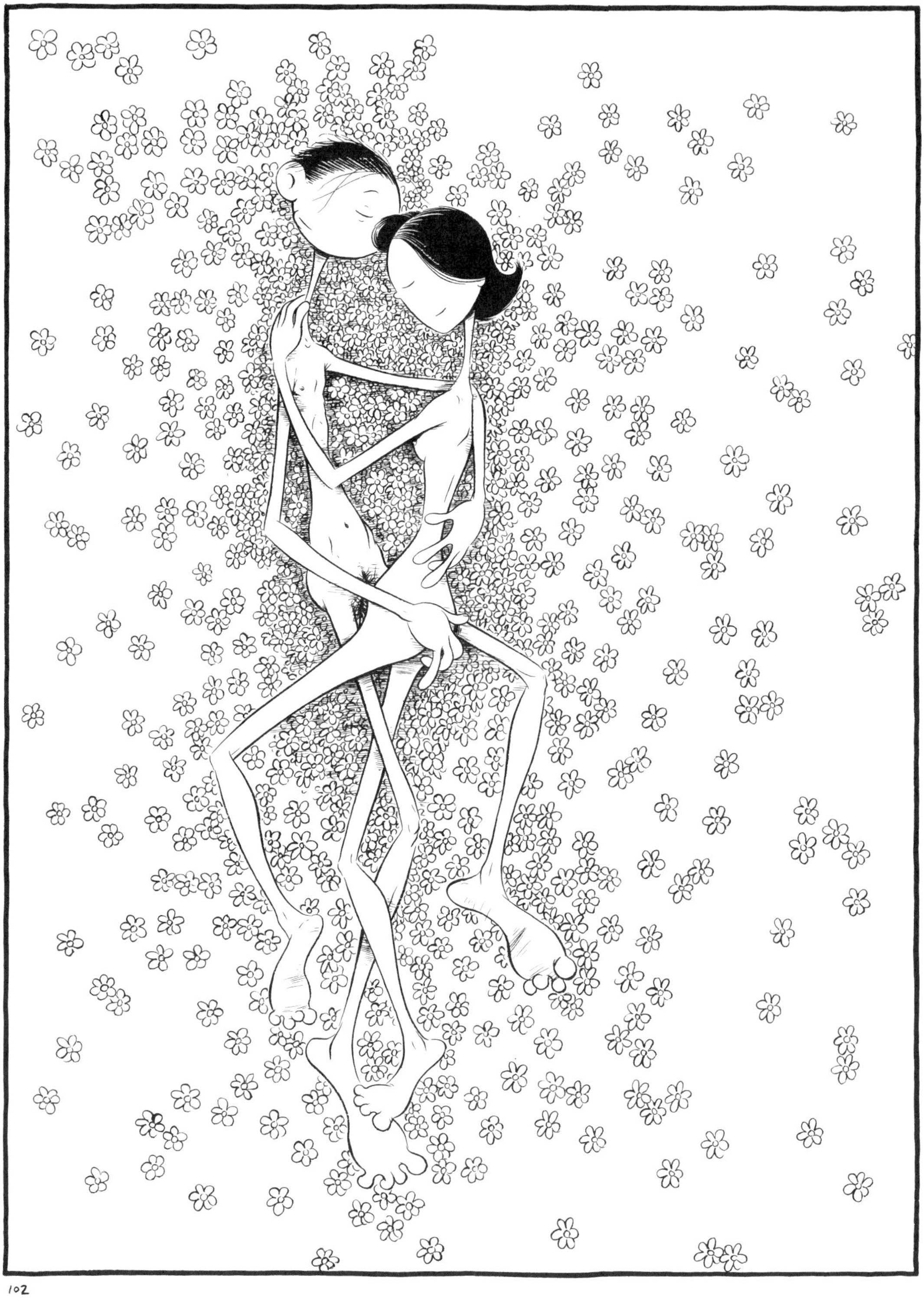

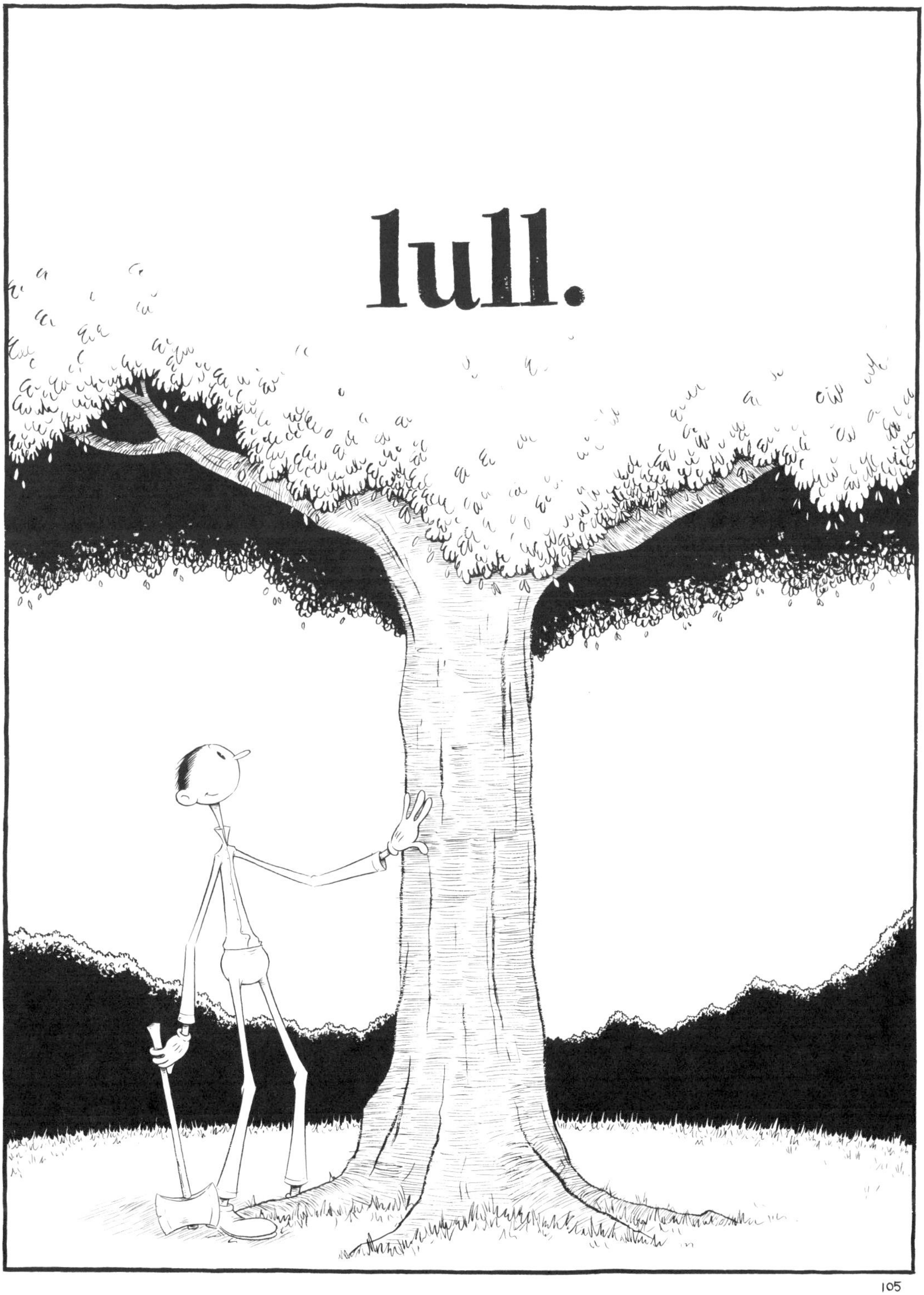
lull.

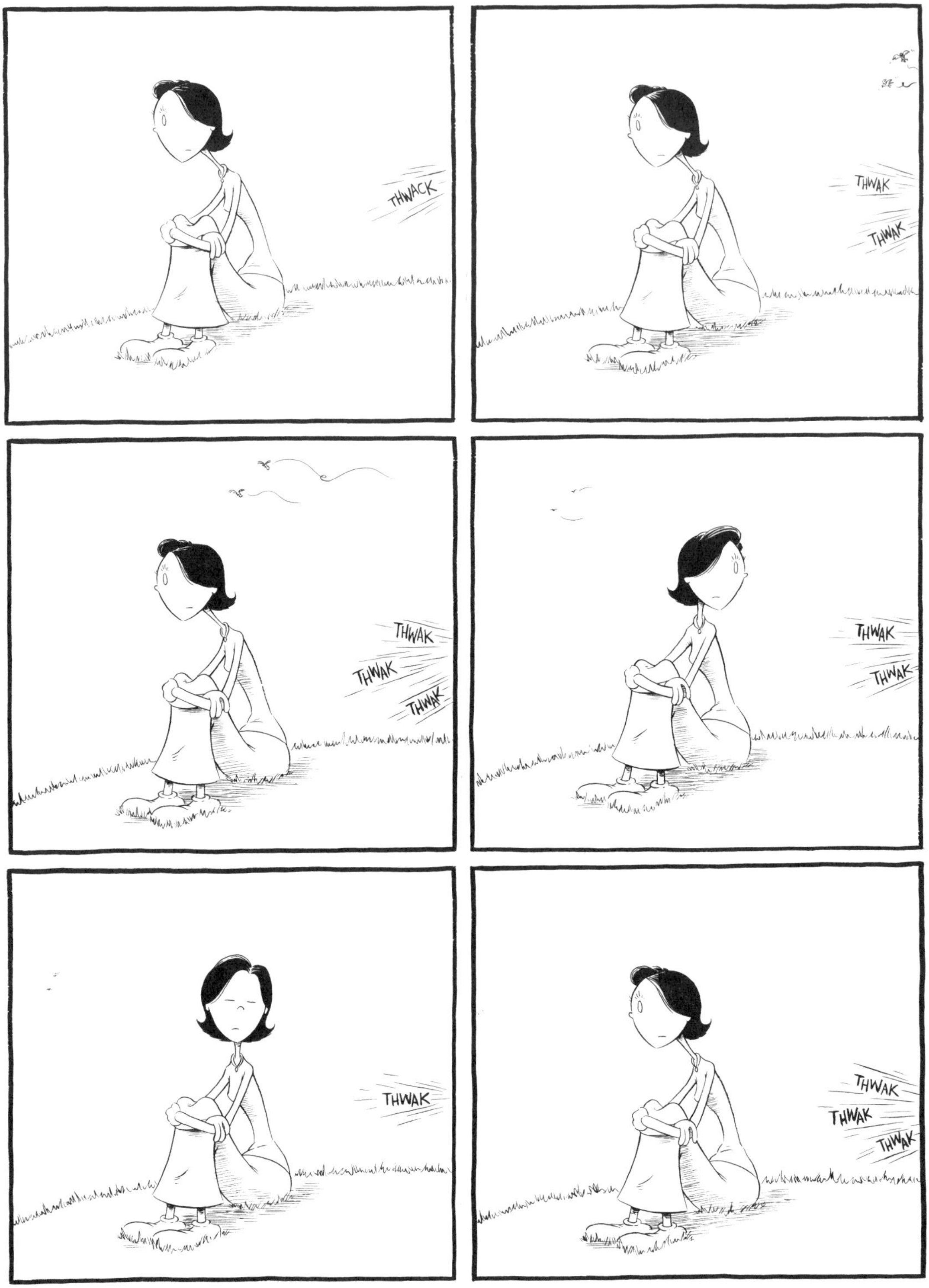
THWACK
THWAK
THWAK
THWAK
THWAK
THWAK
THWAK
THWAK
THWAK
THWAK
THWAK
THWAK

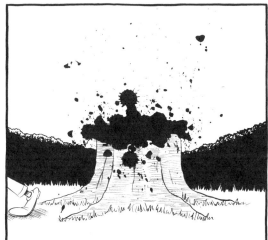

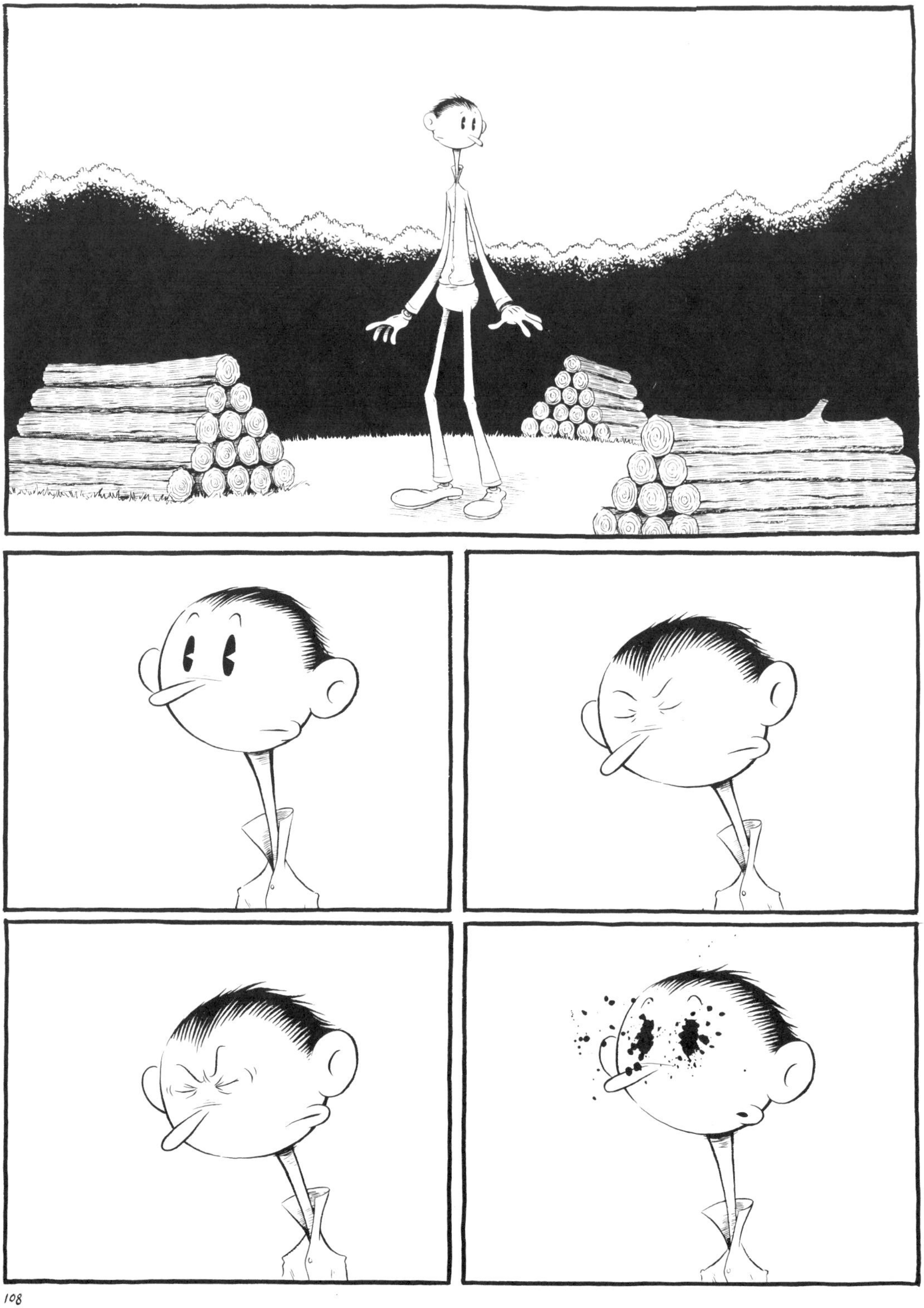

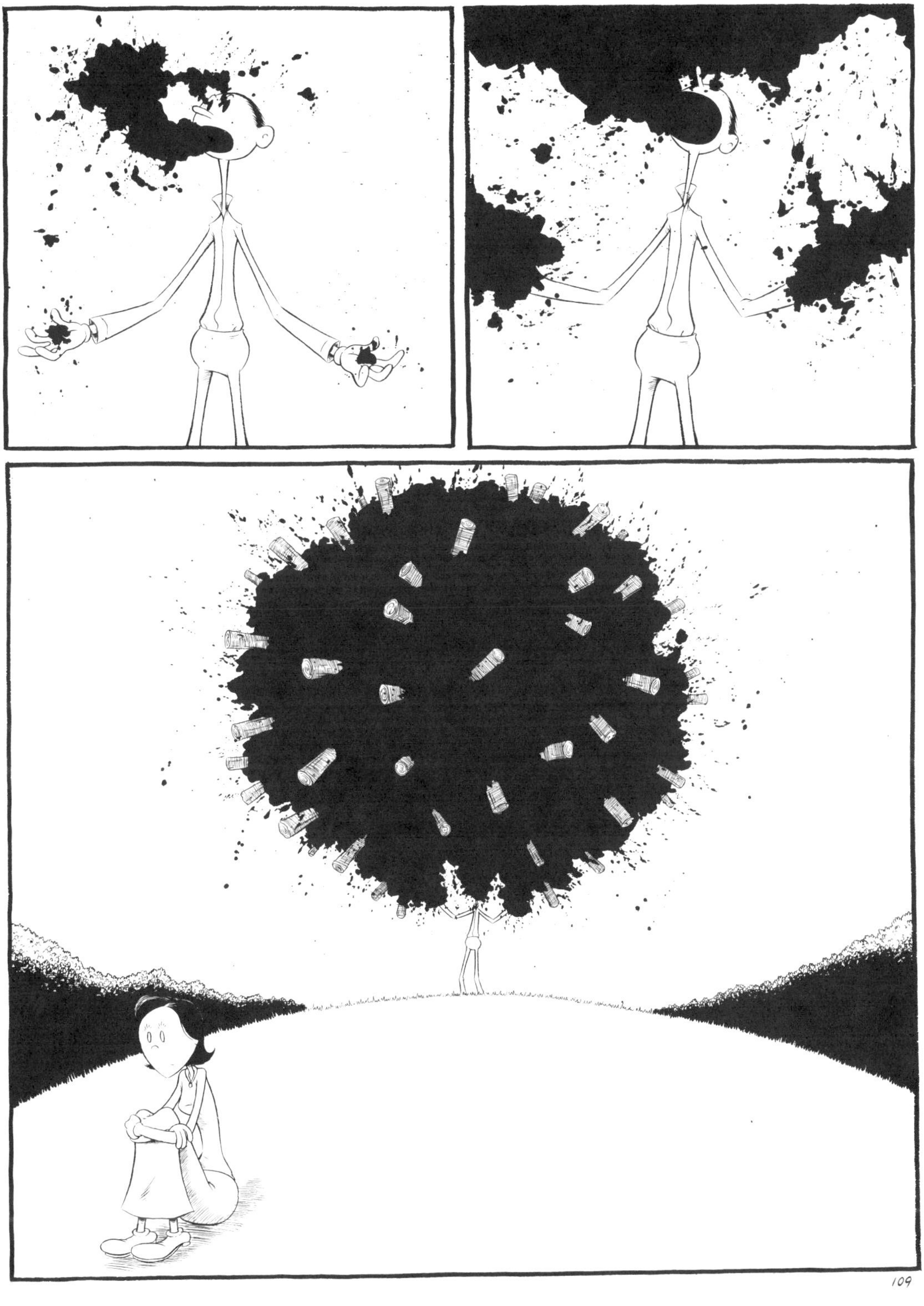

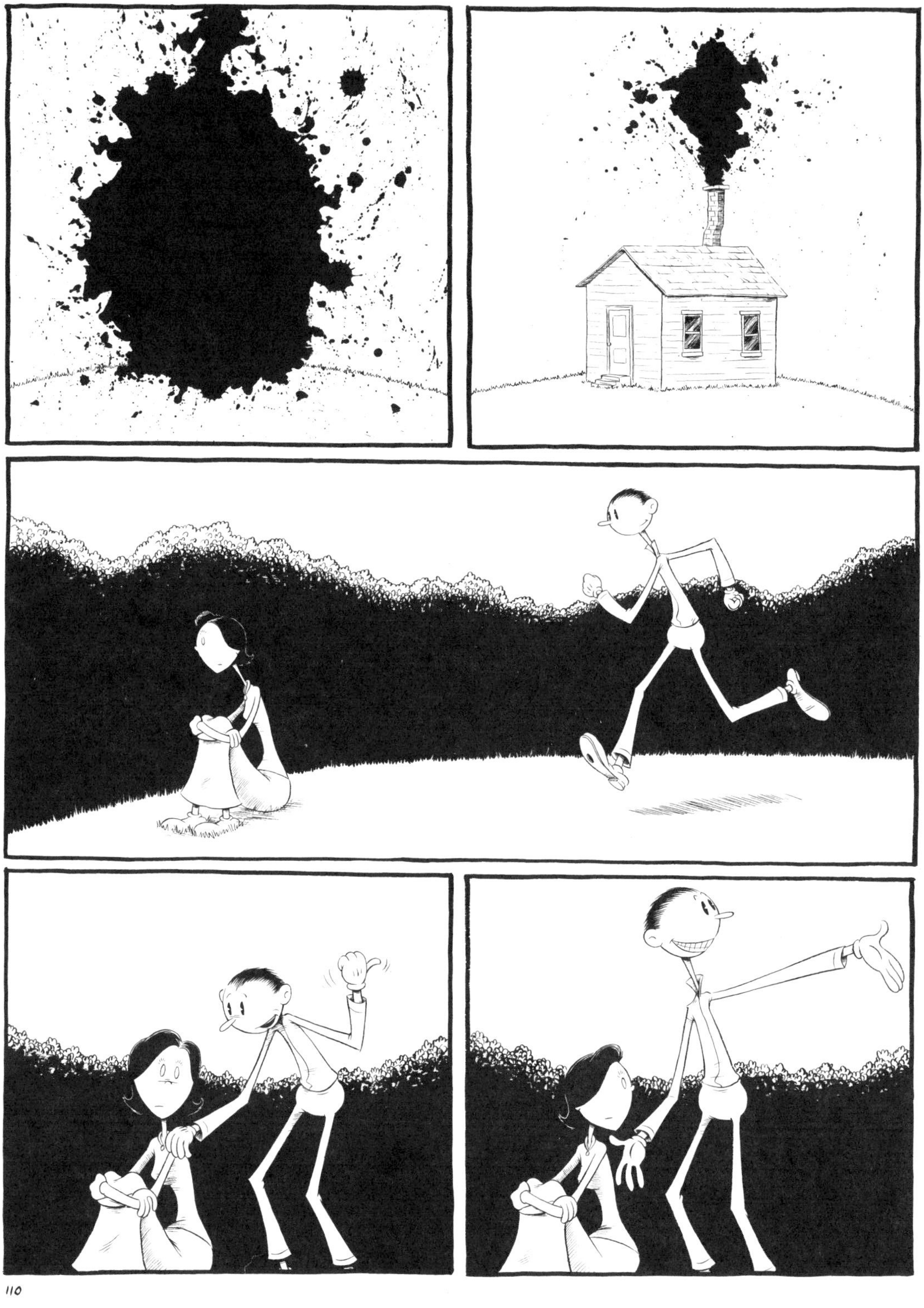

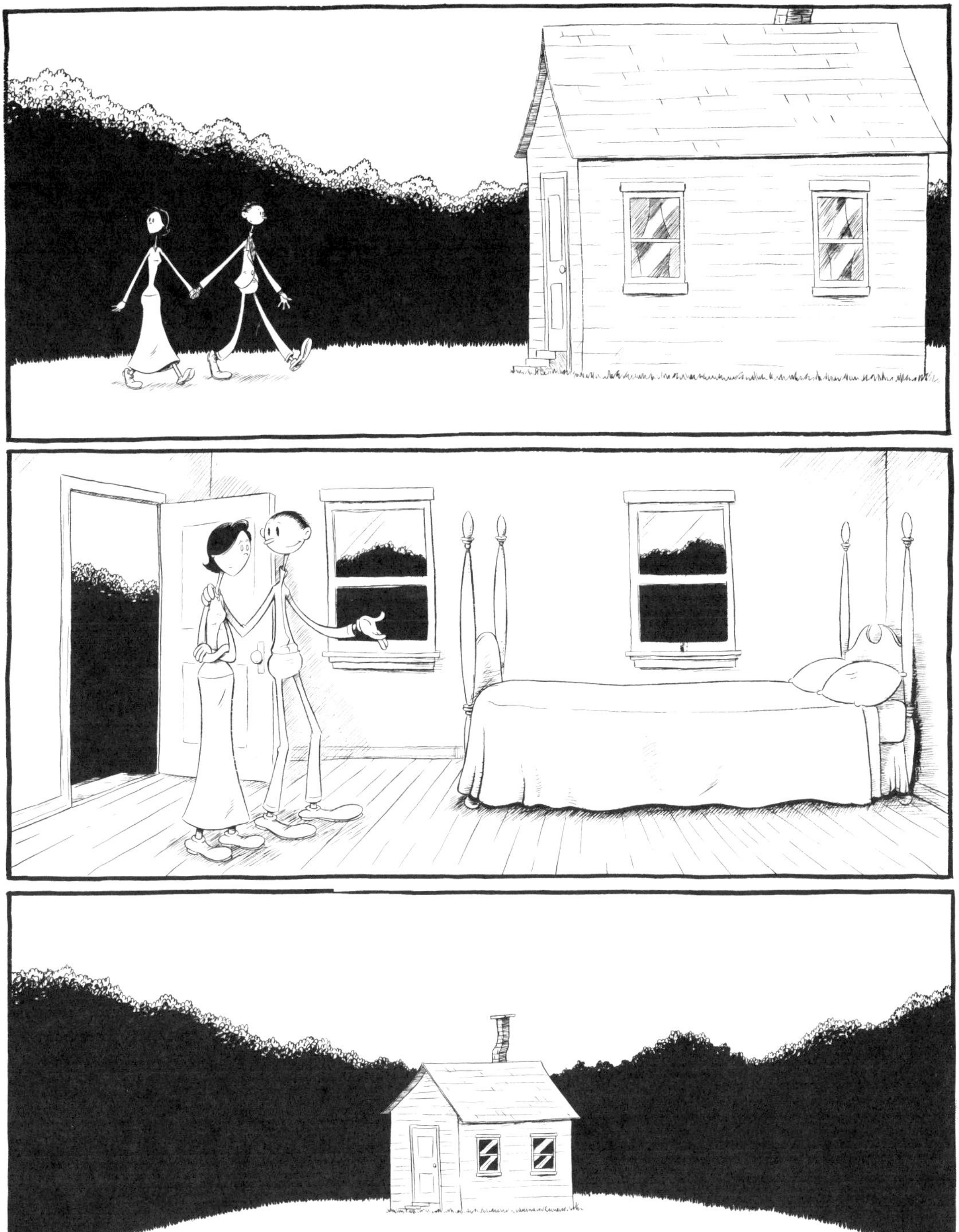

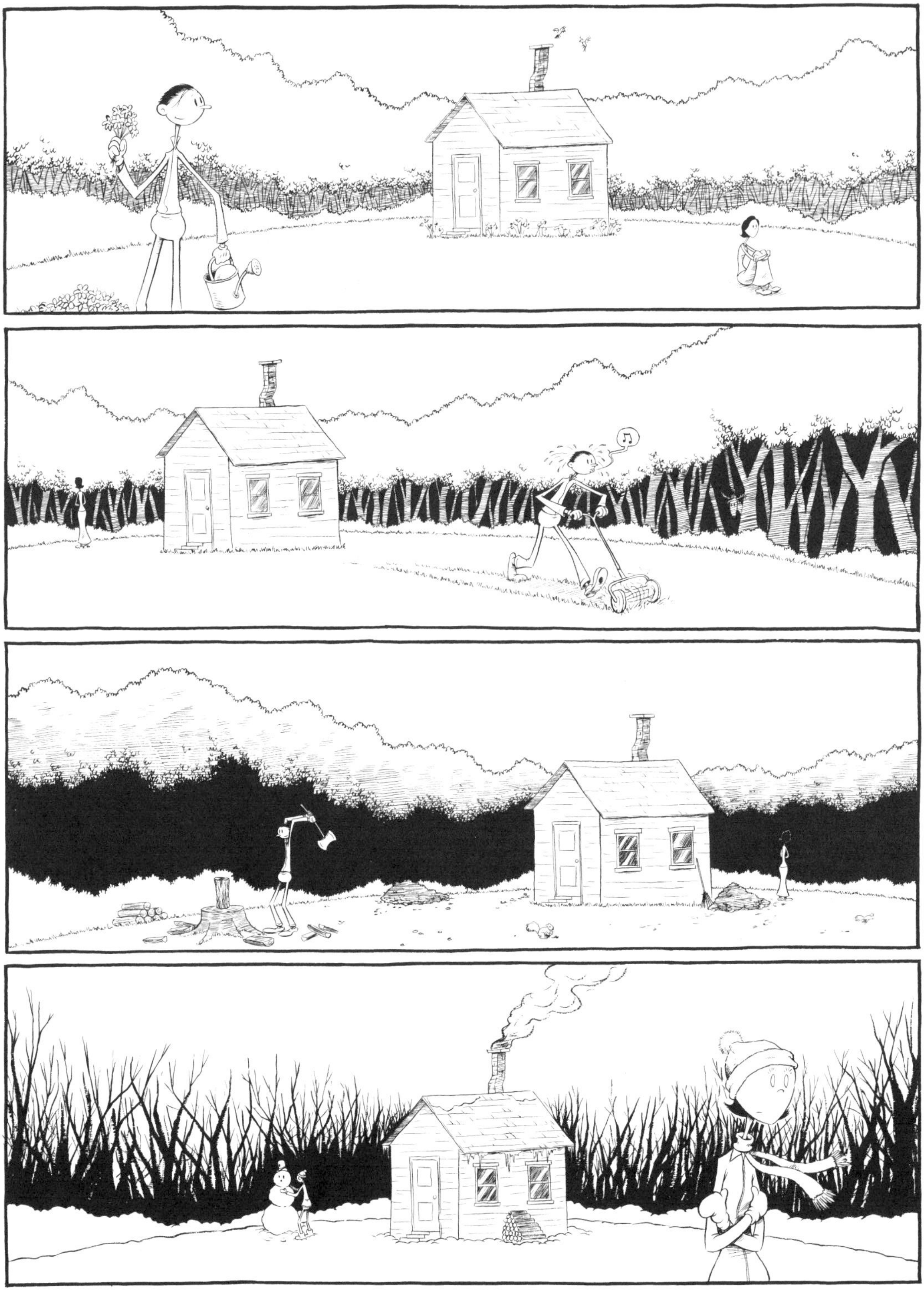

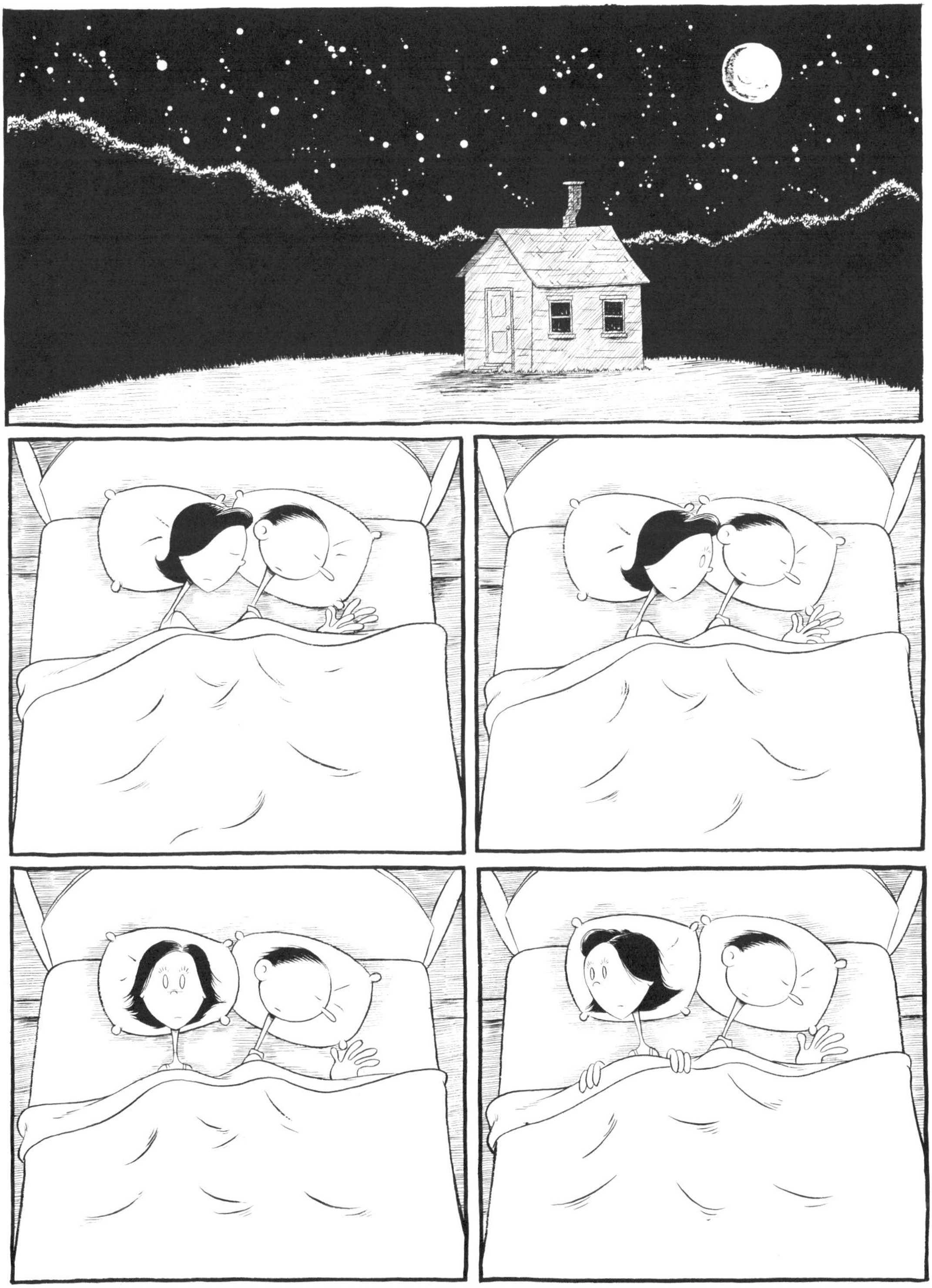

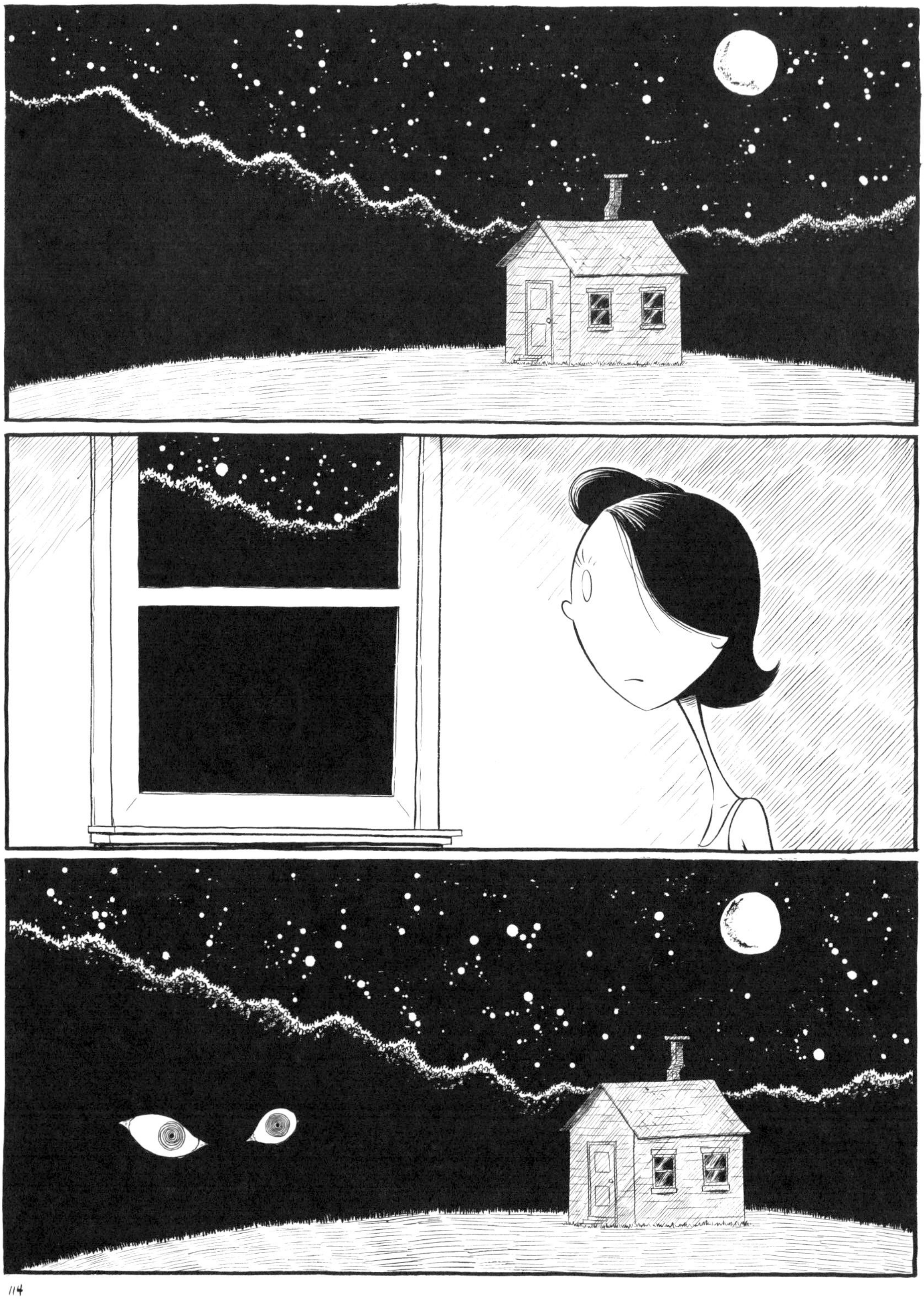

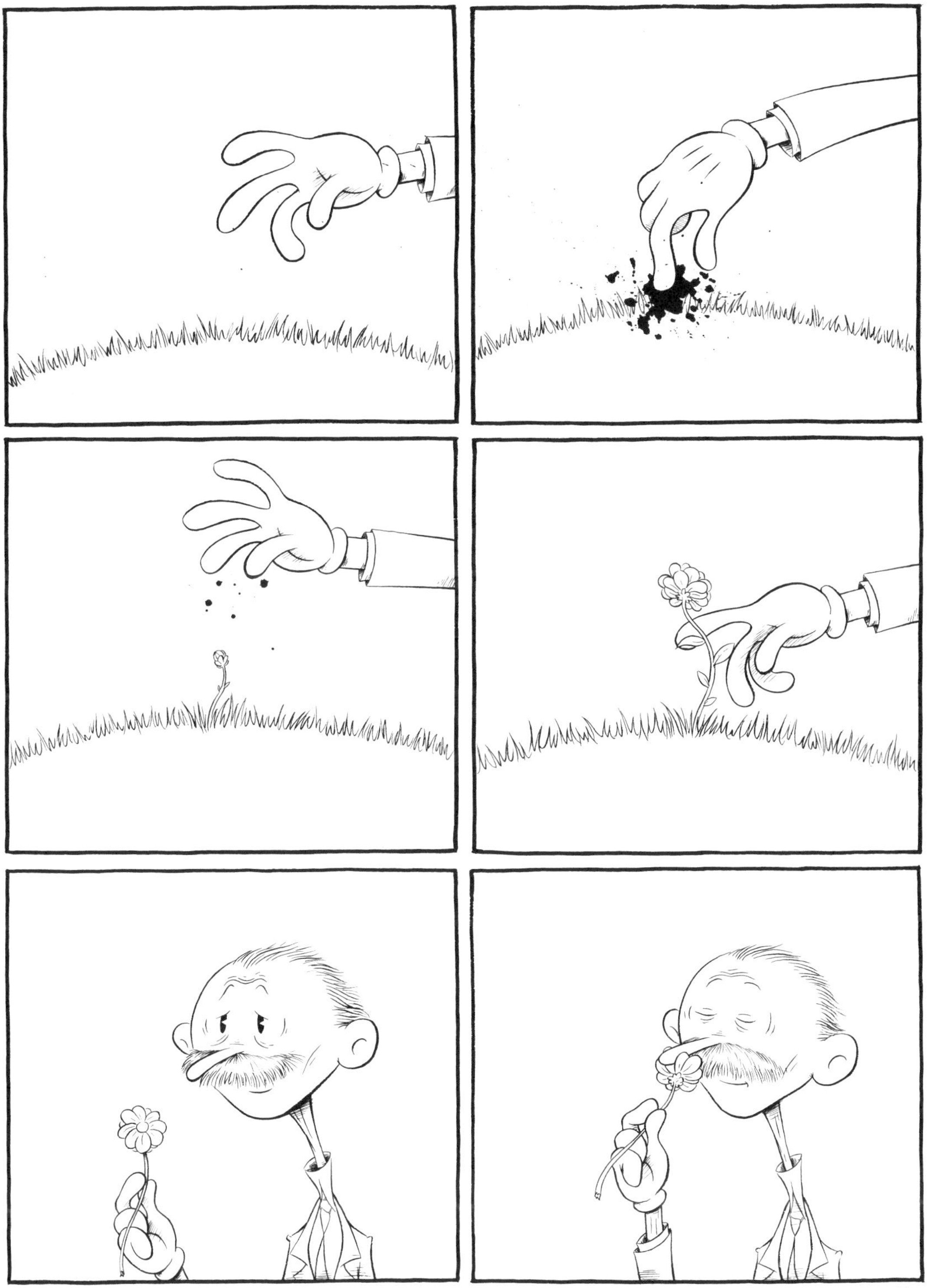

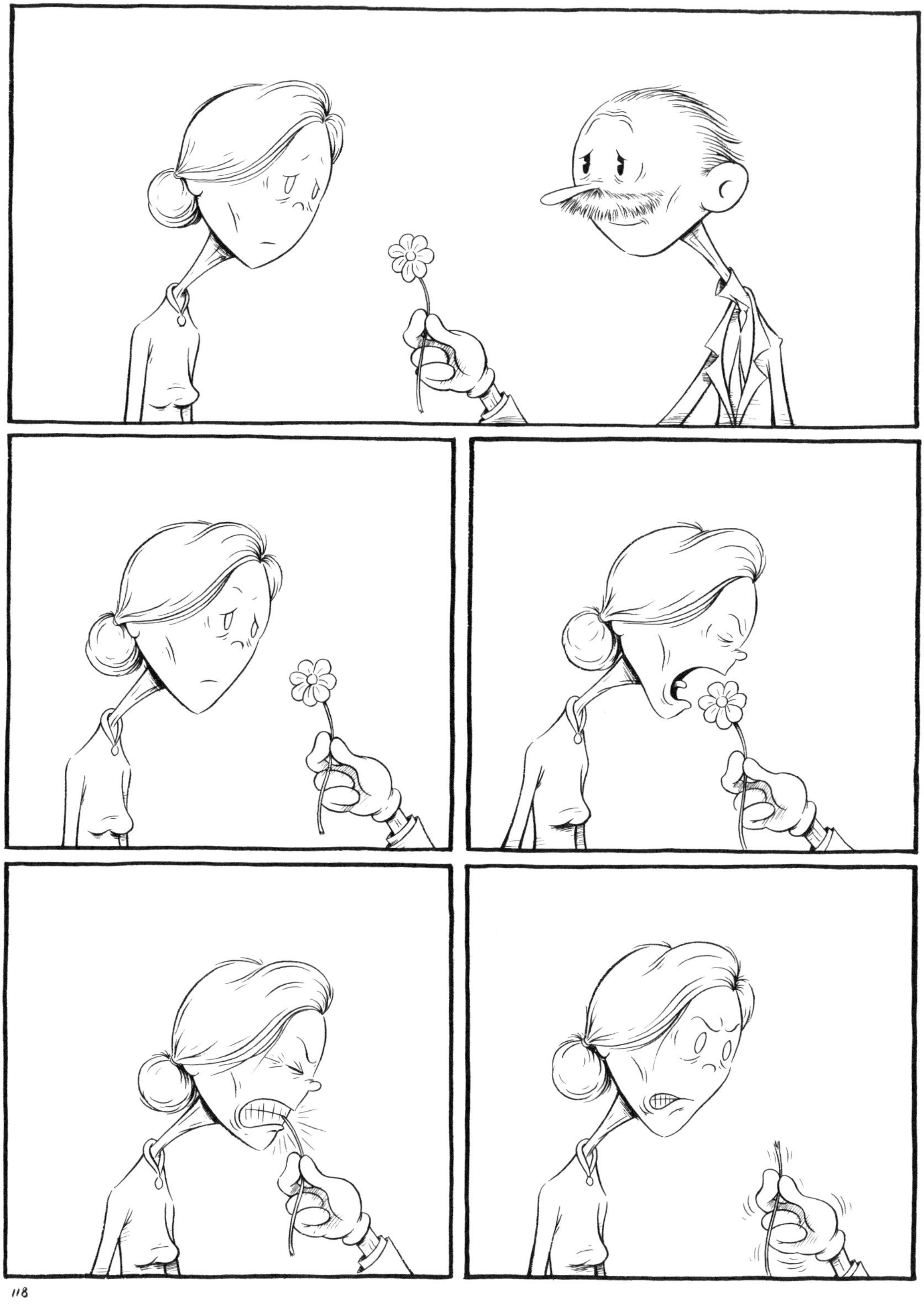

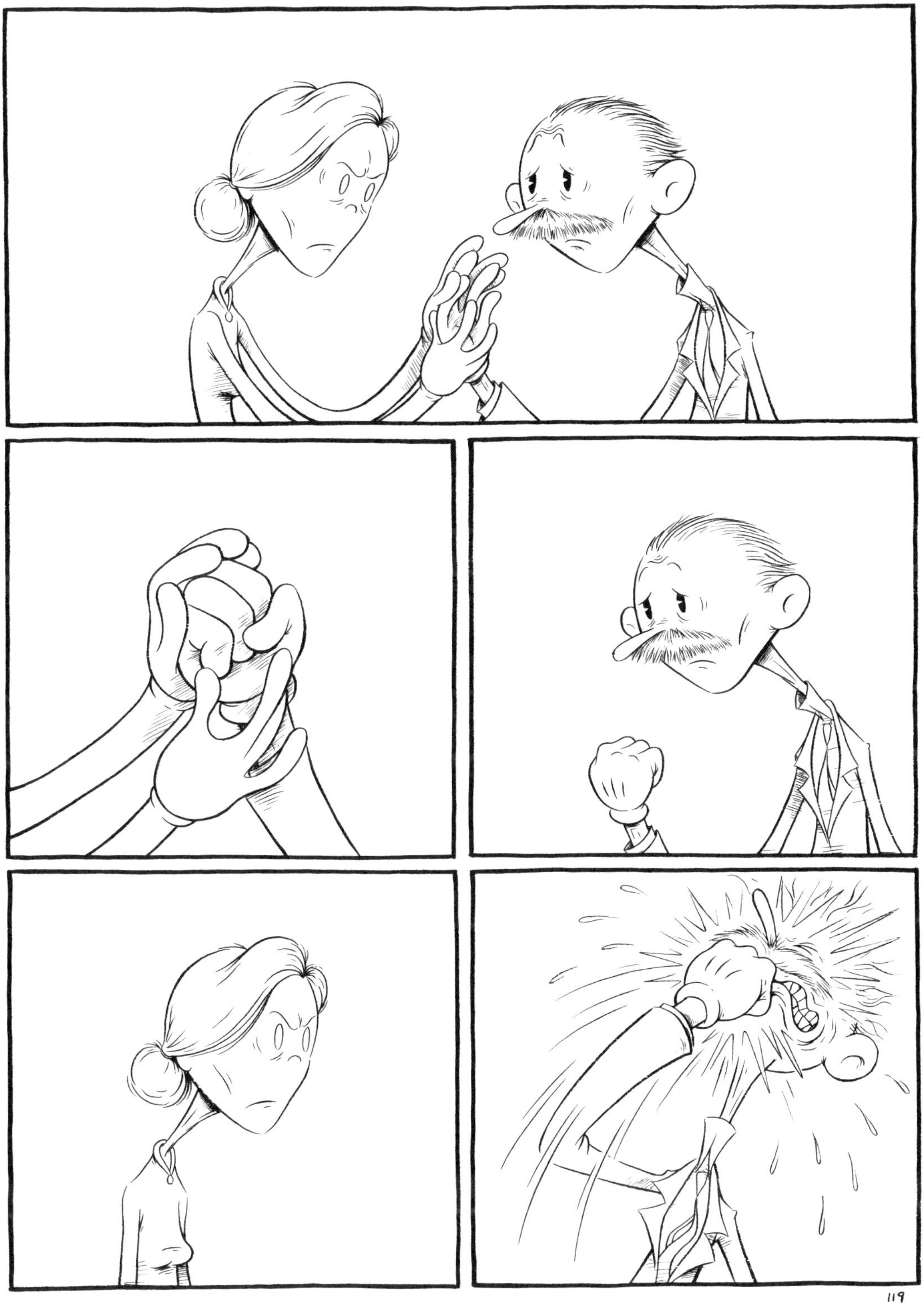

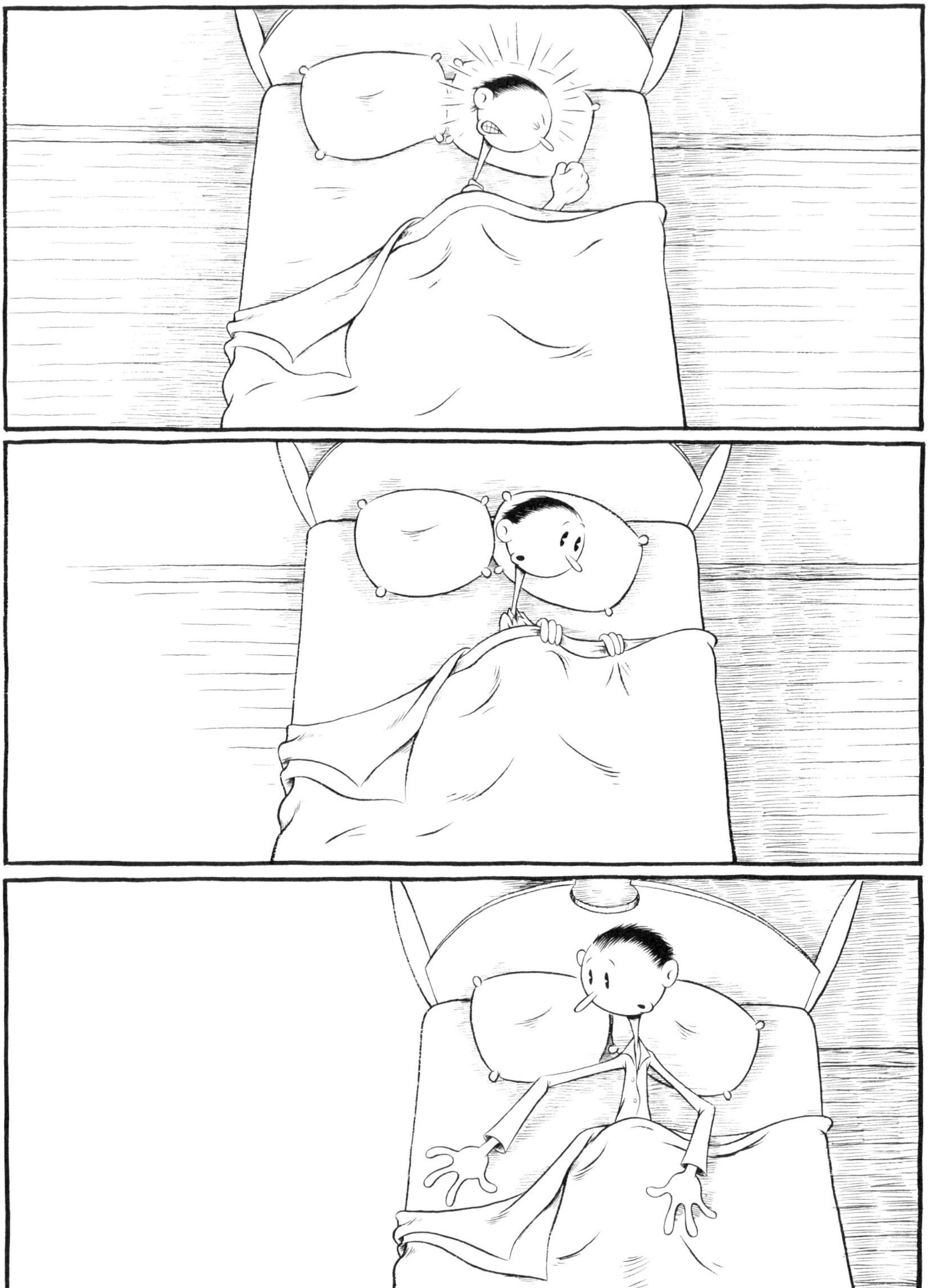

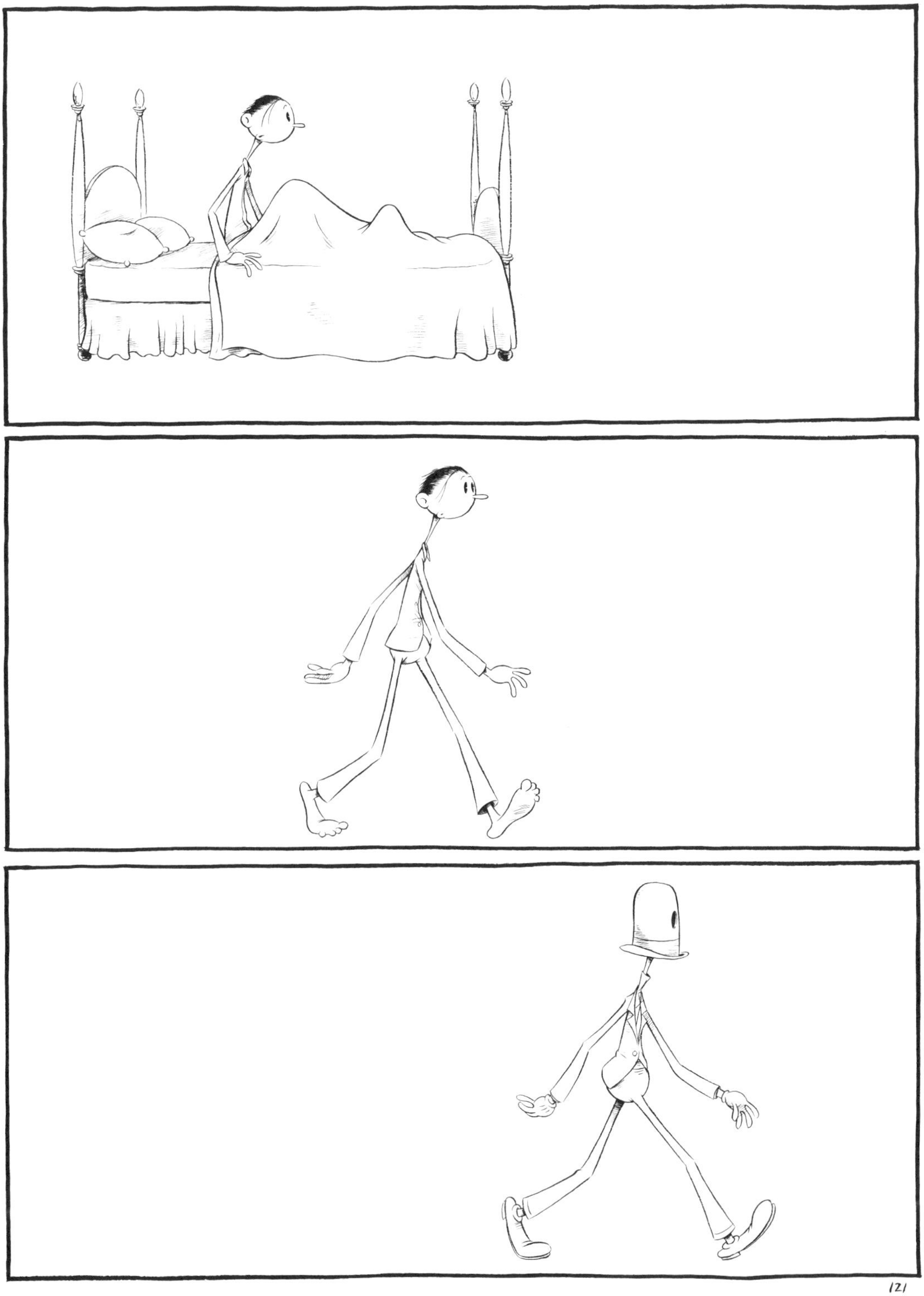

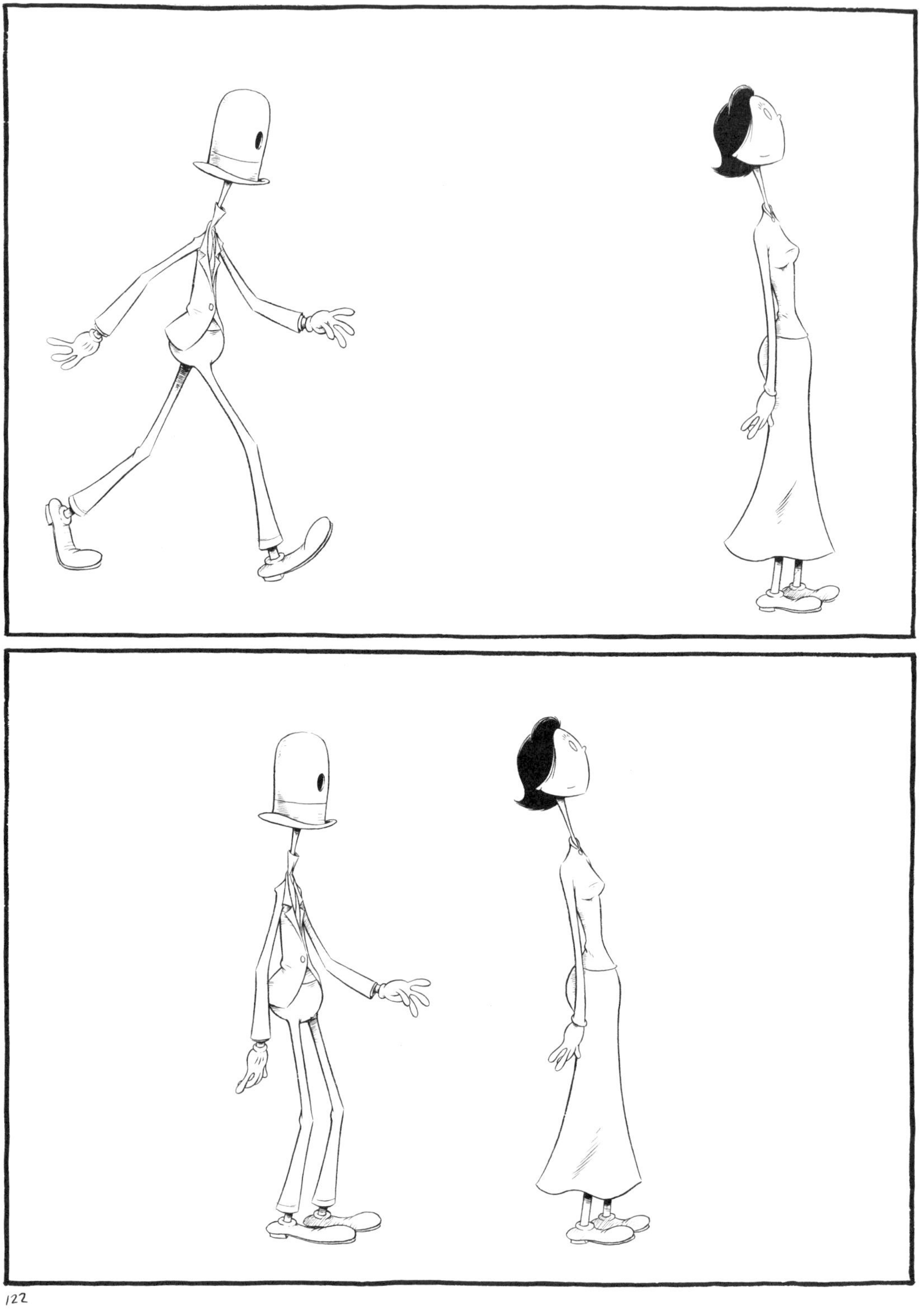

wanton.

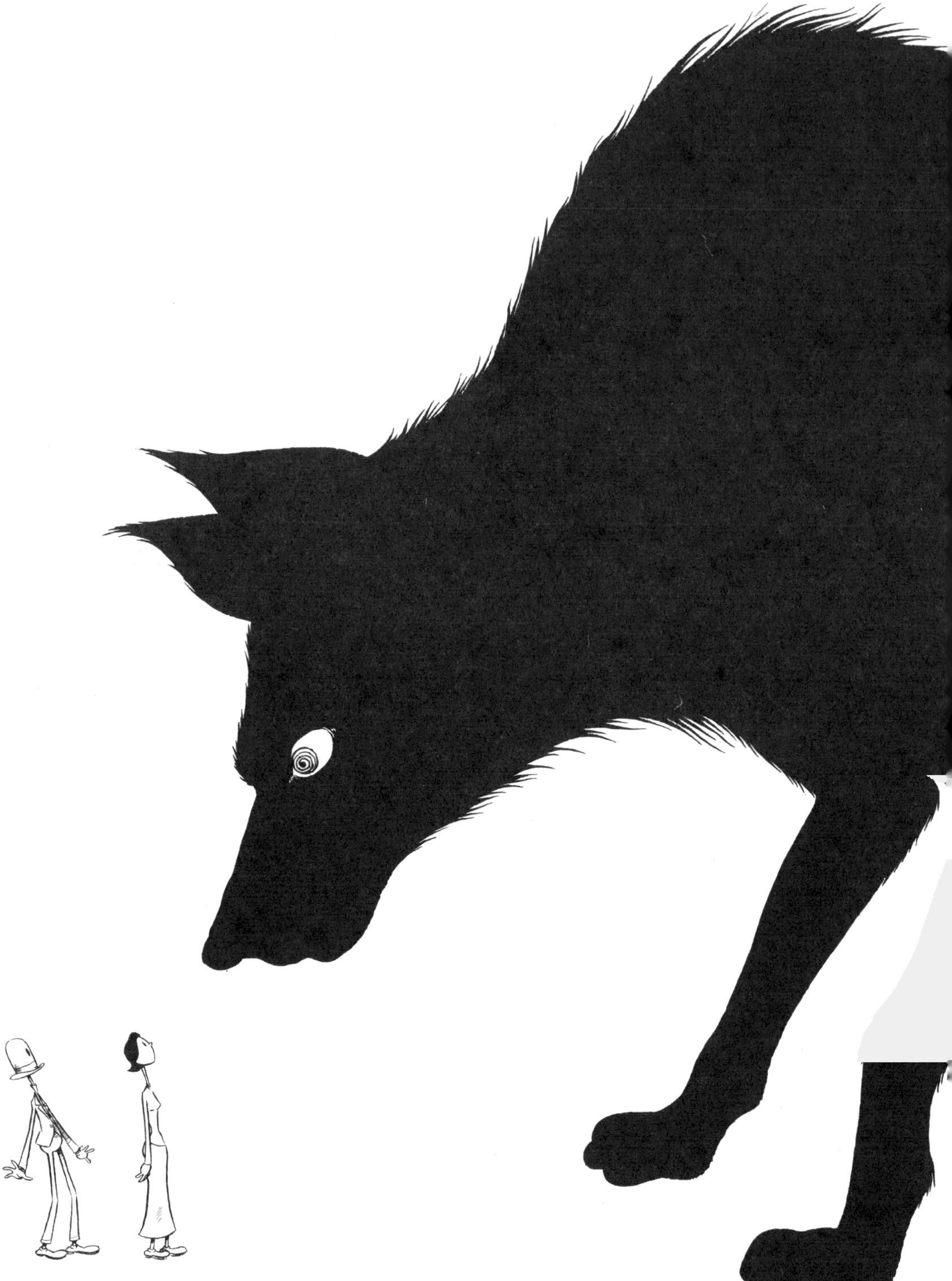

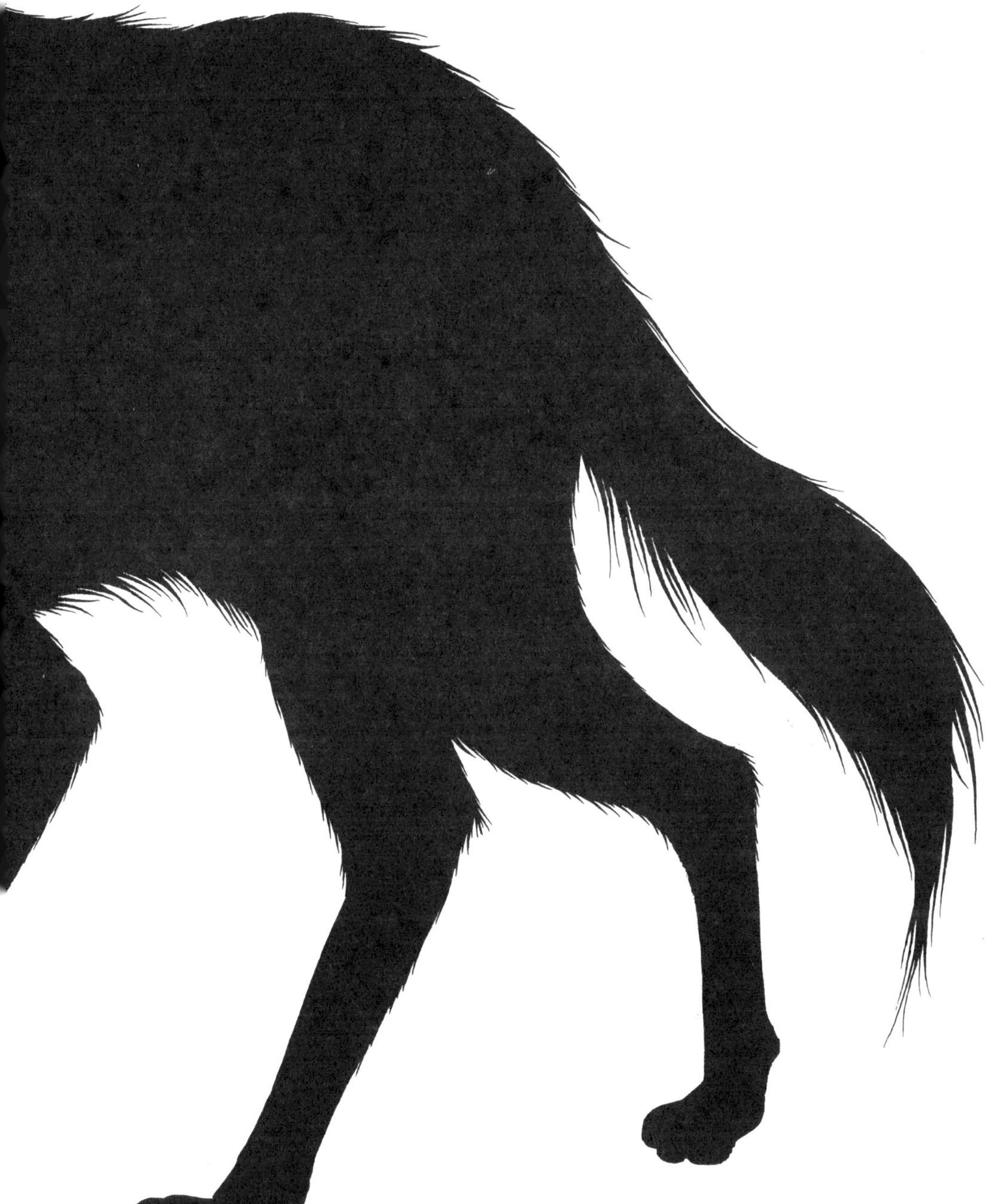

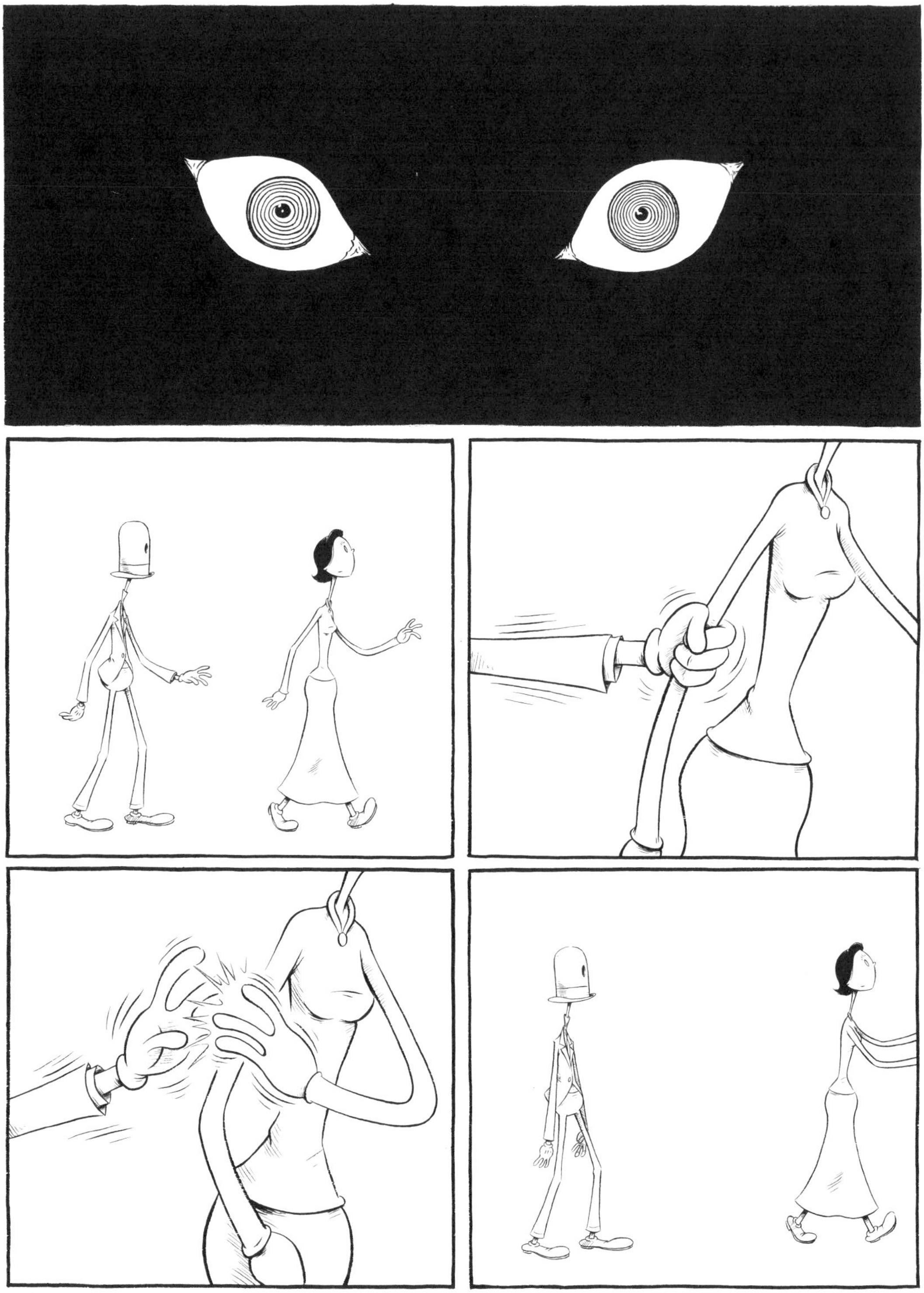

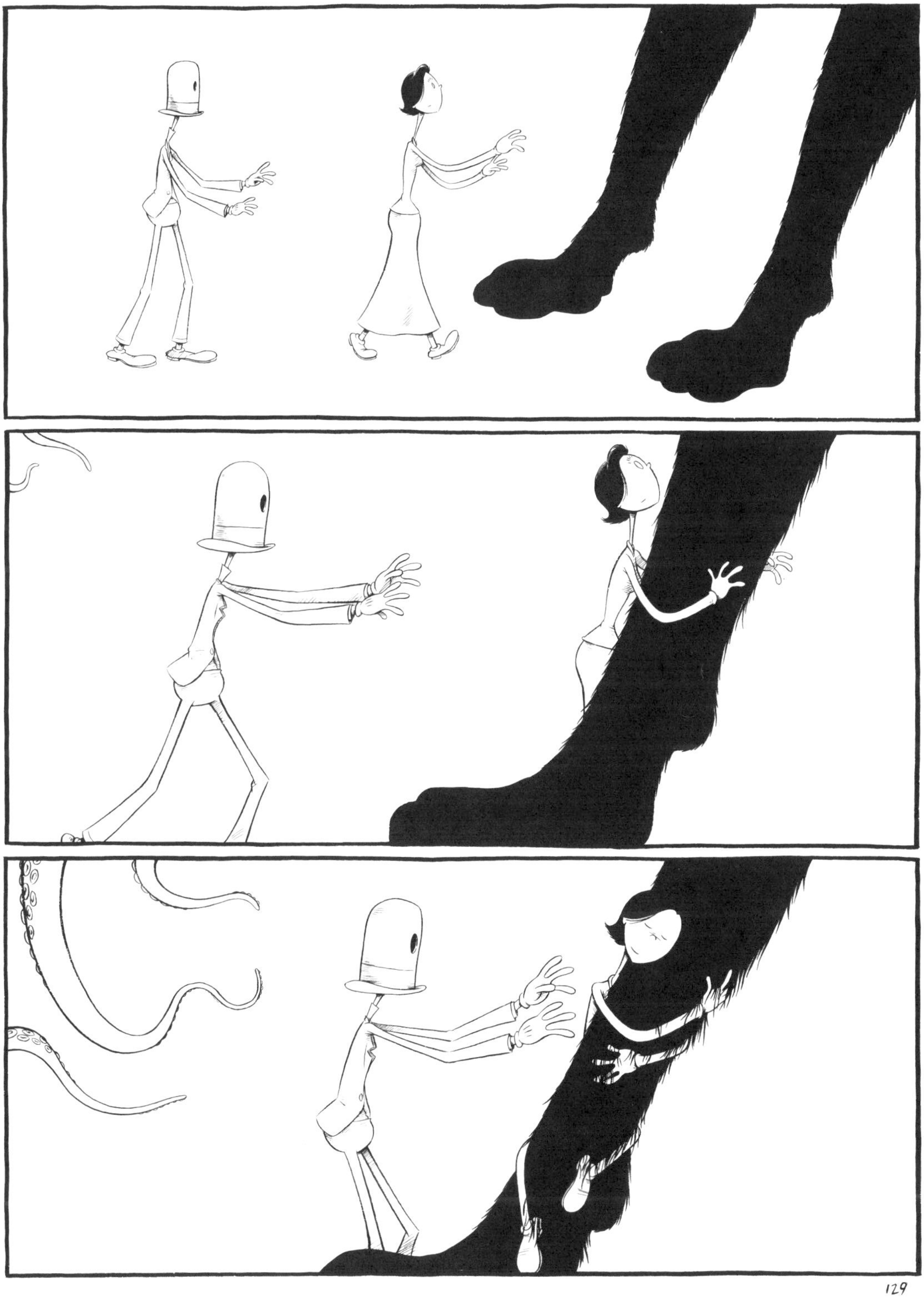

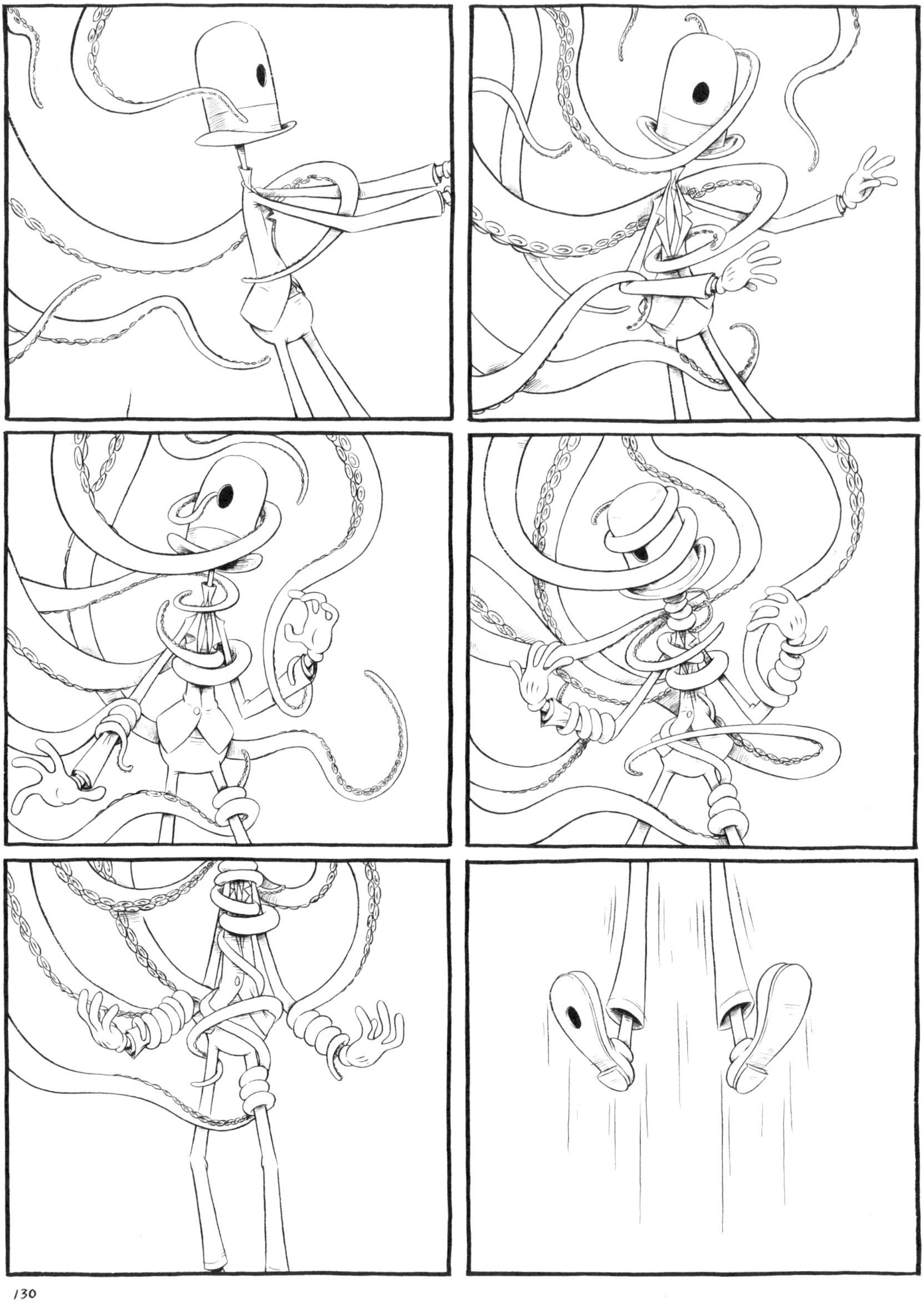

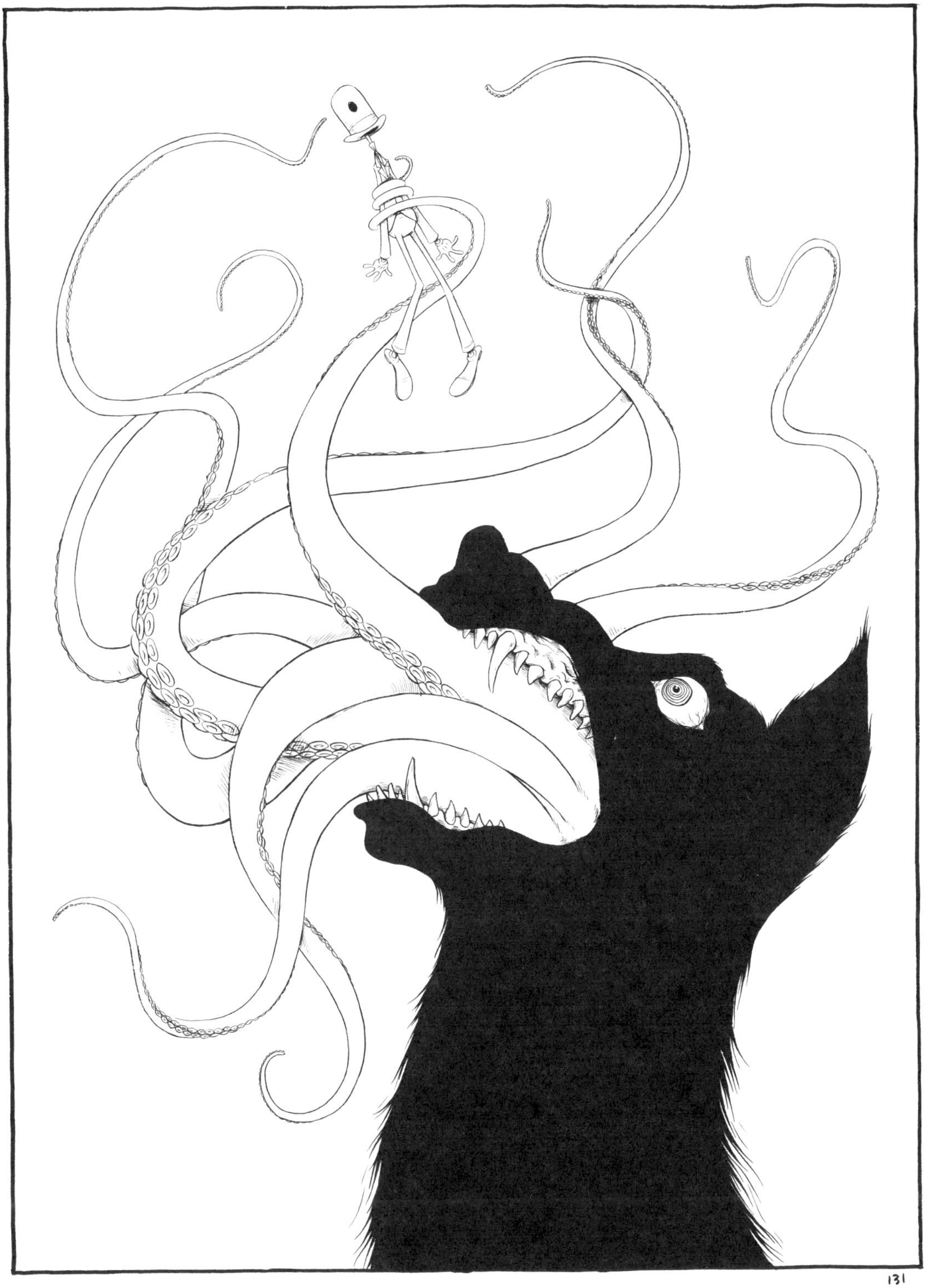

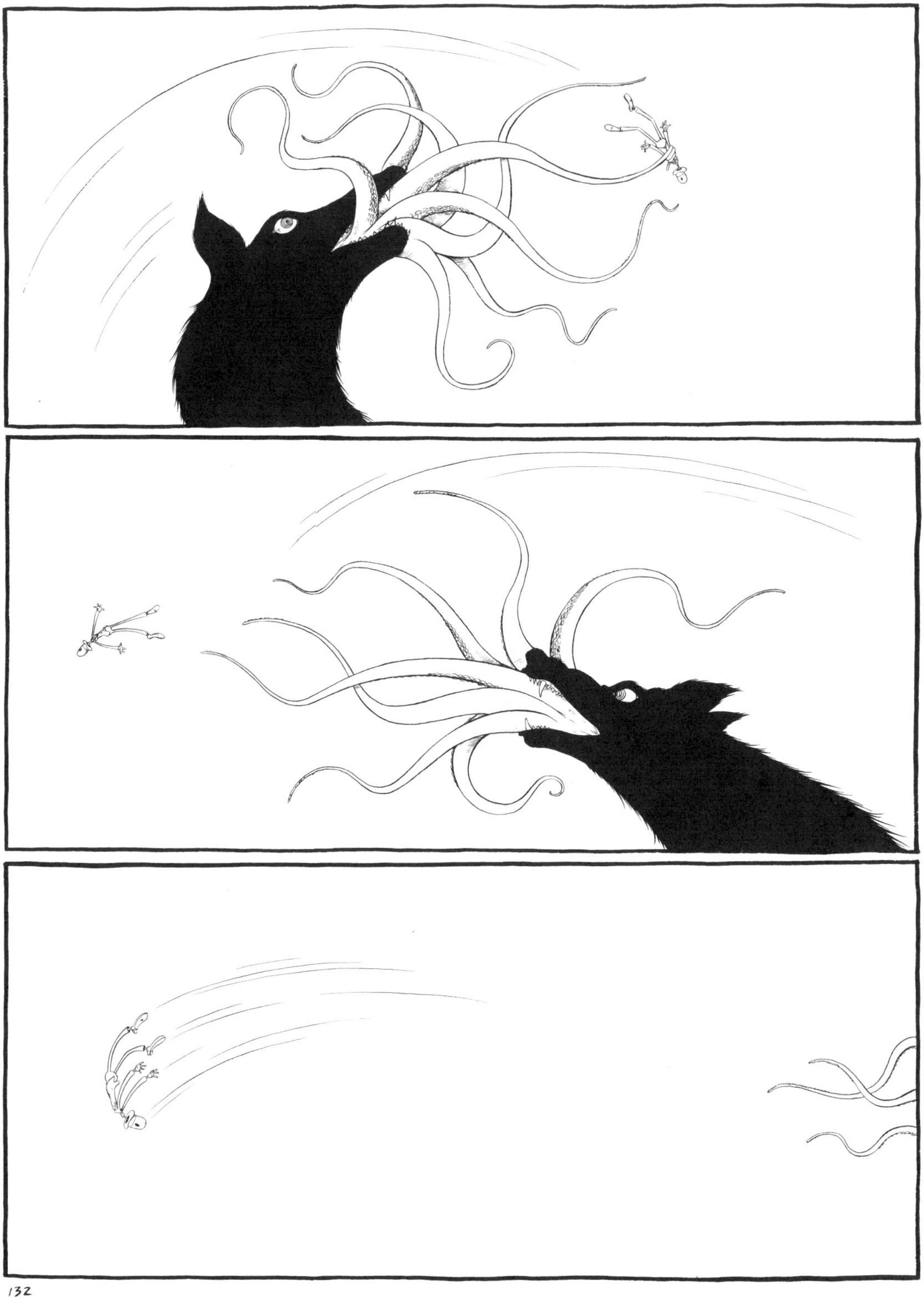

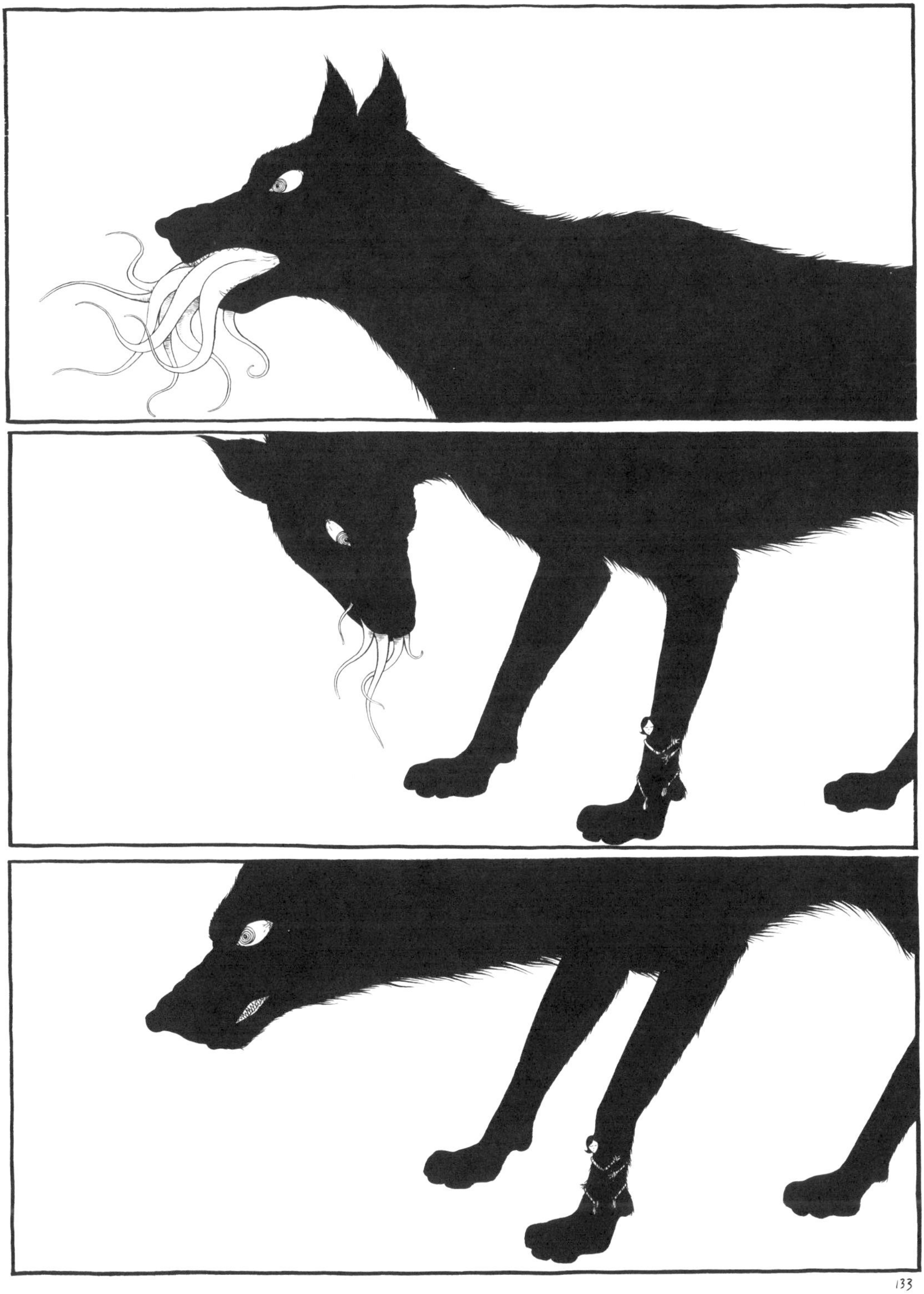

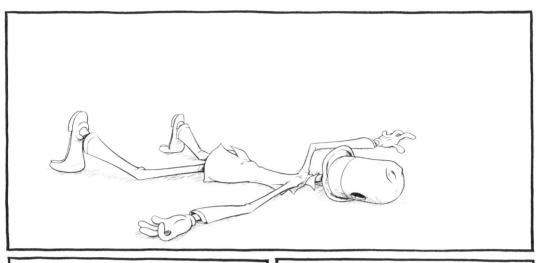

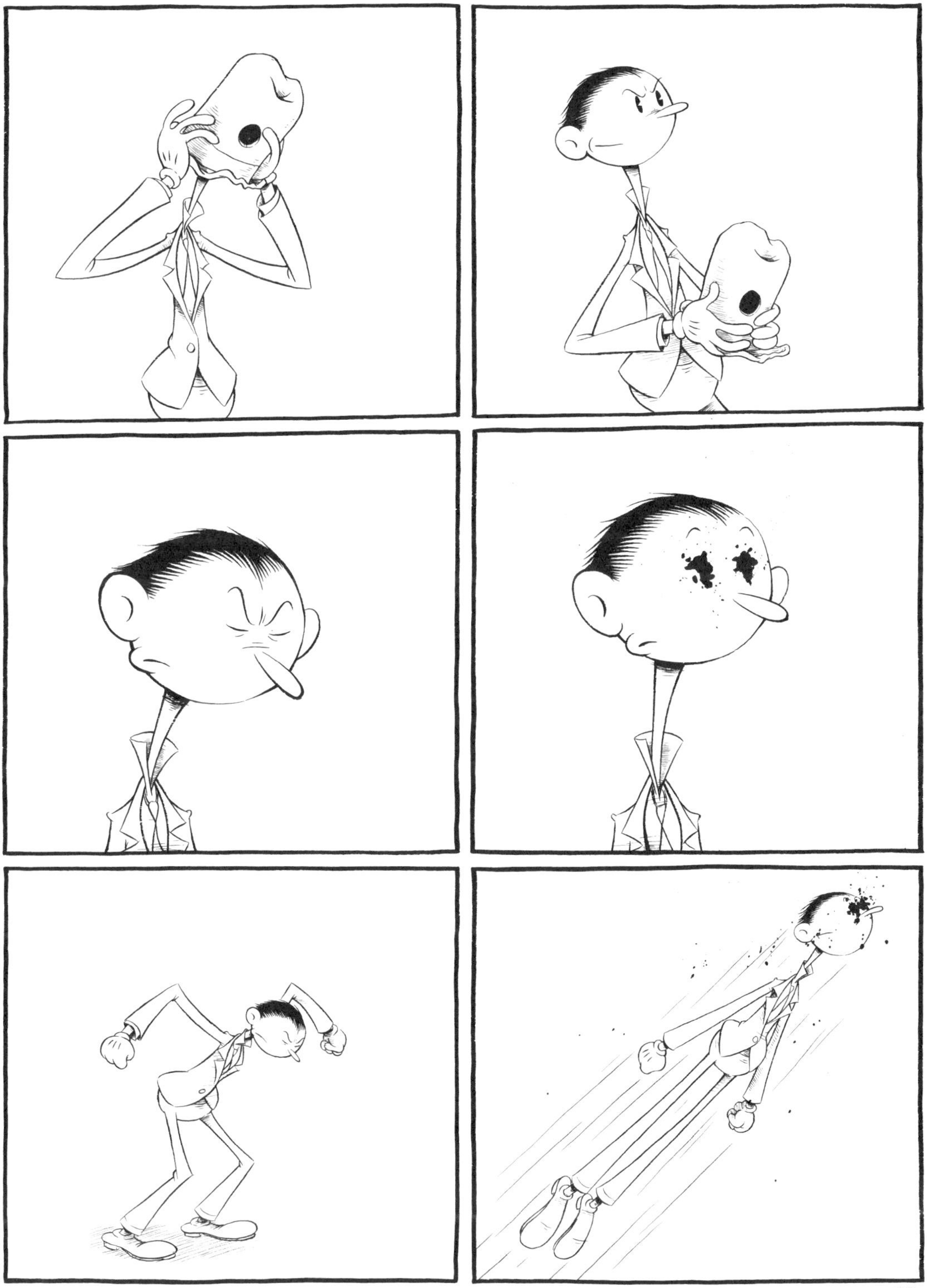

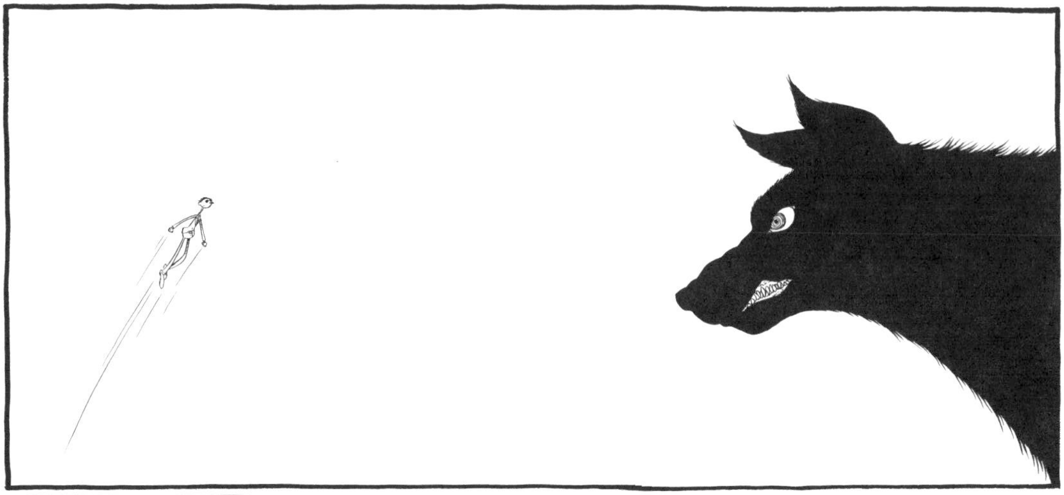

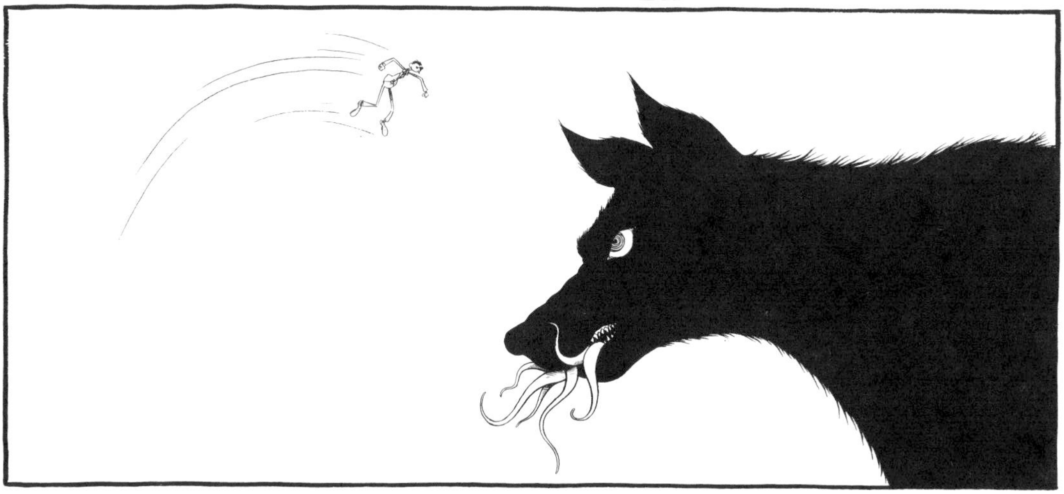

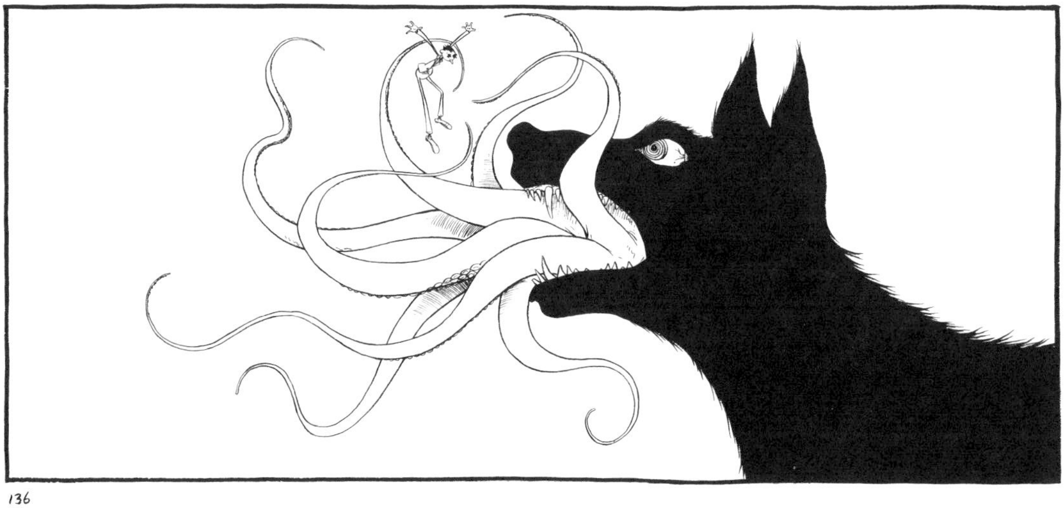

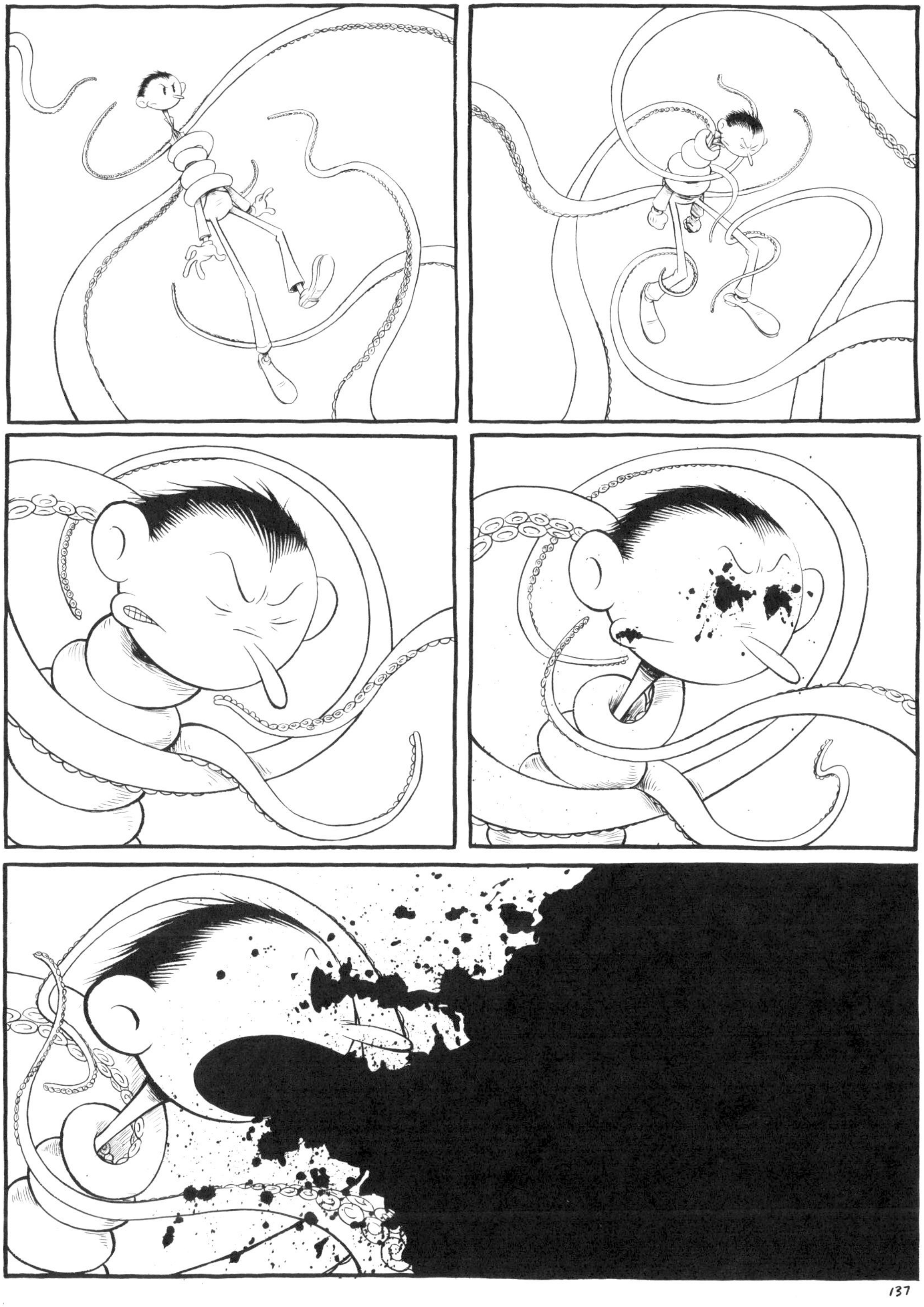

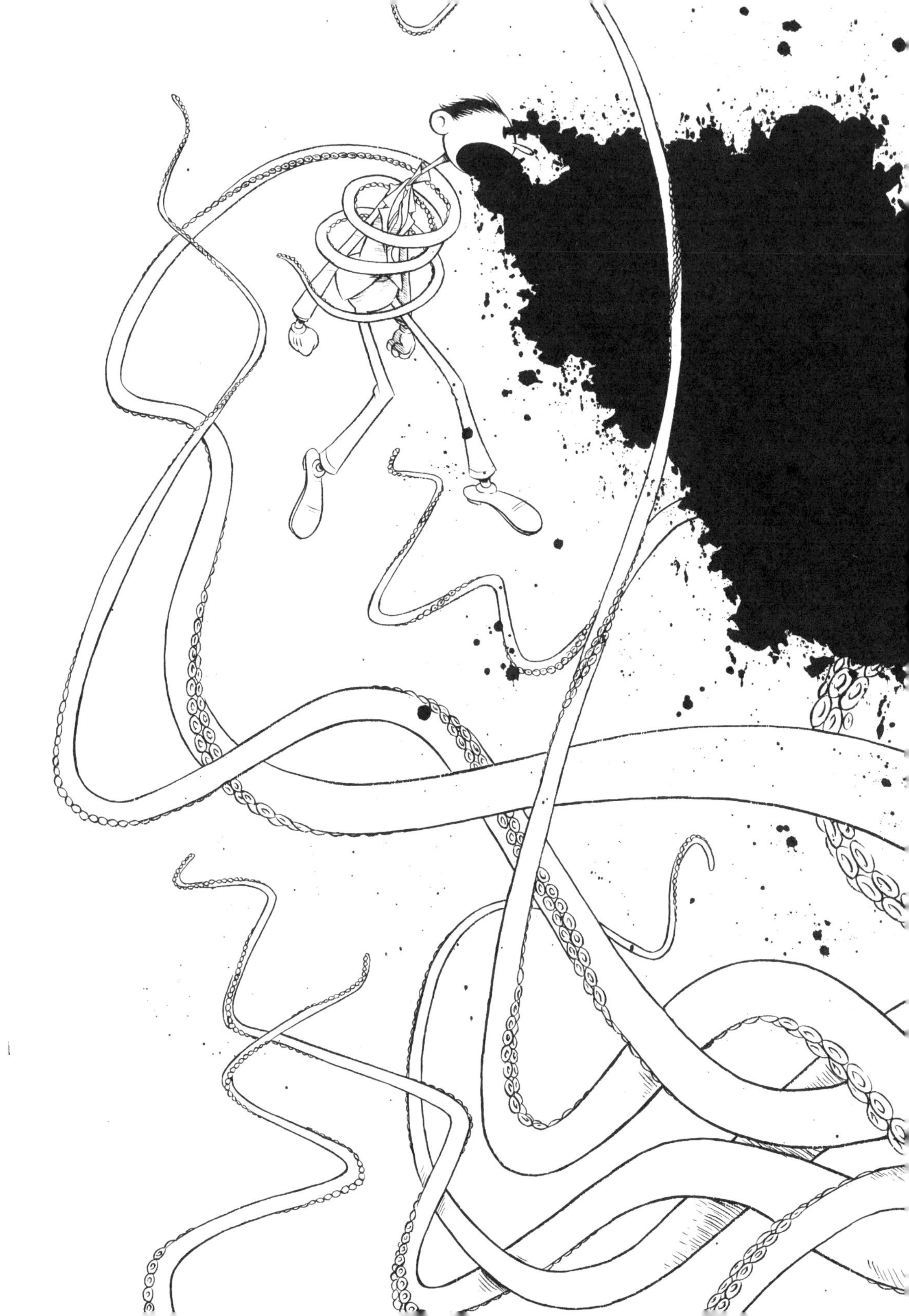

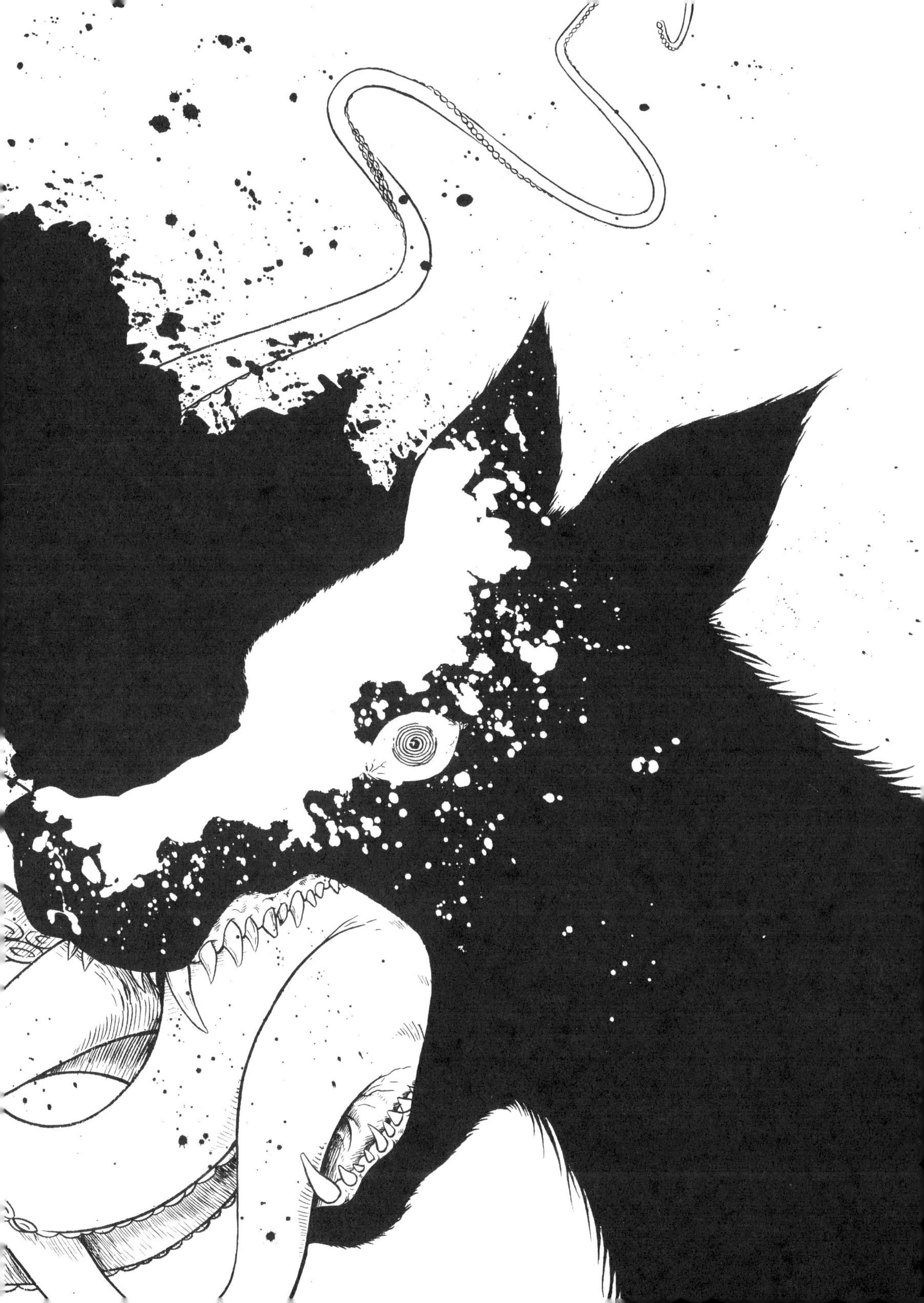

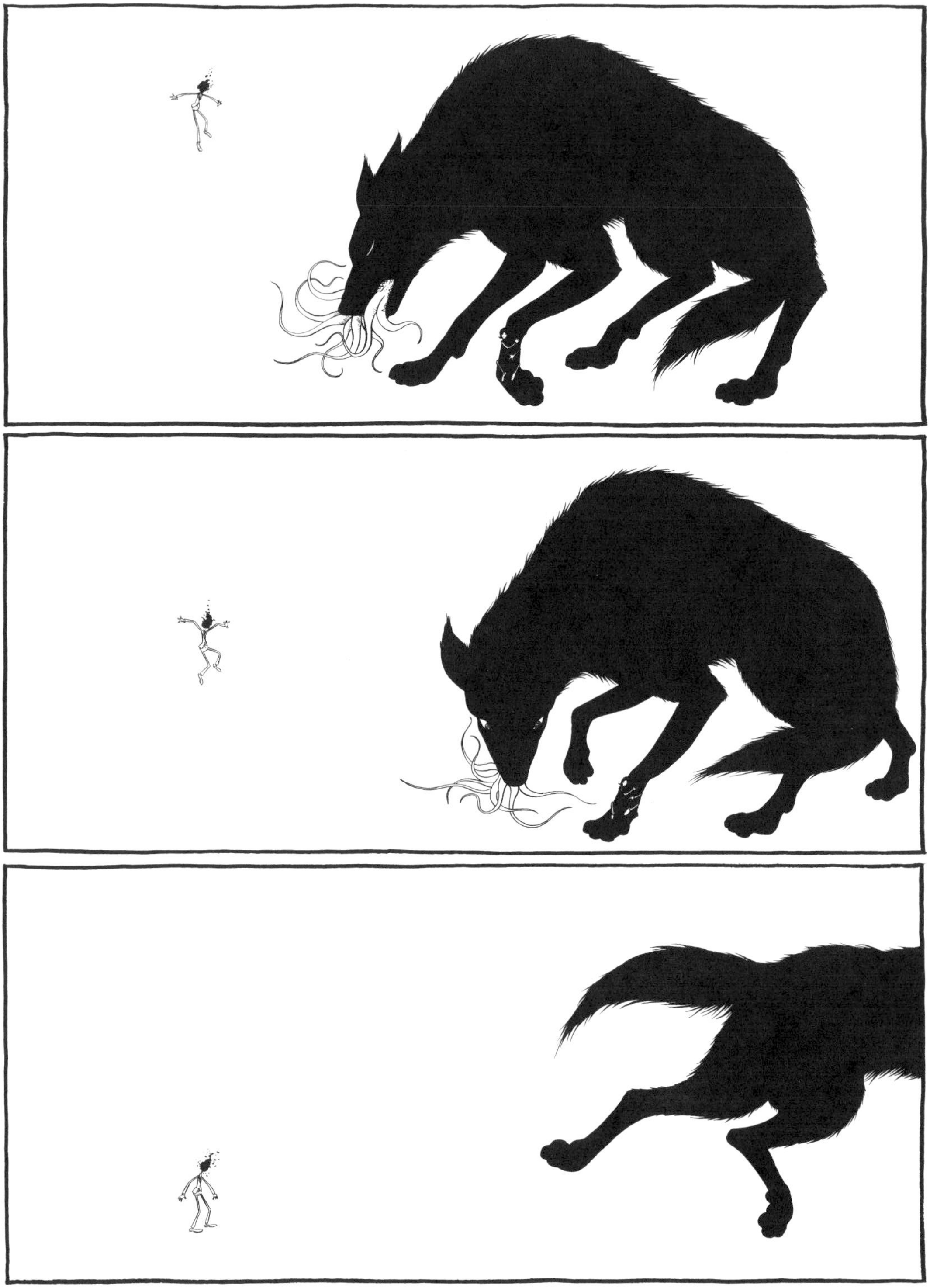

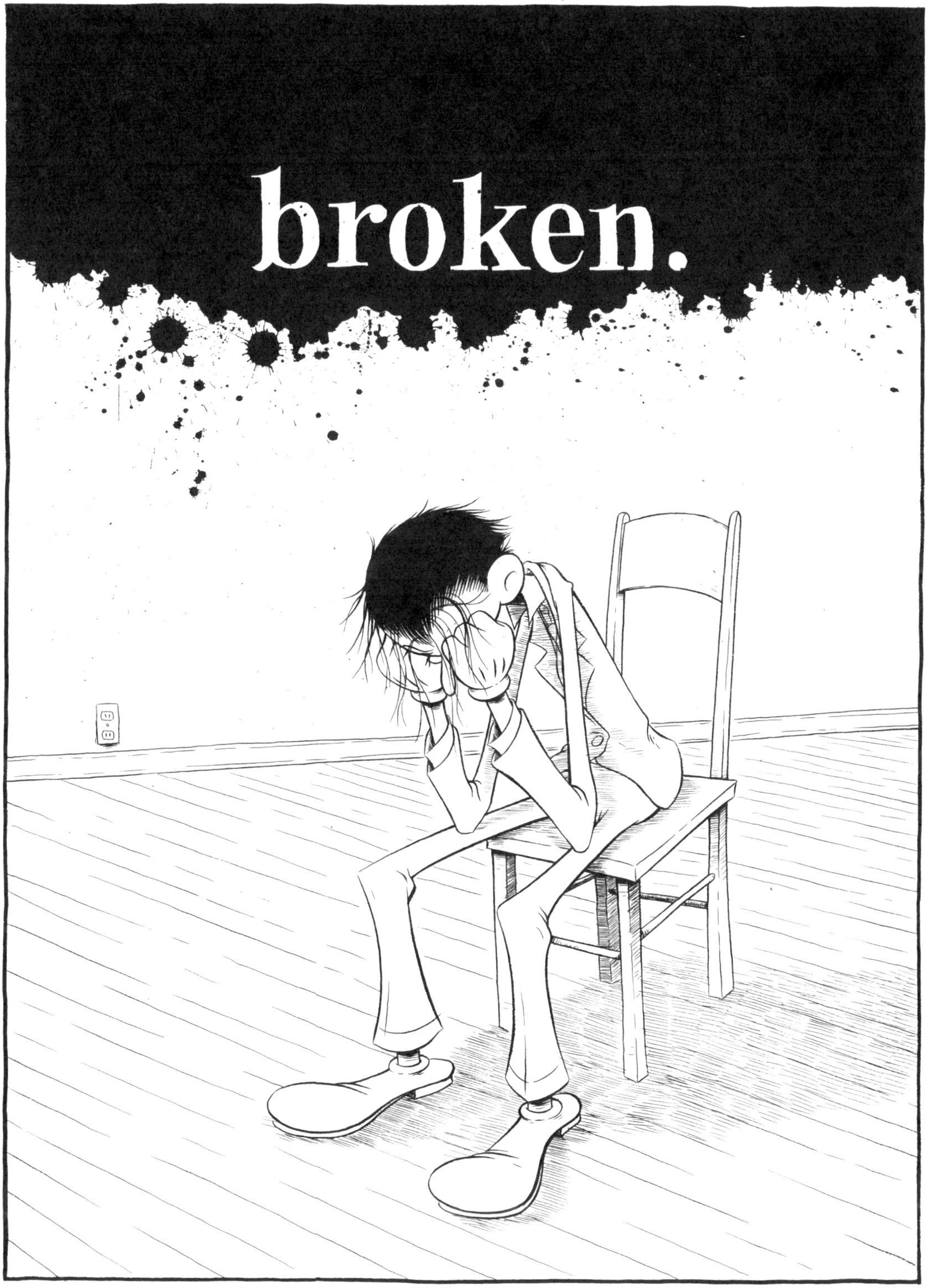
broken.

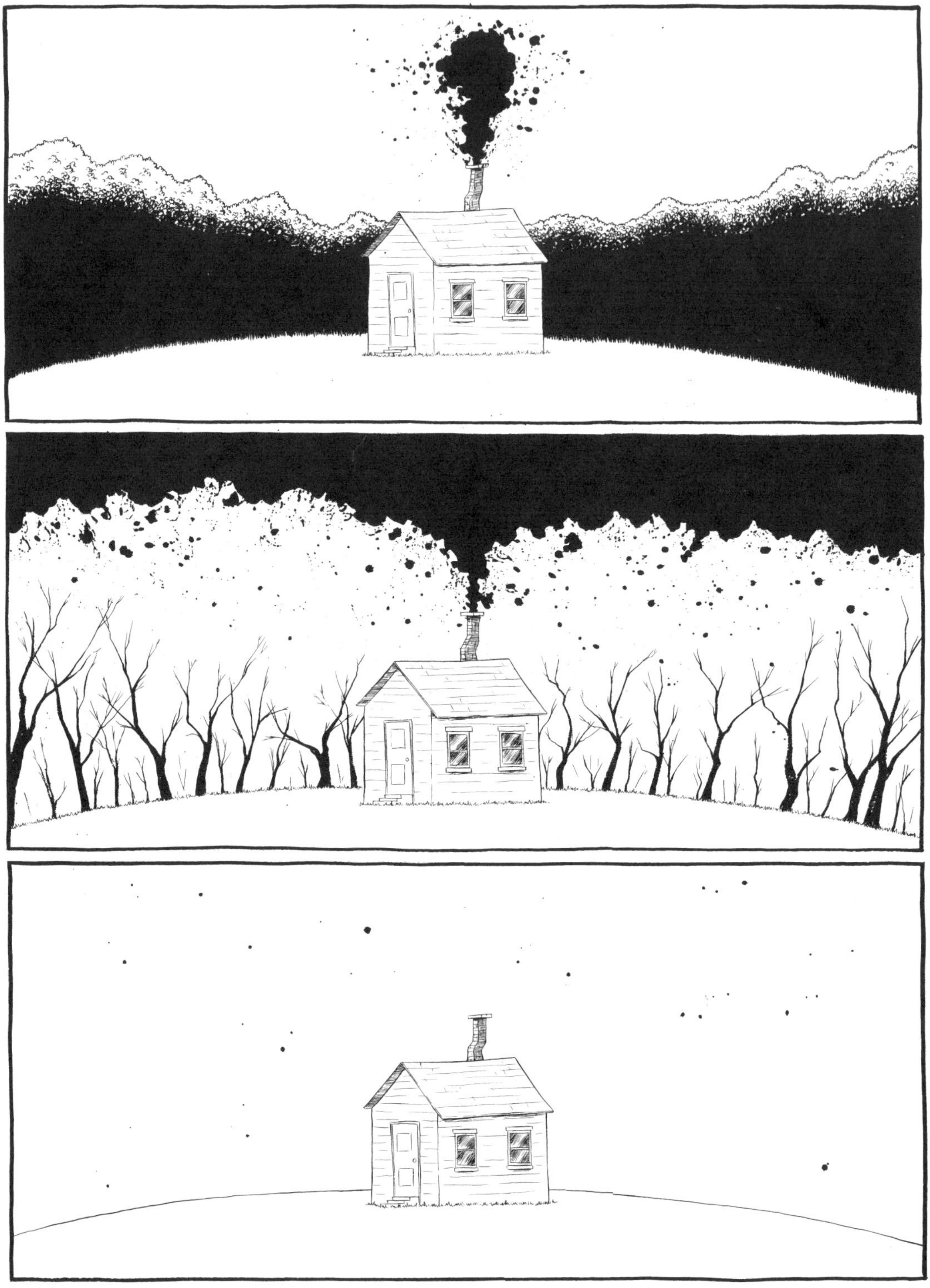

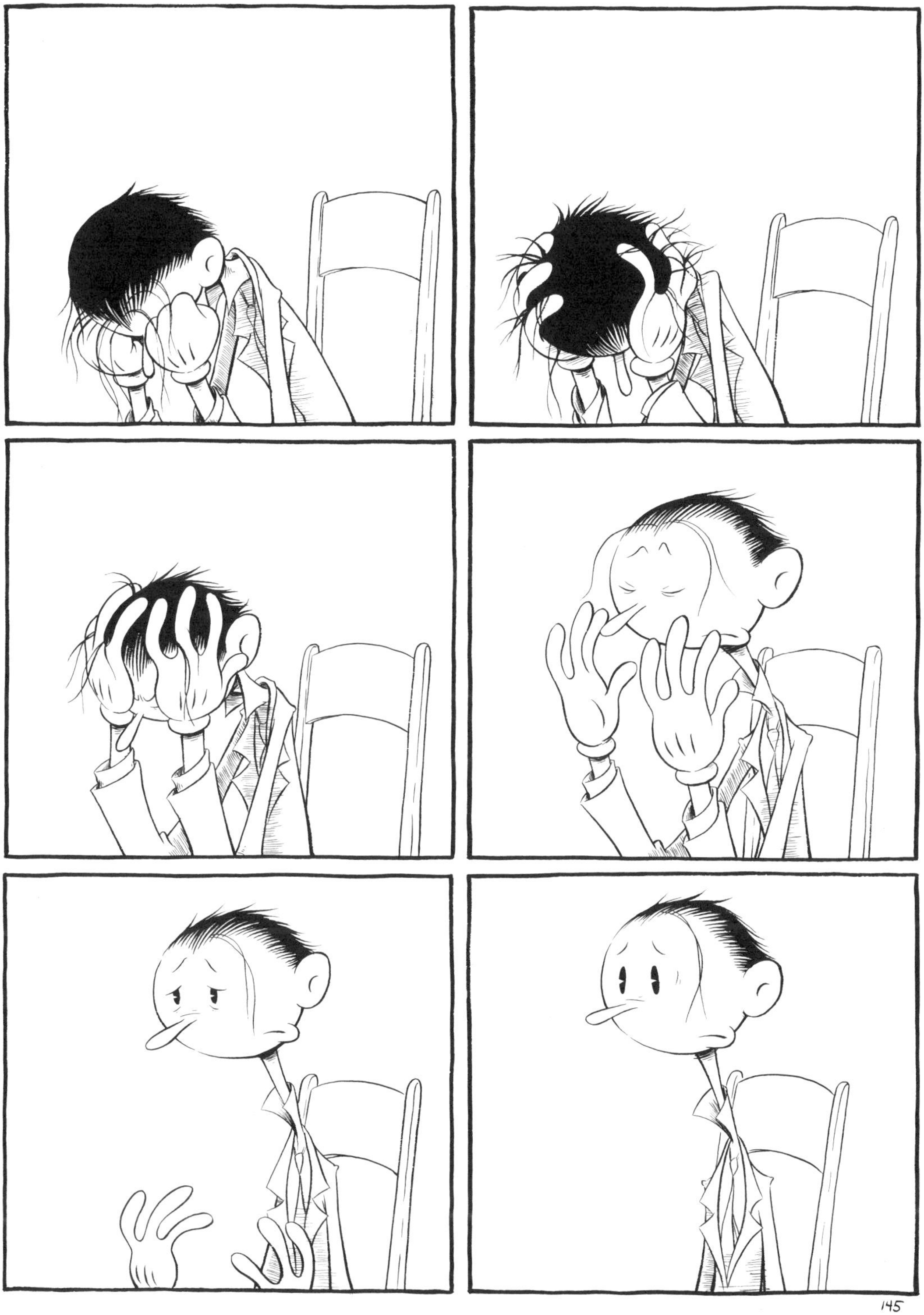

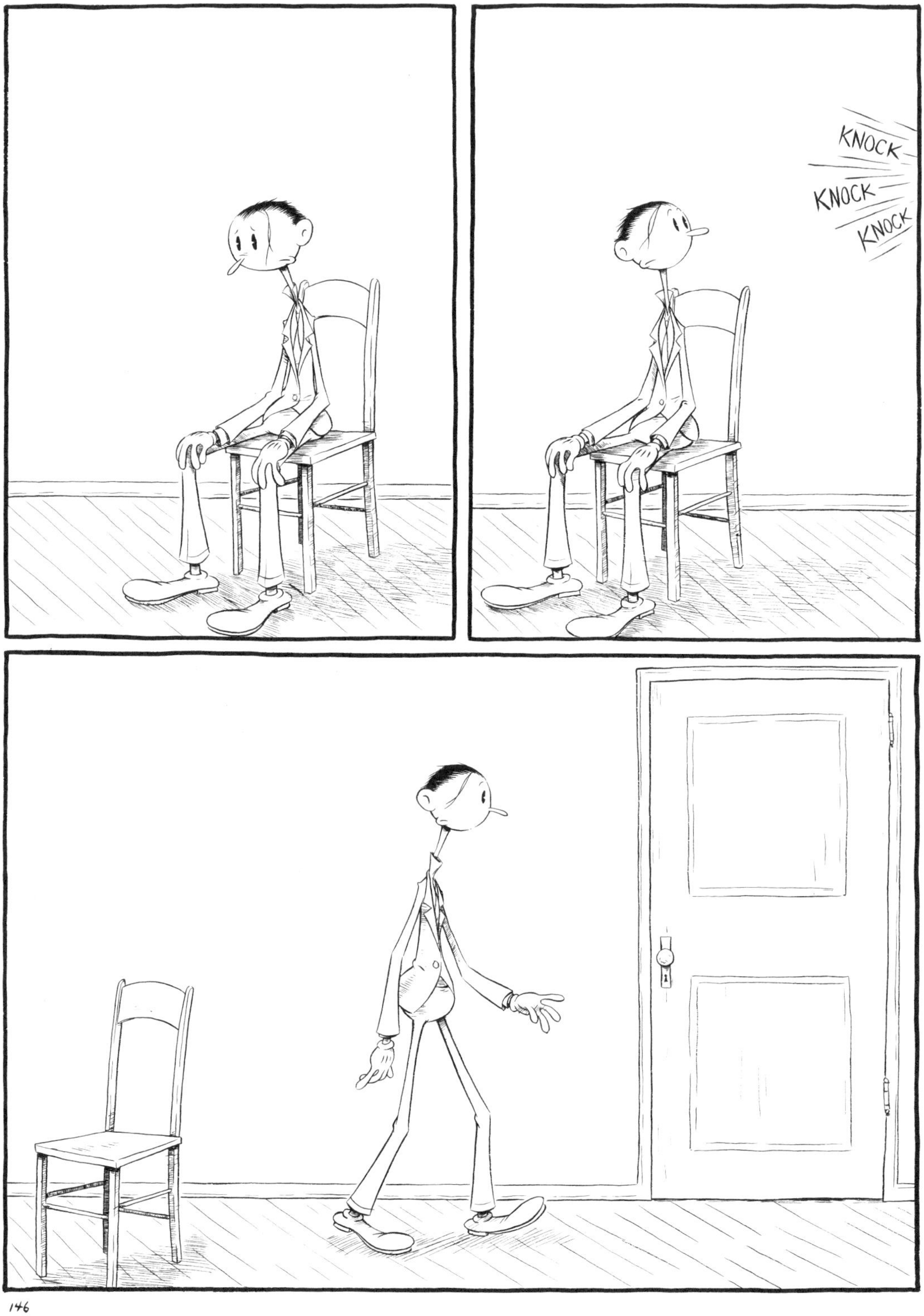
KNOCK
KNOCK
KNOCK

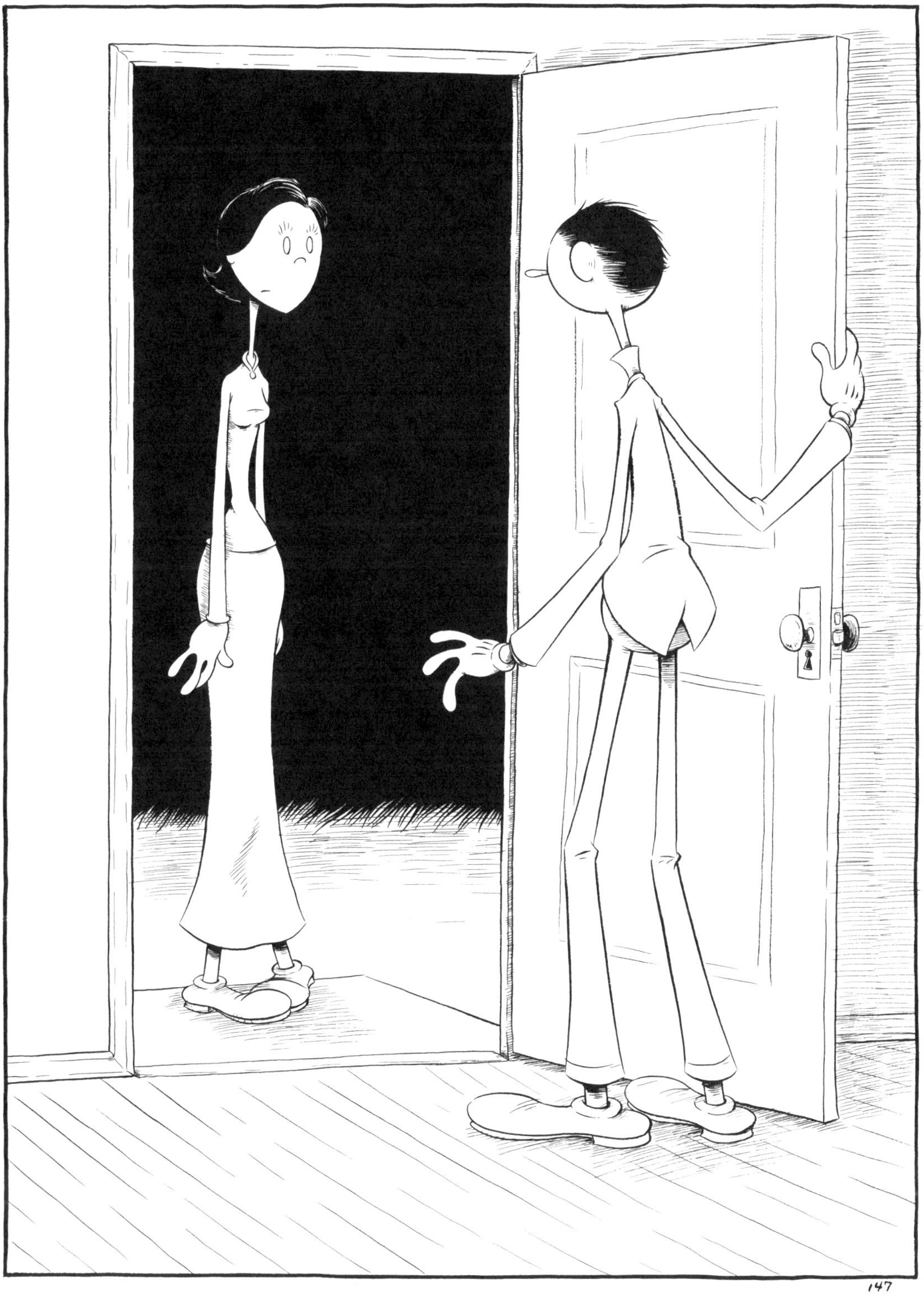

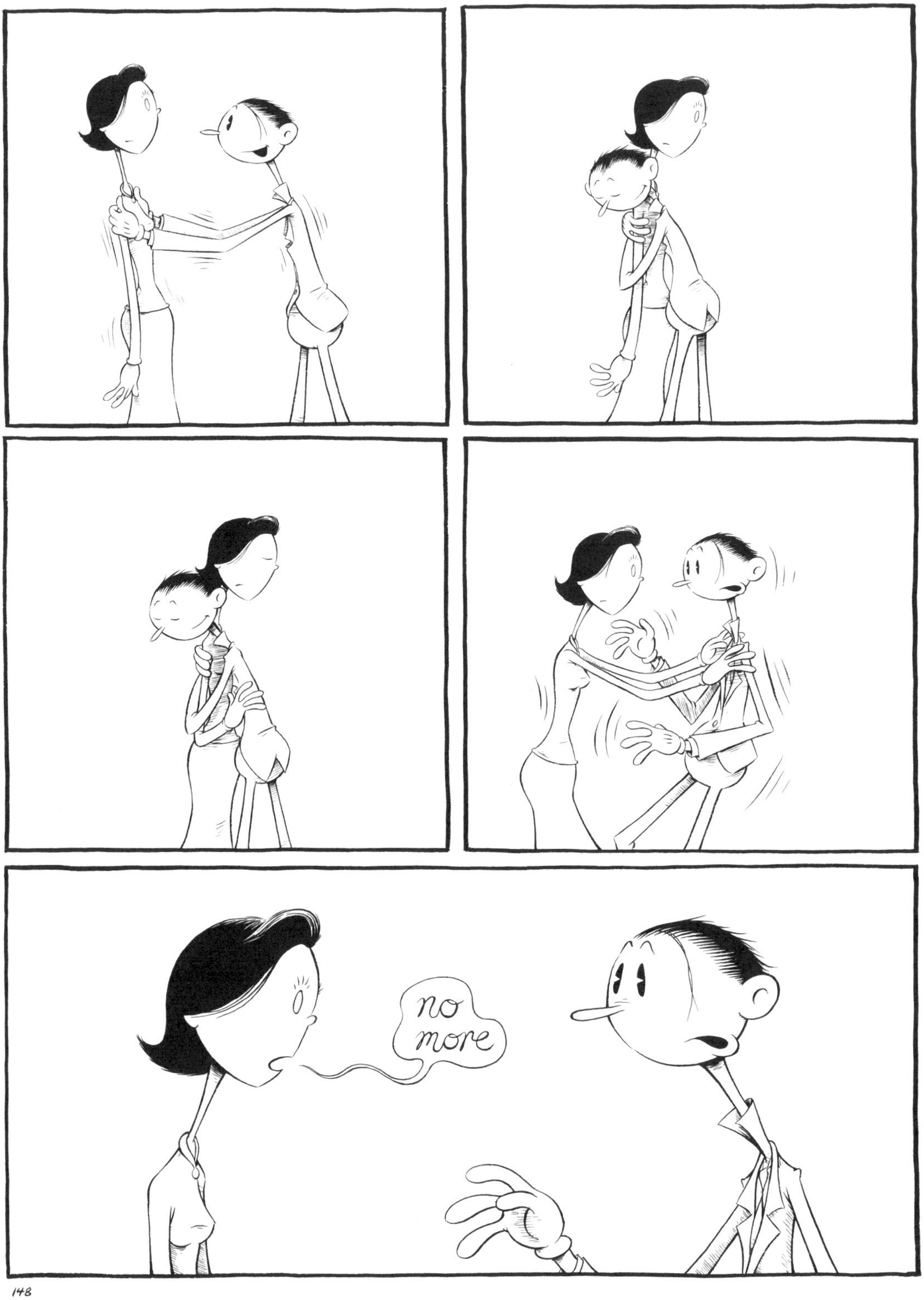
no more

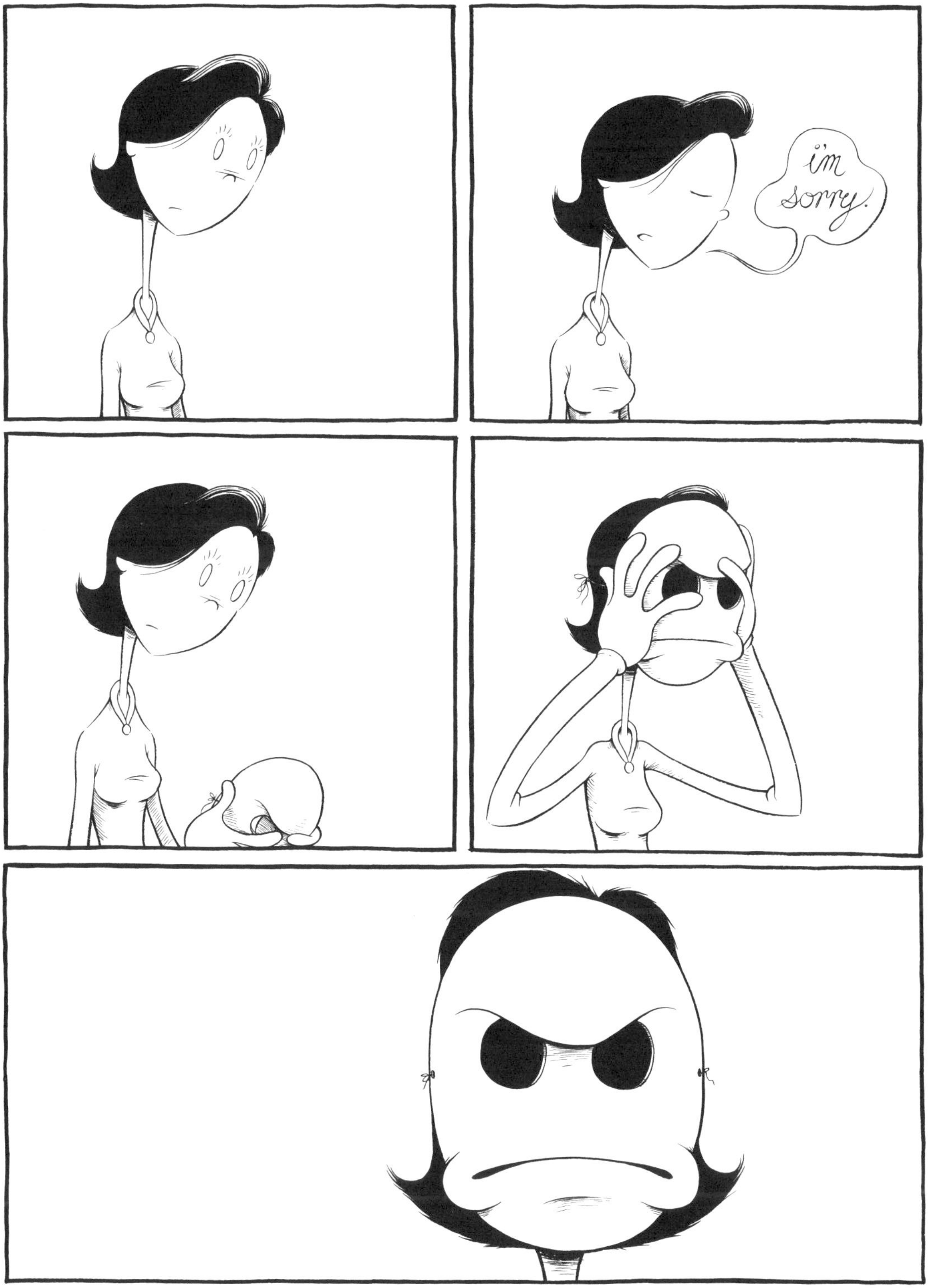
i'm sorry.

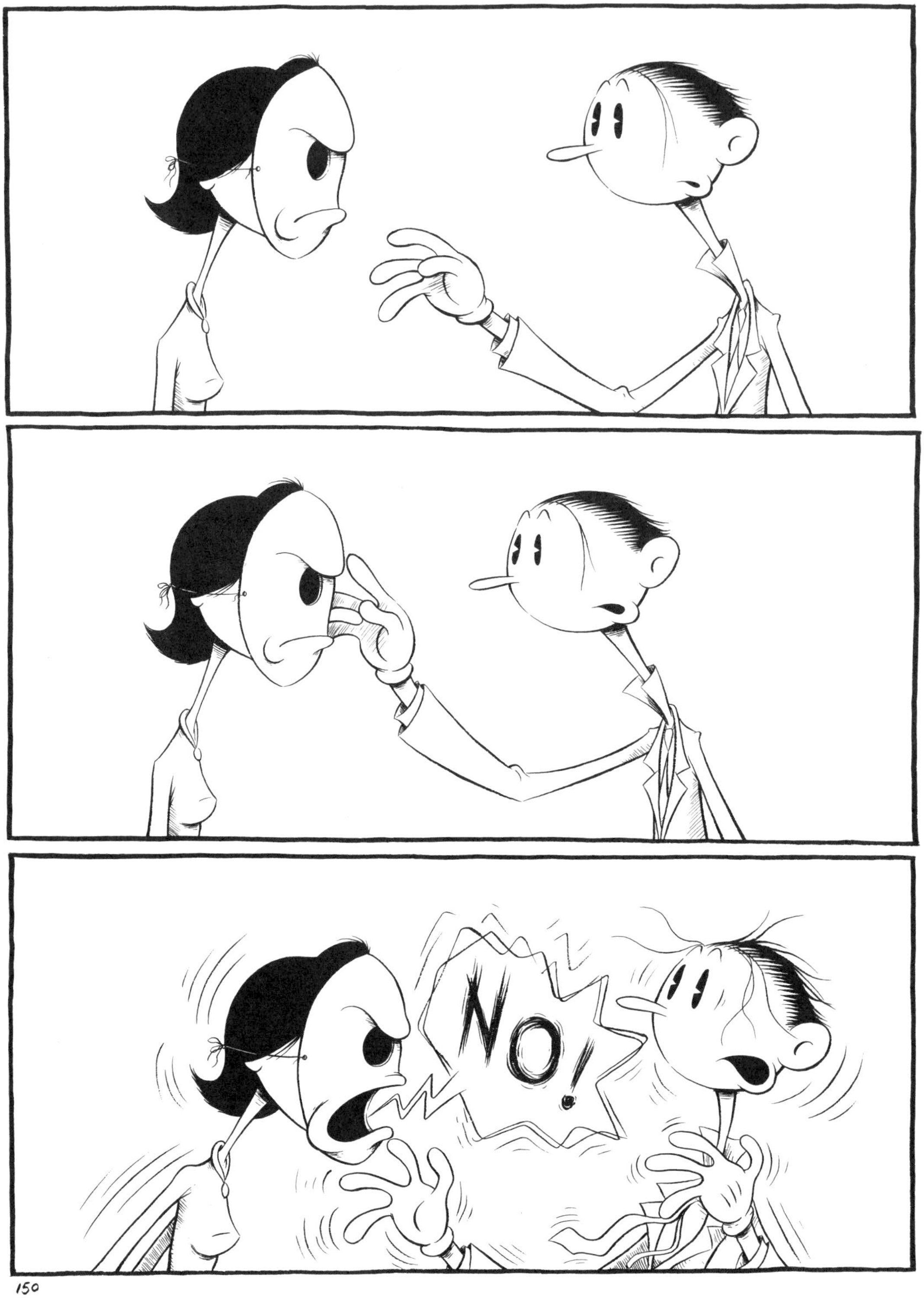
NO!

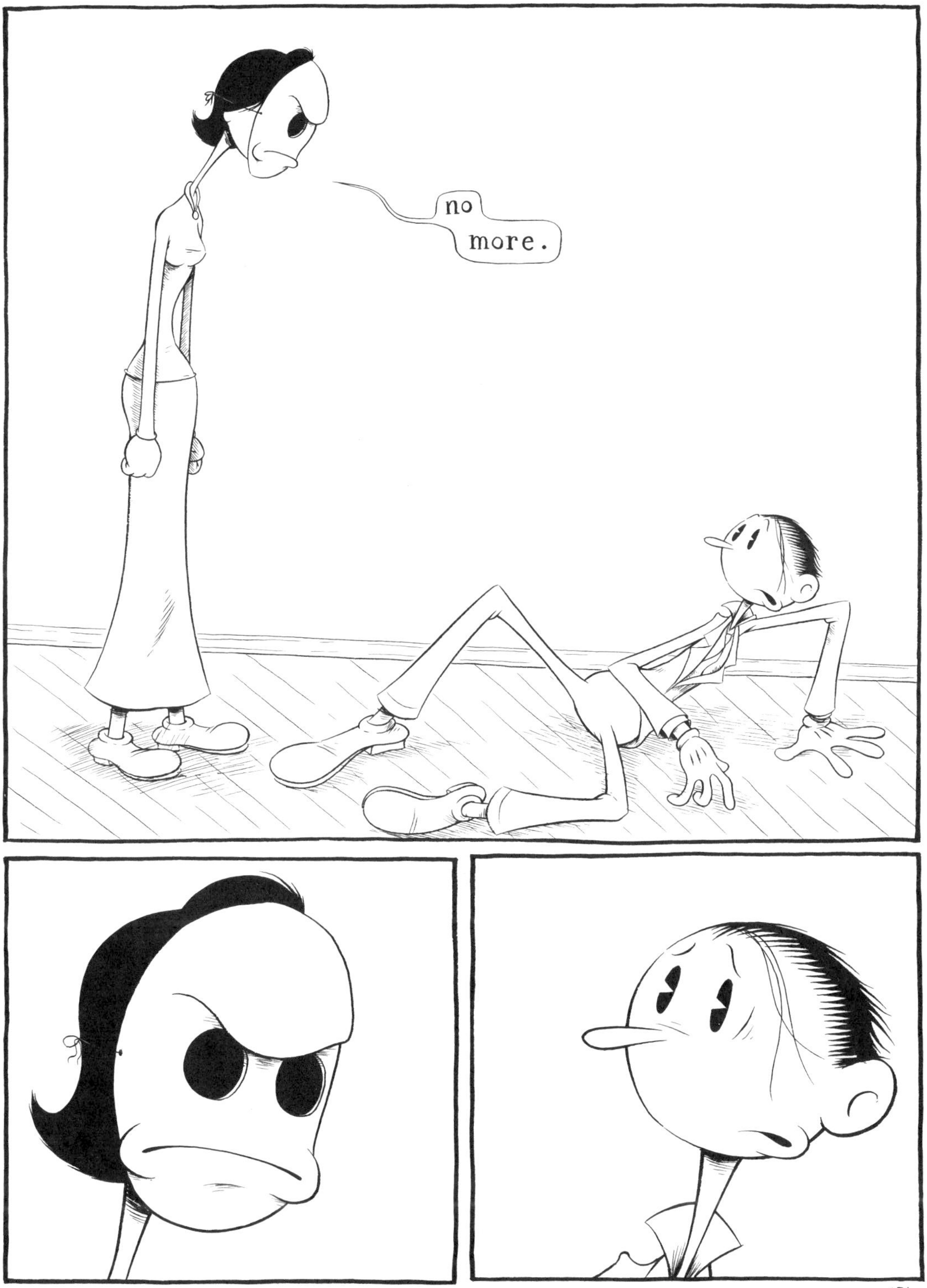
no more.

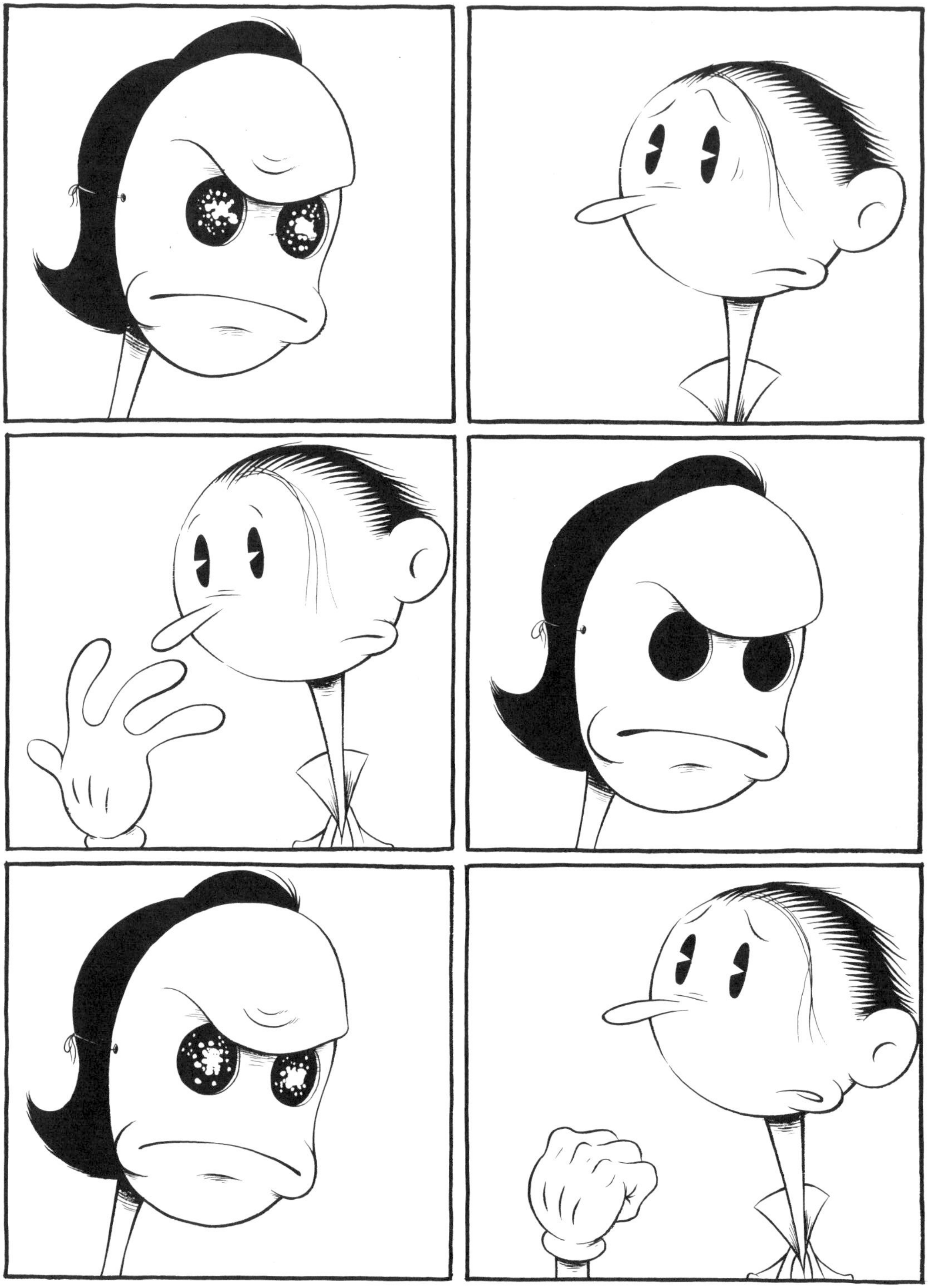

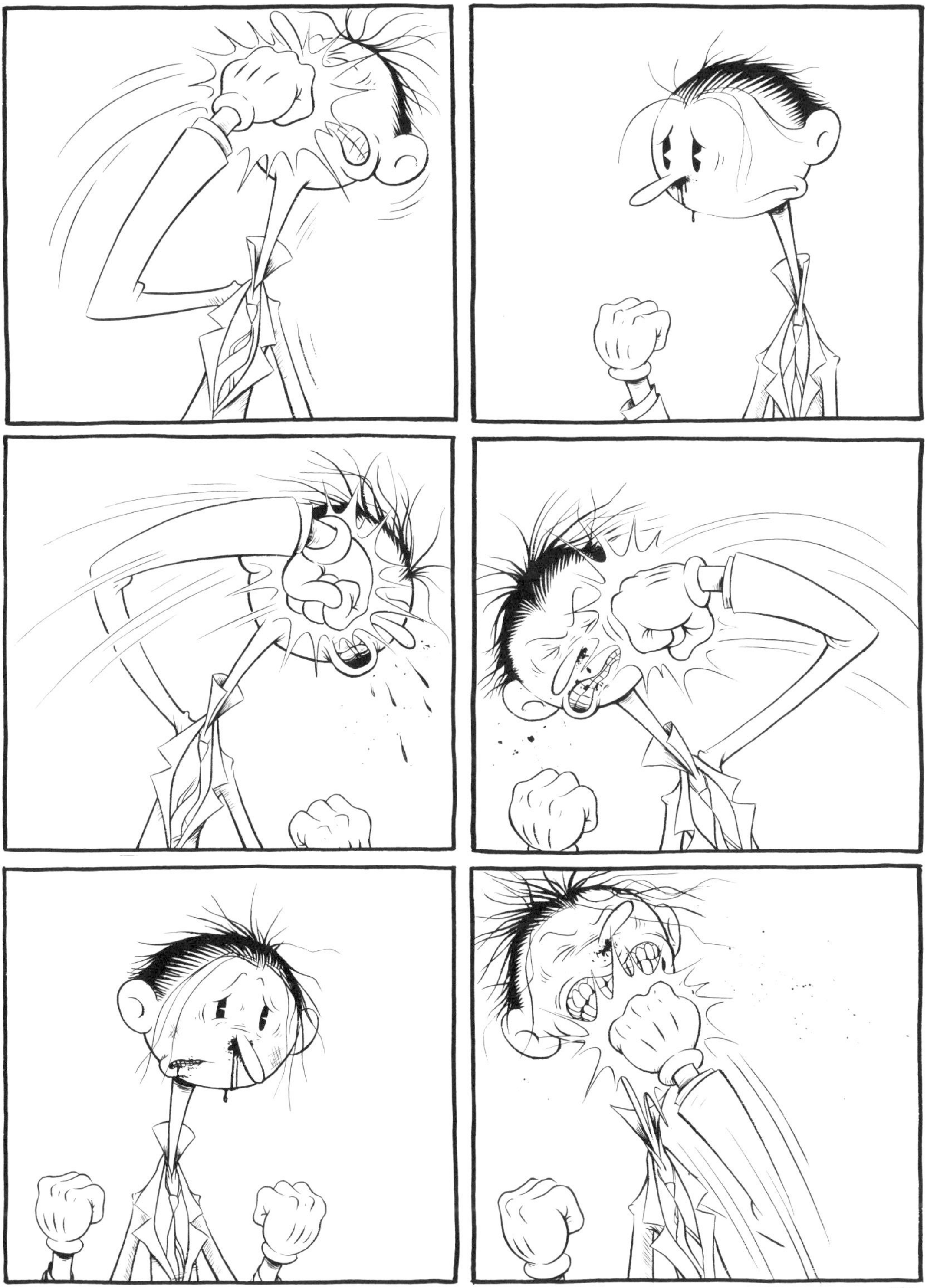

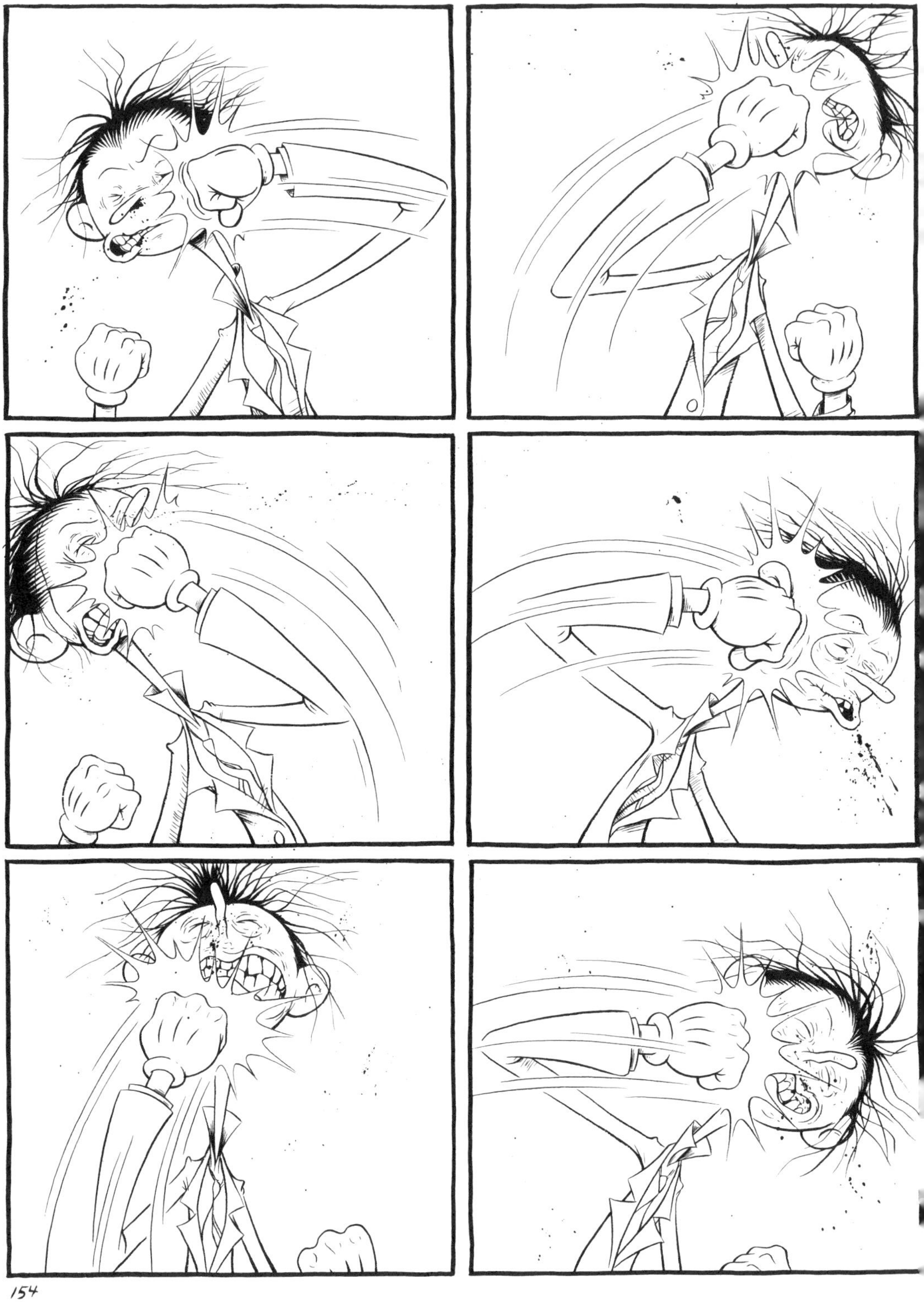

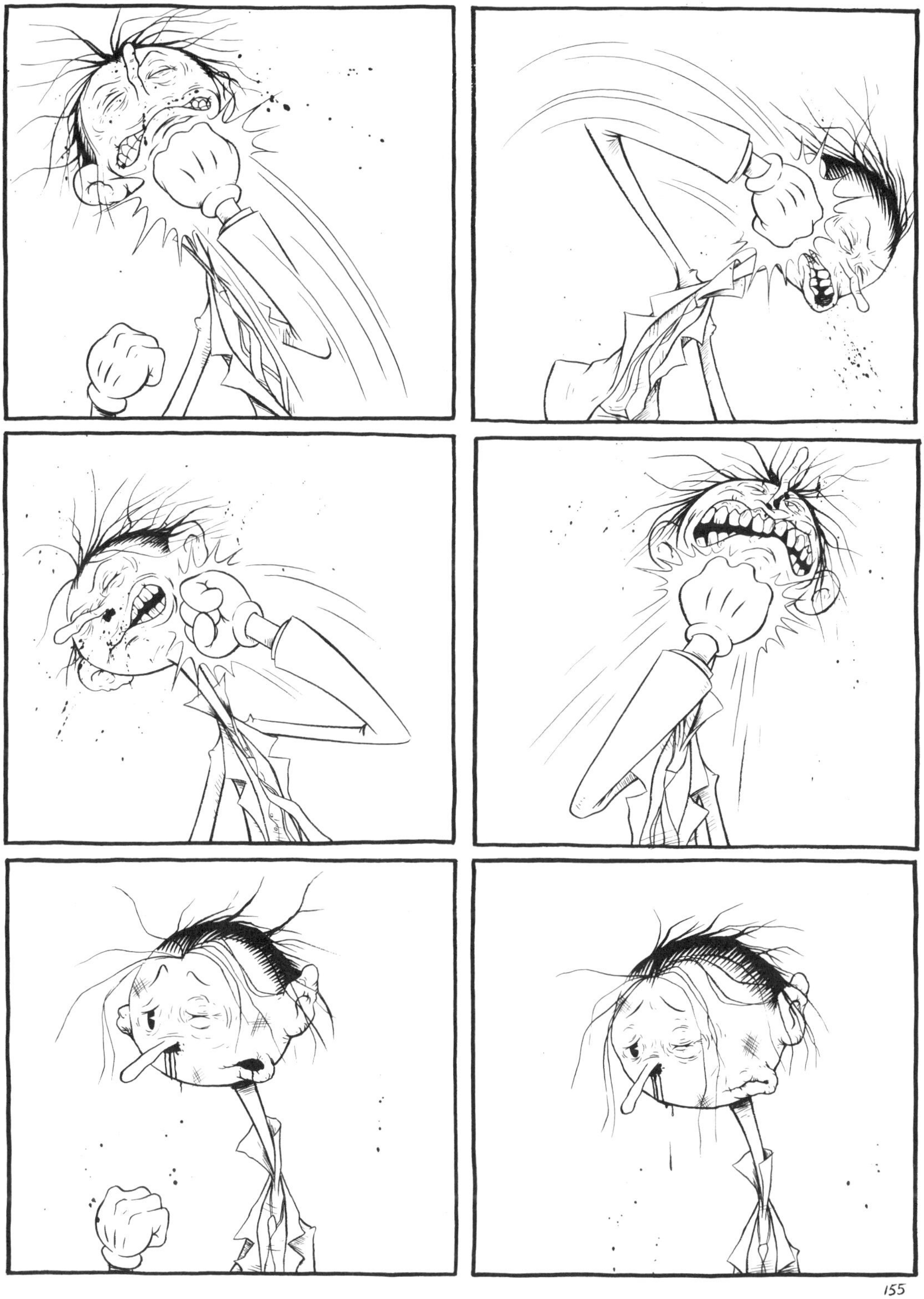

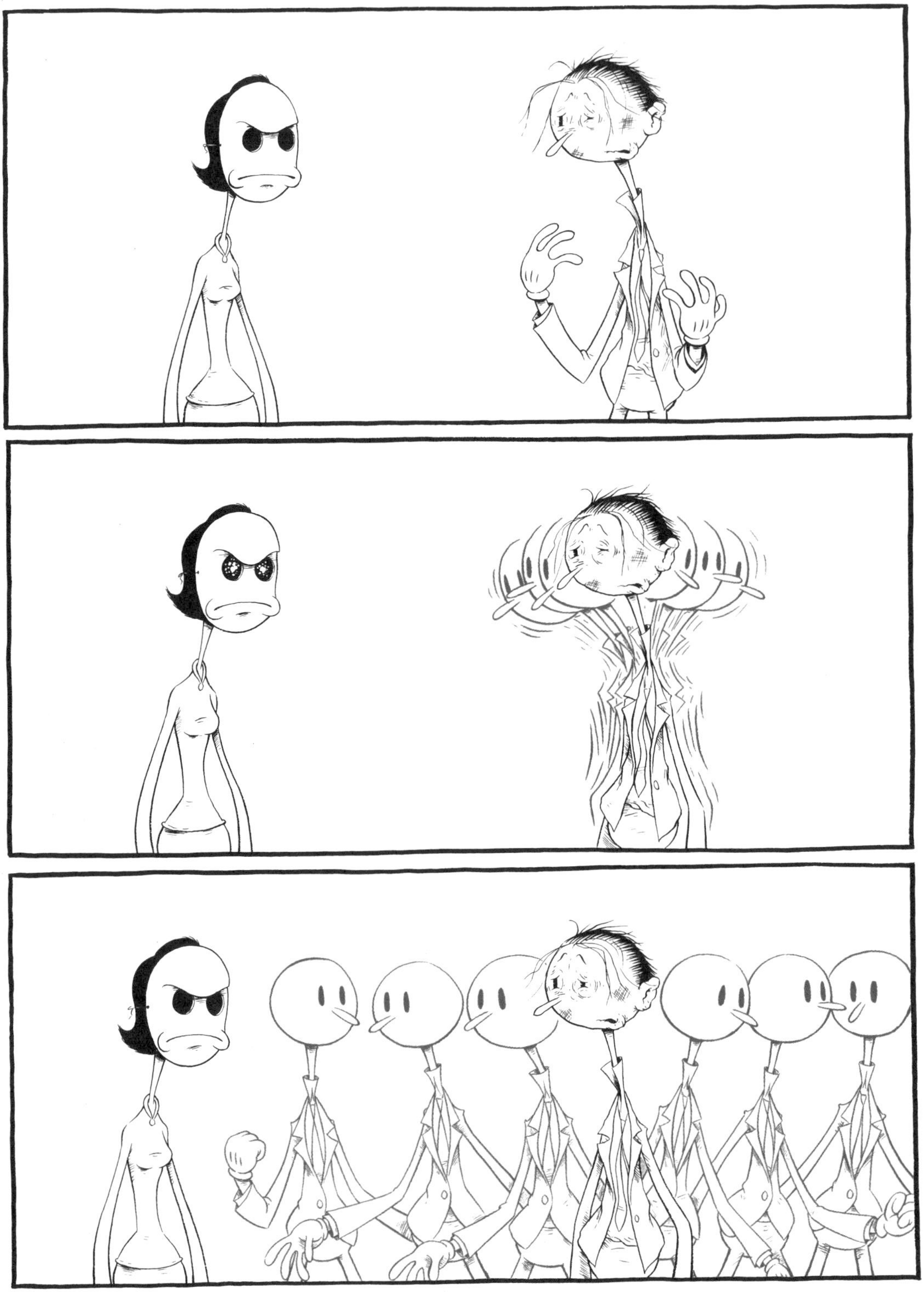

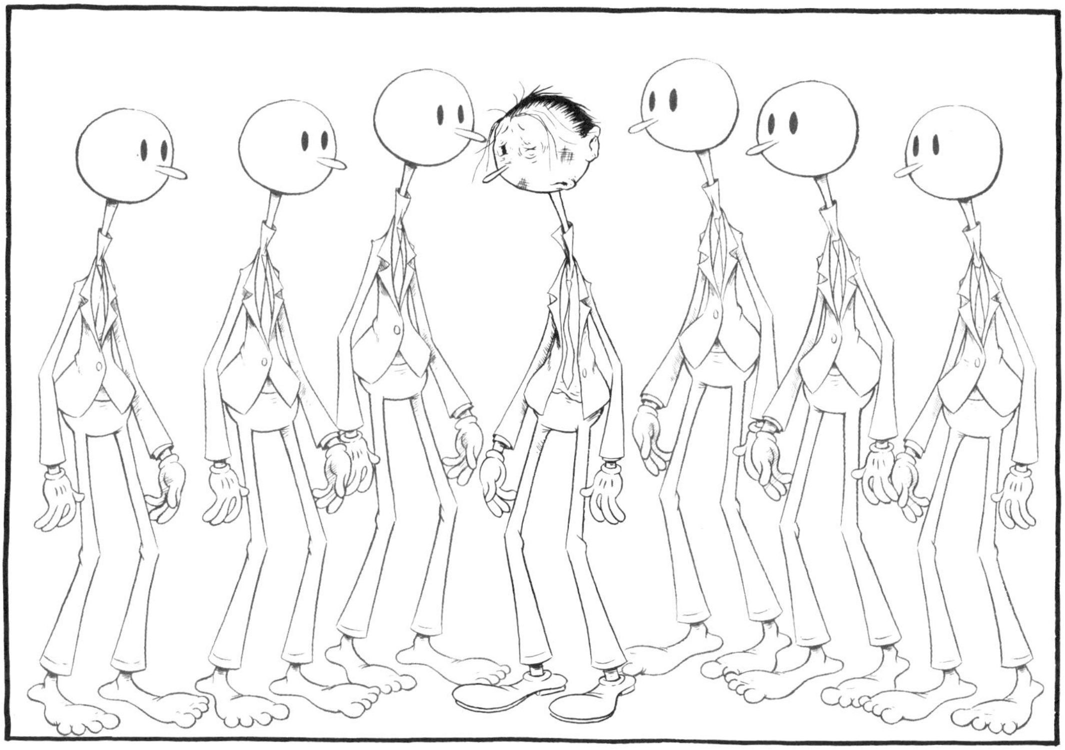

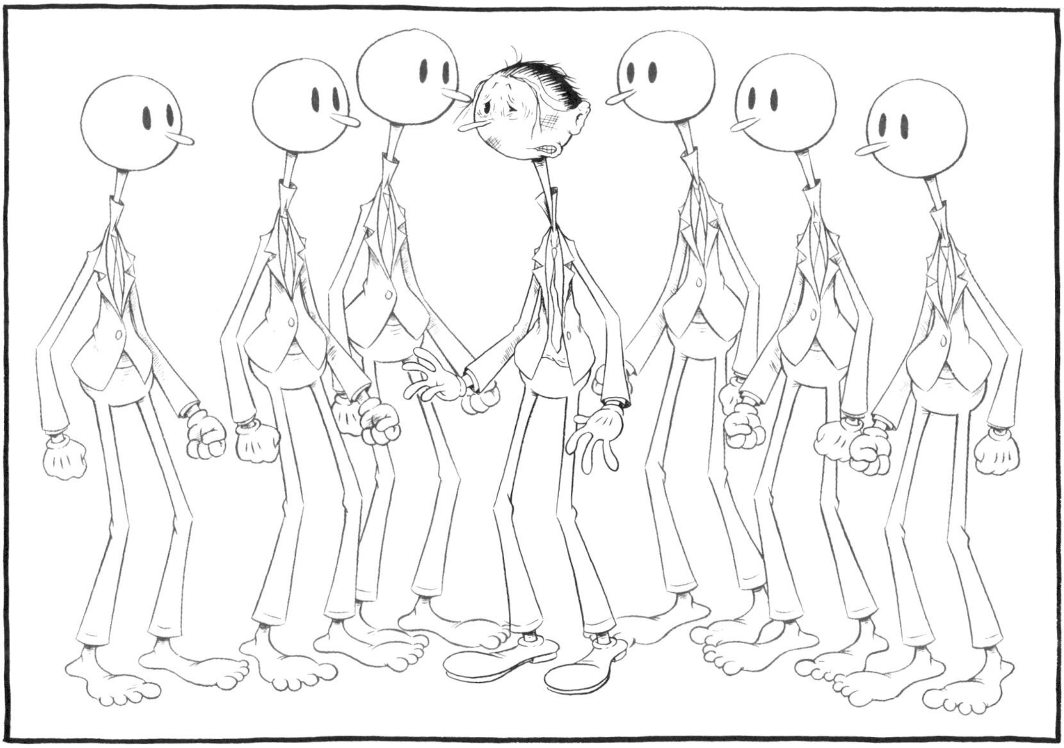

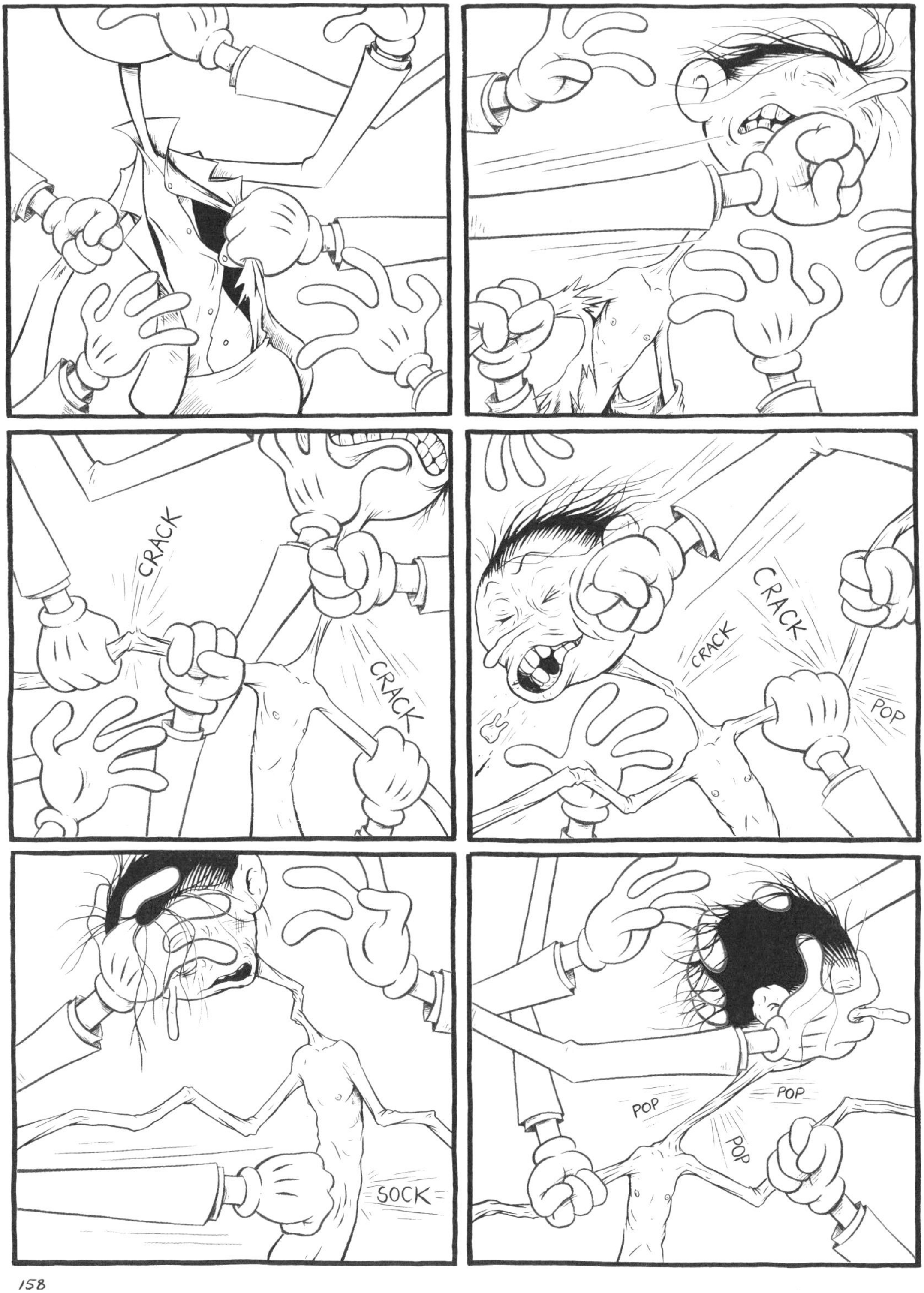
CRACK
CRACK
CRACK
CRACK
POP
SOCK
POP
POP
POP

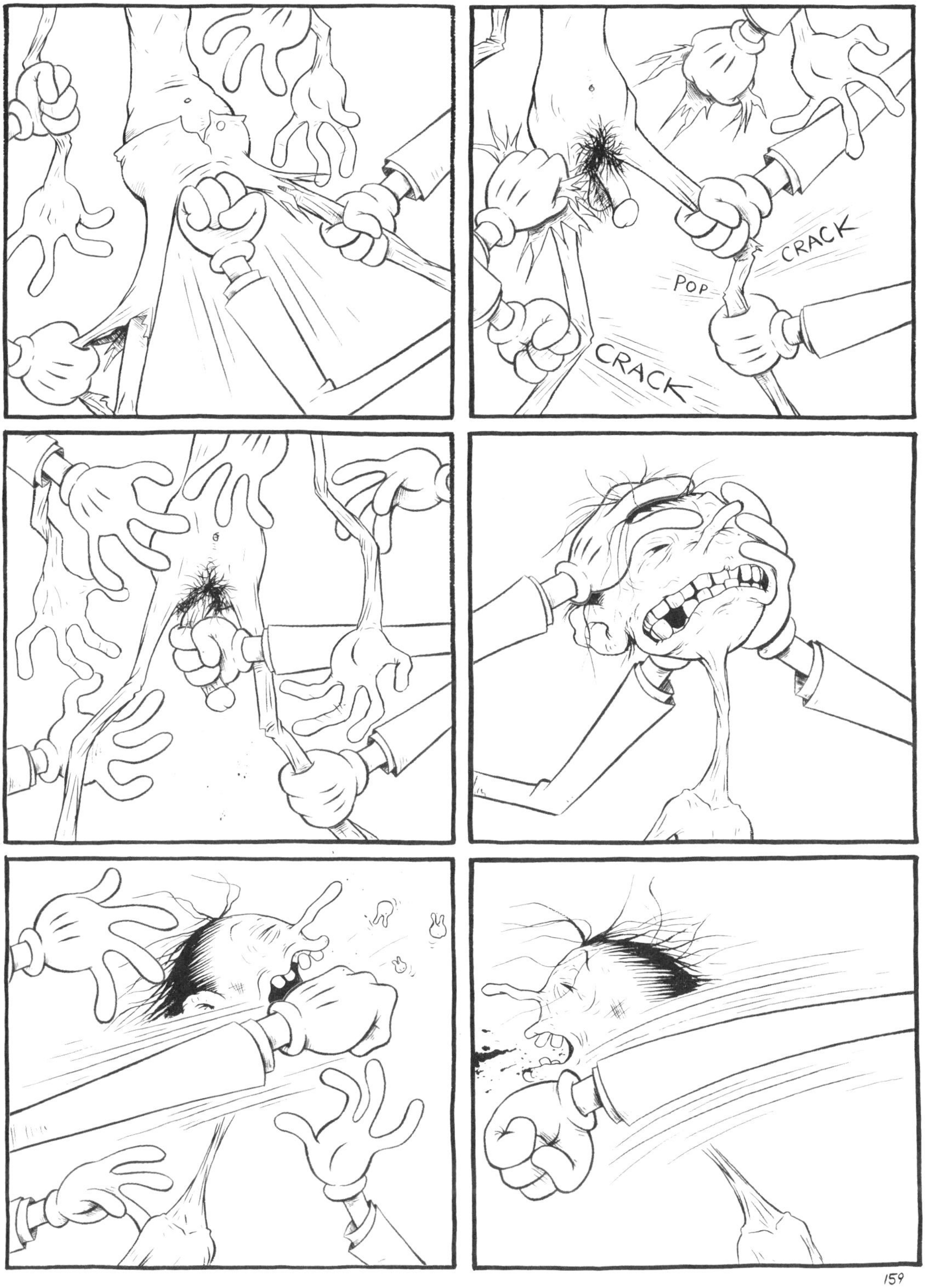
CRACK
POP
CRACK

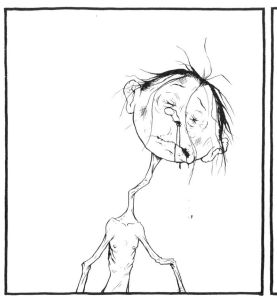
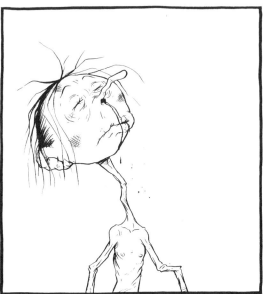
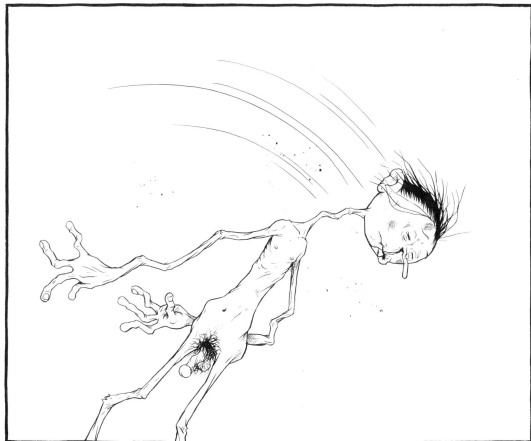

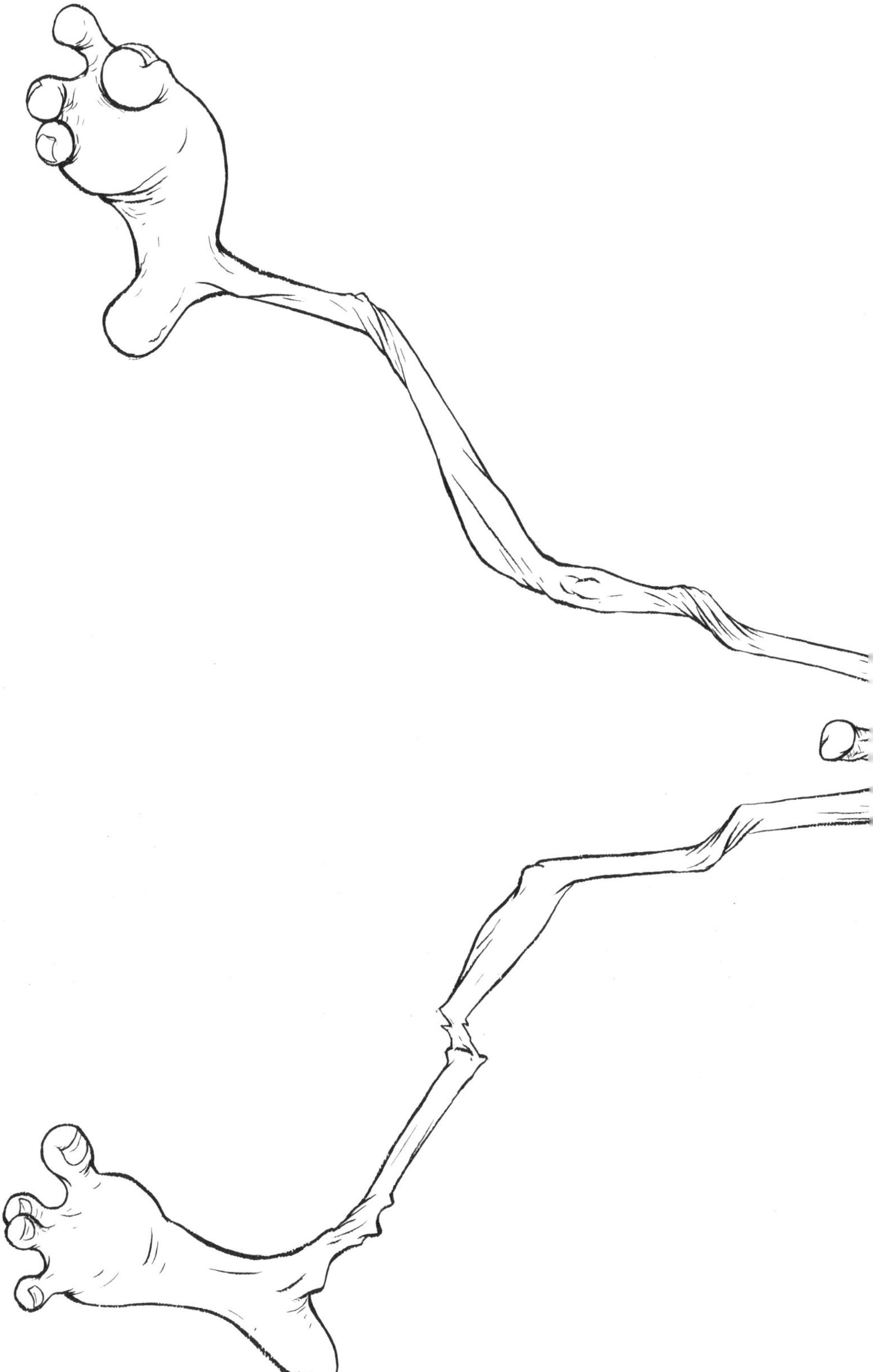

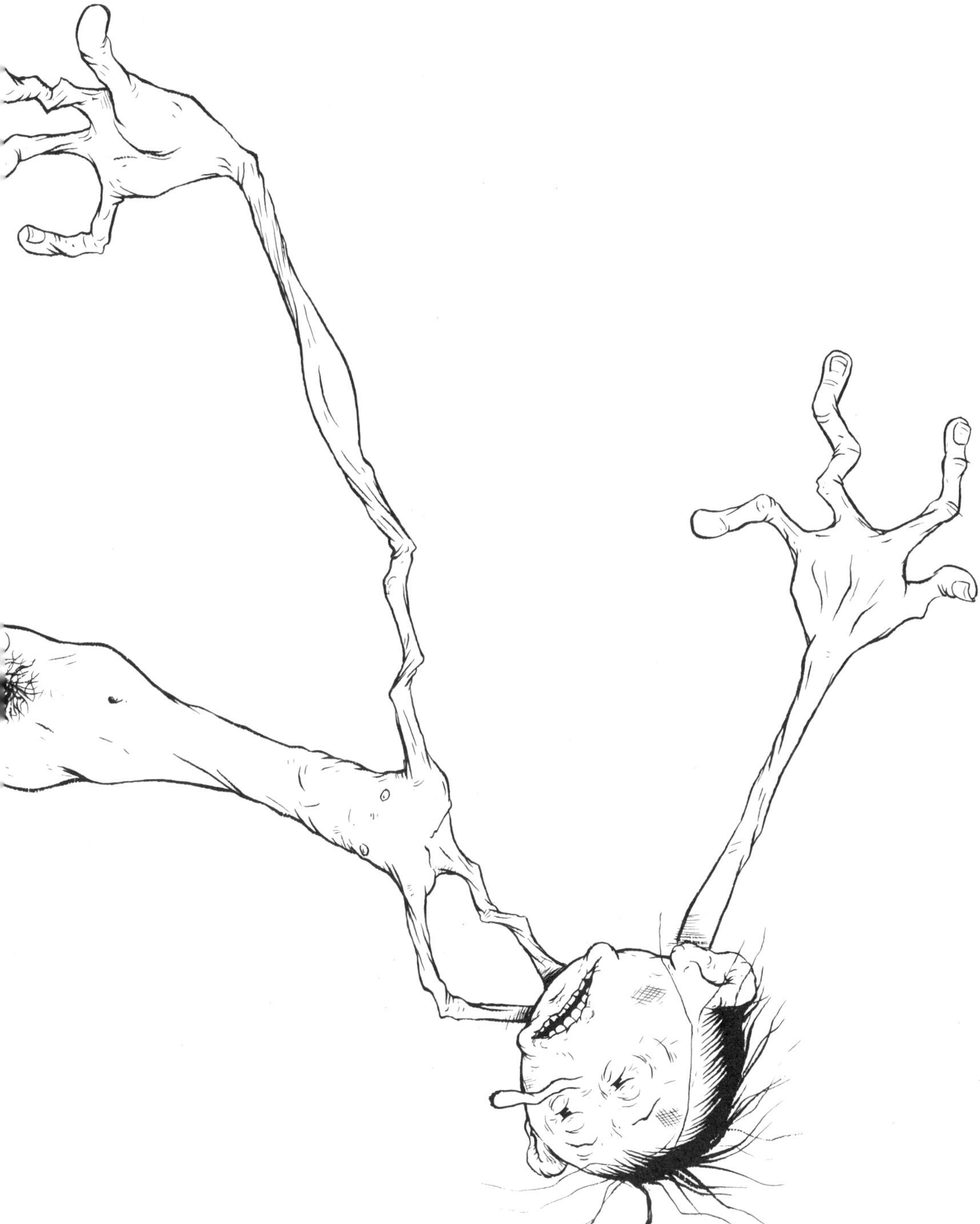

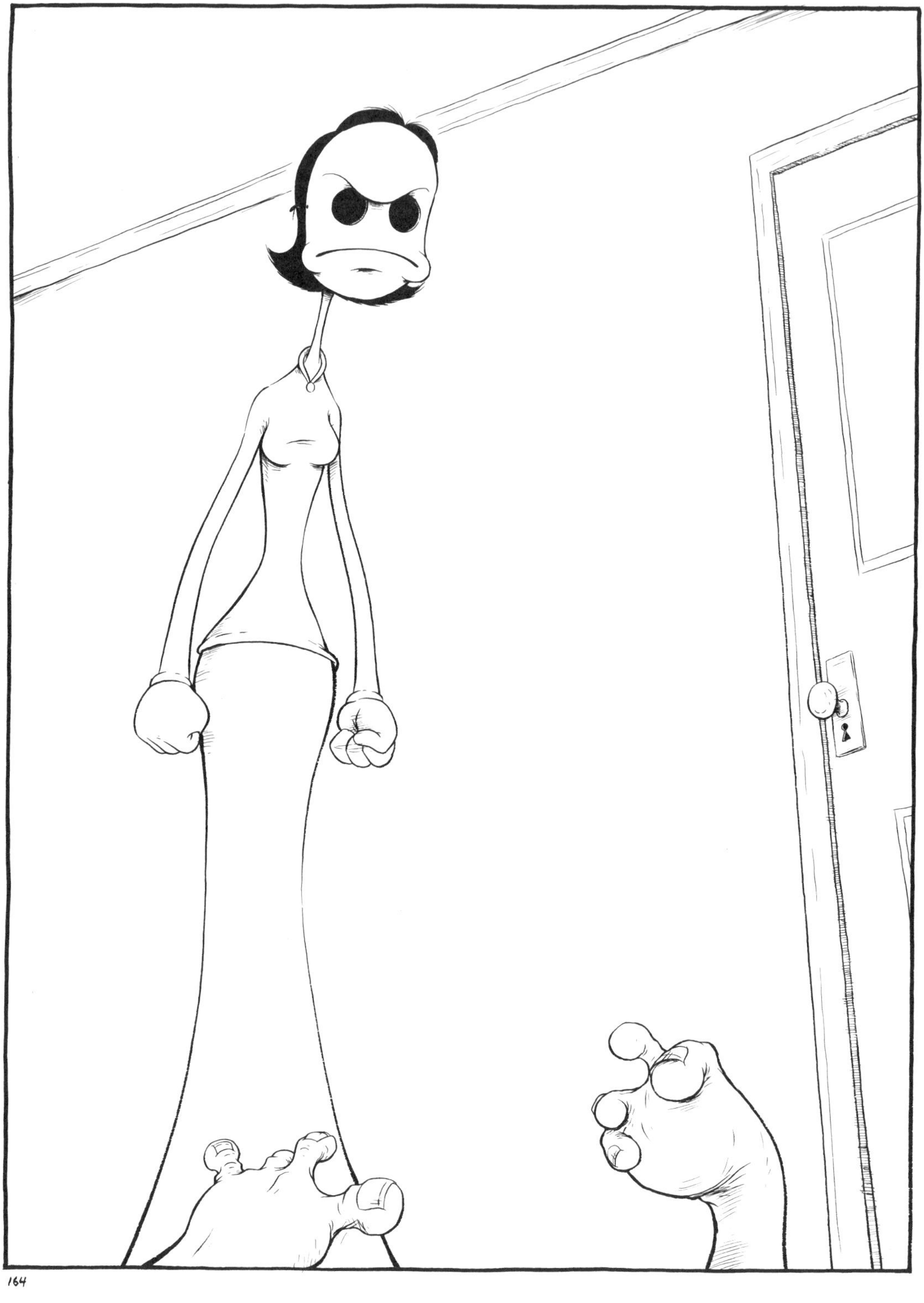

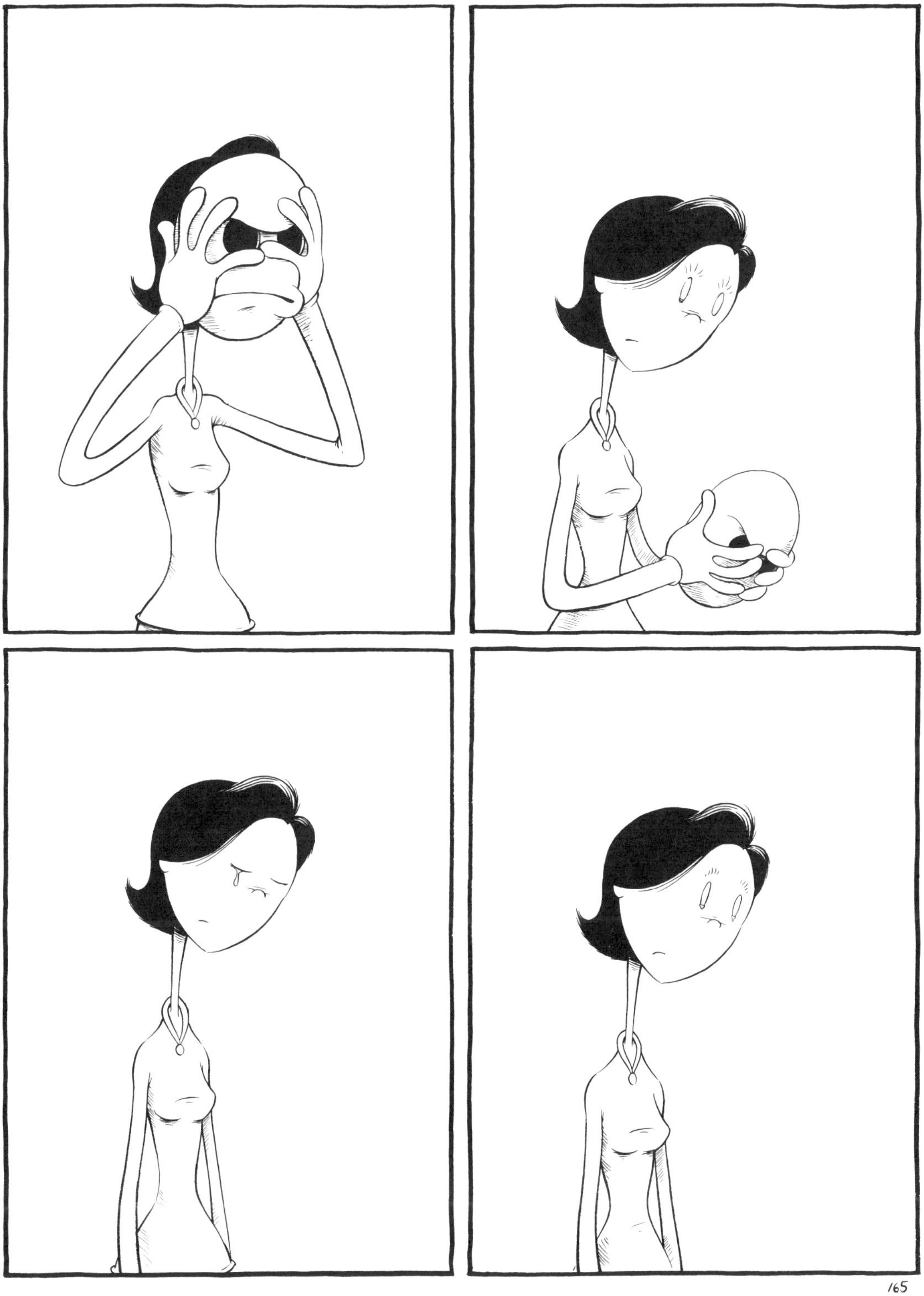

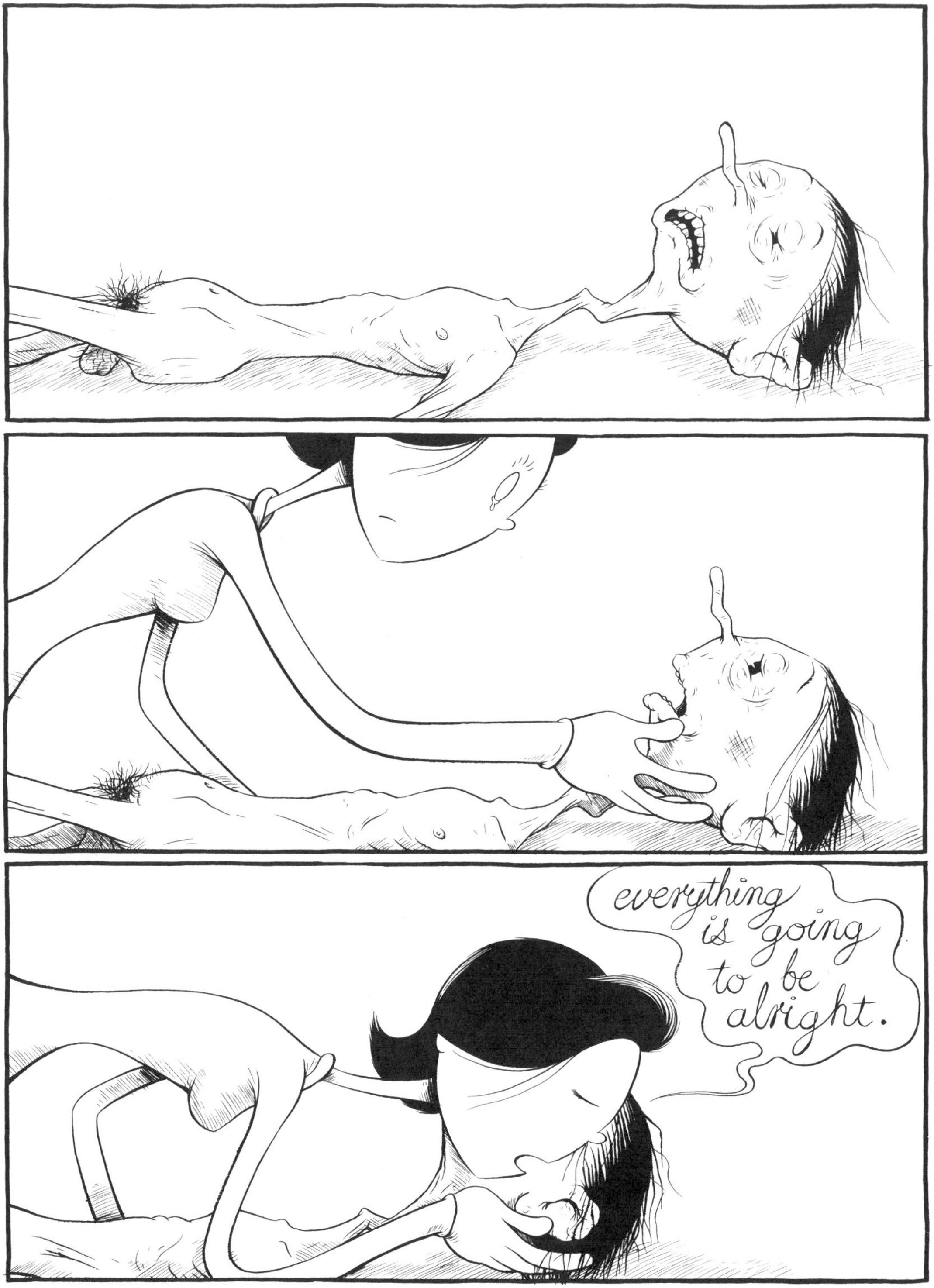
everything is going to be alright.

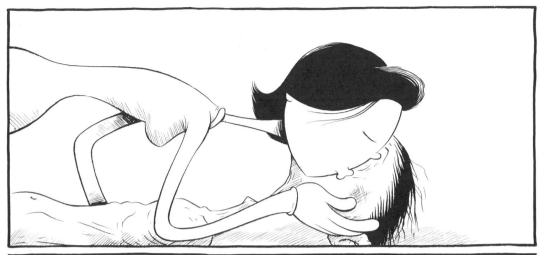

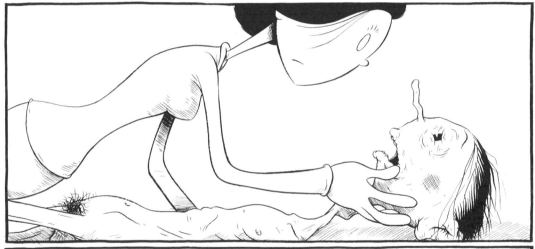

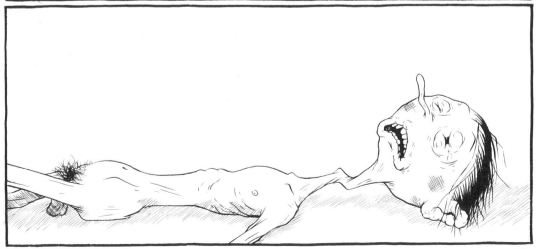

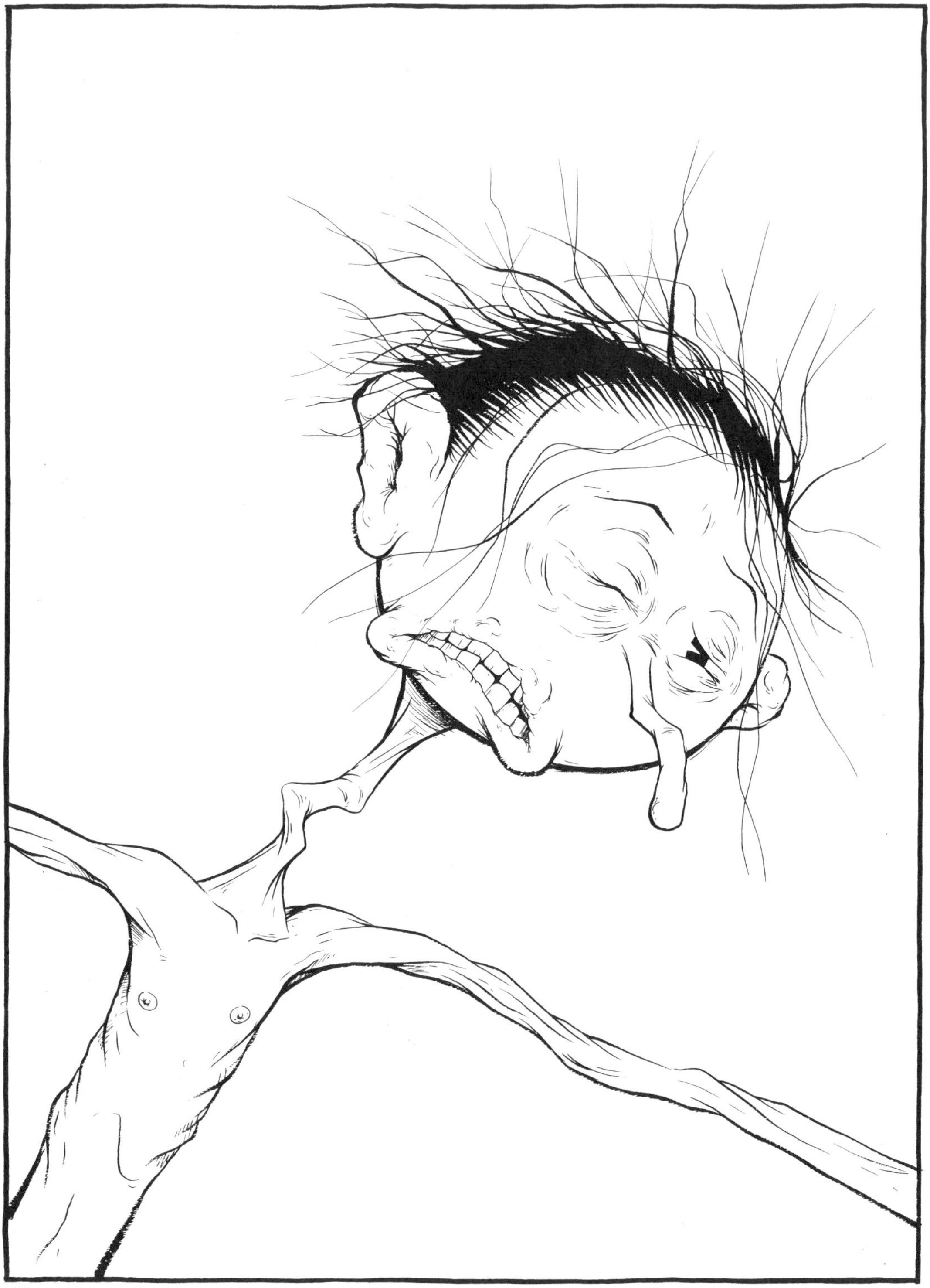

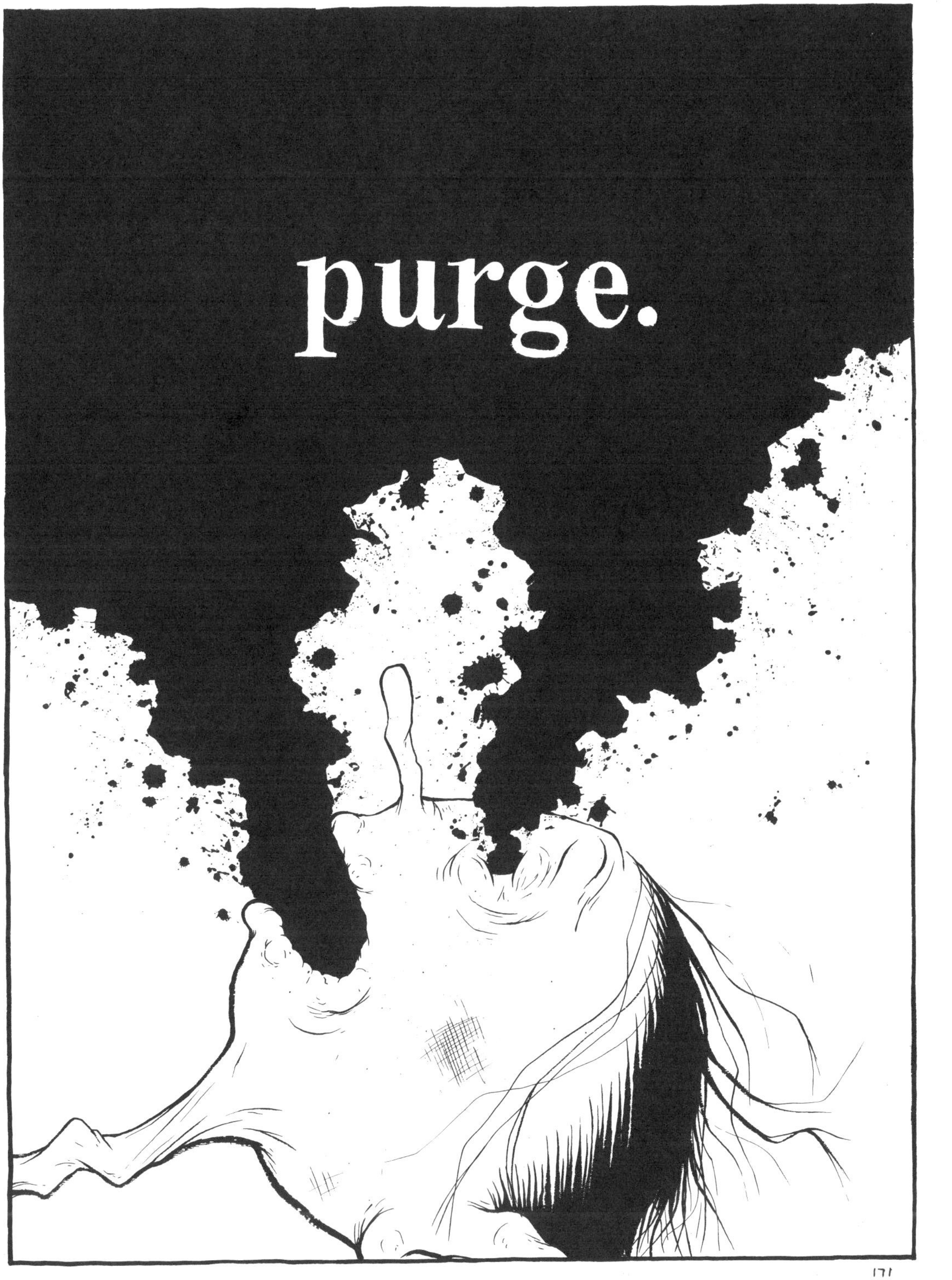
purge.

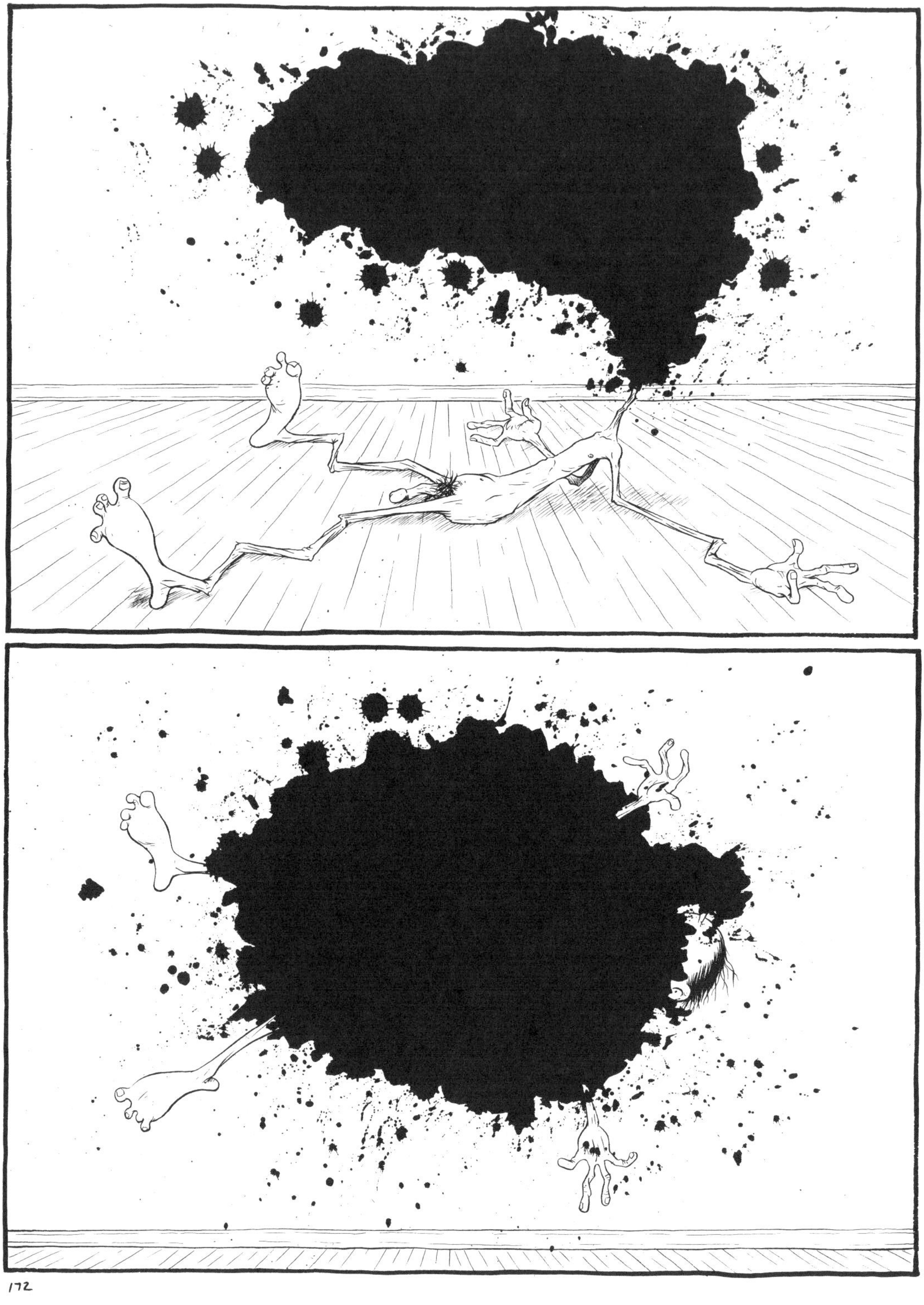

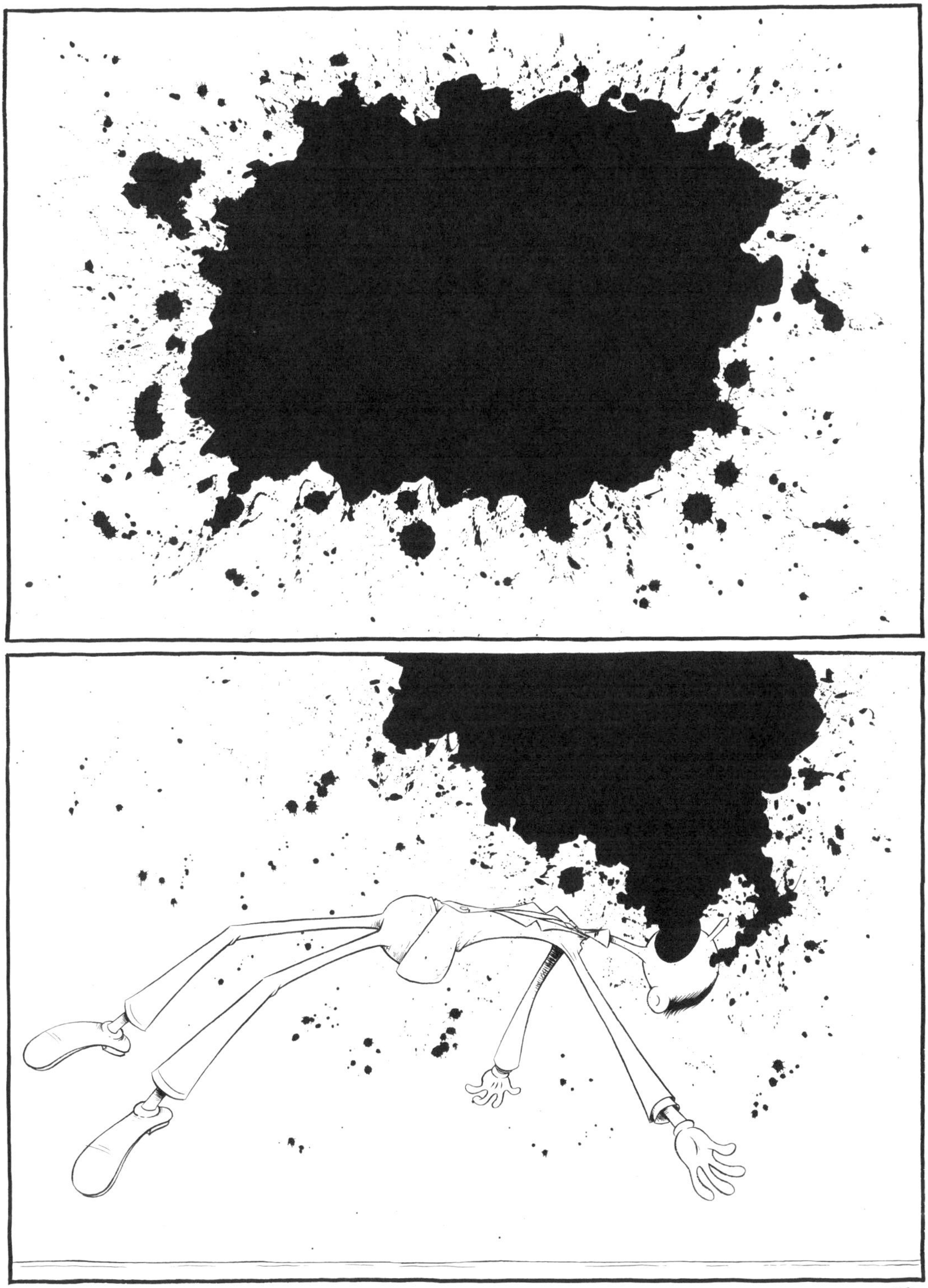

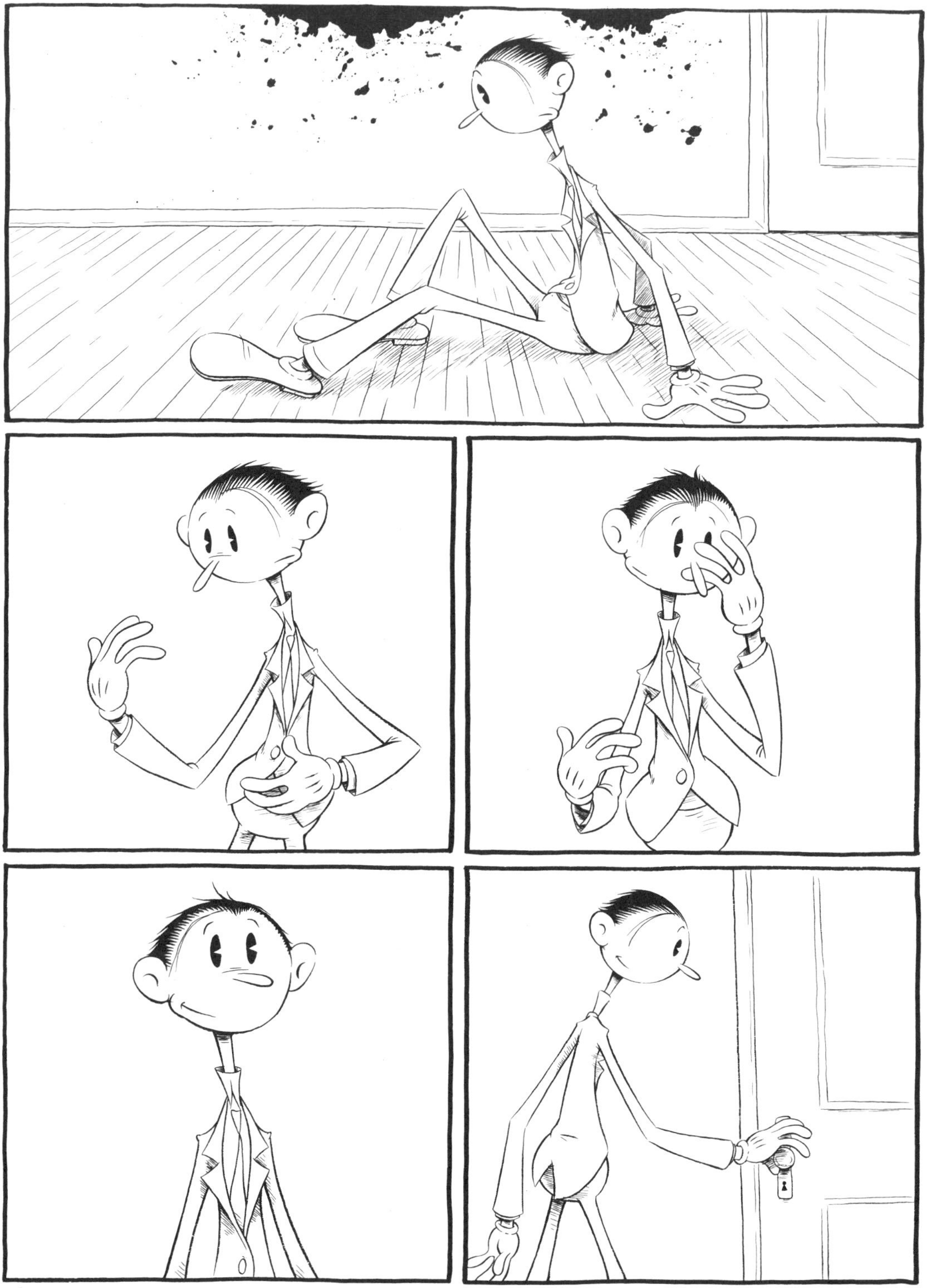

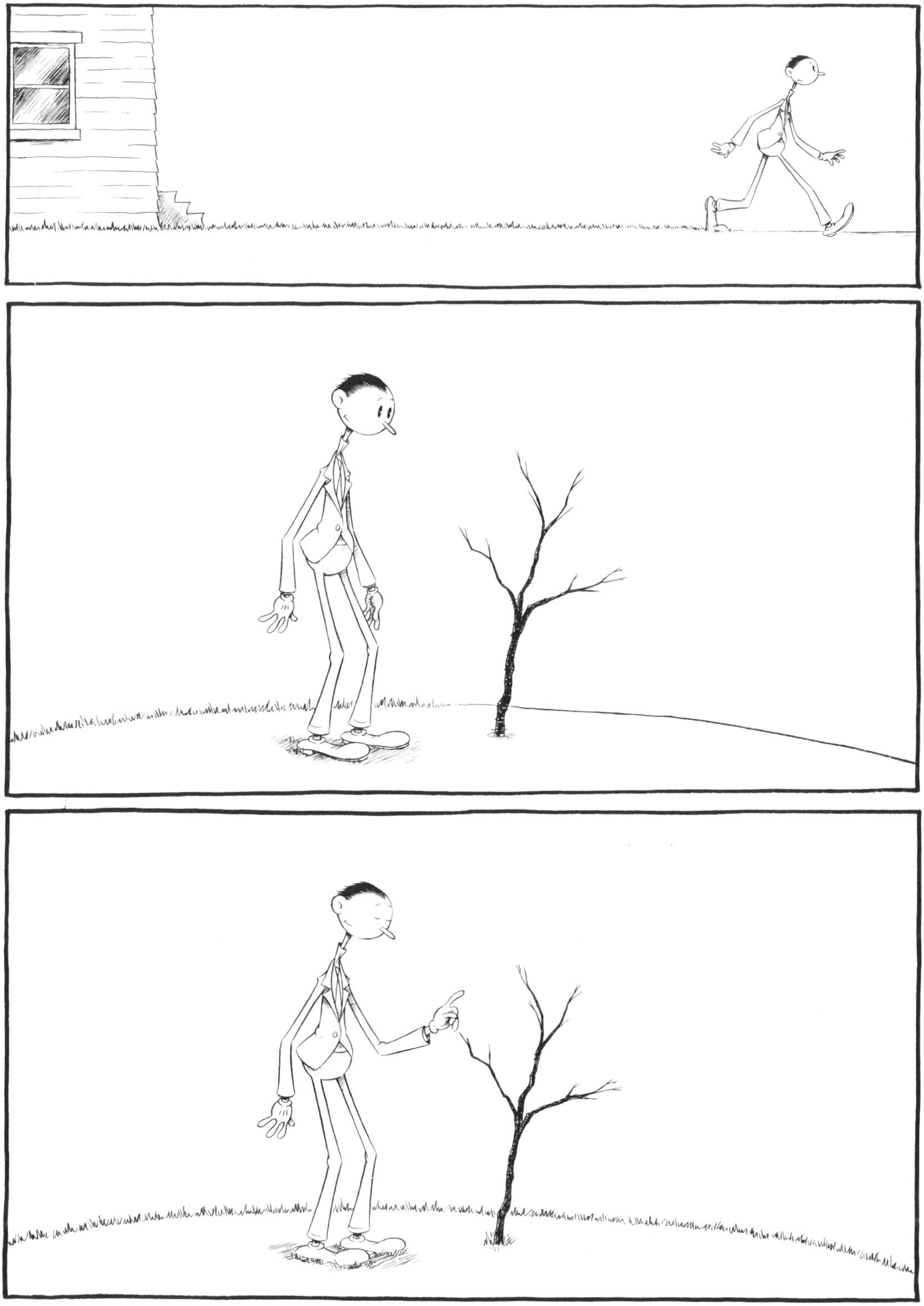

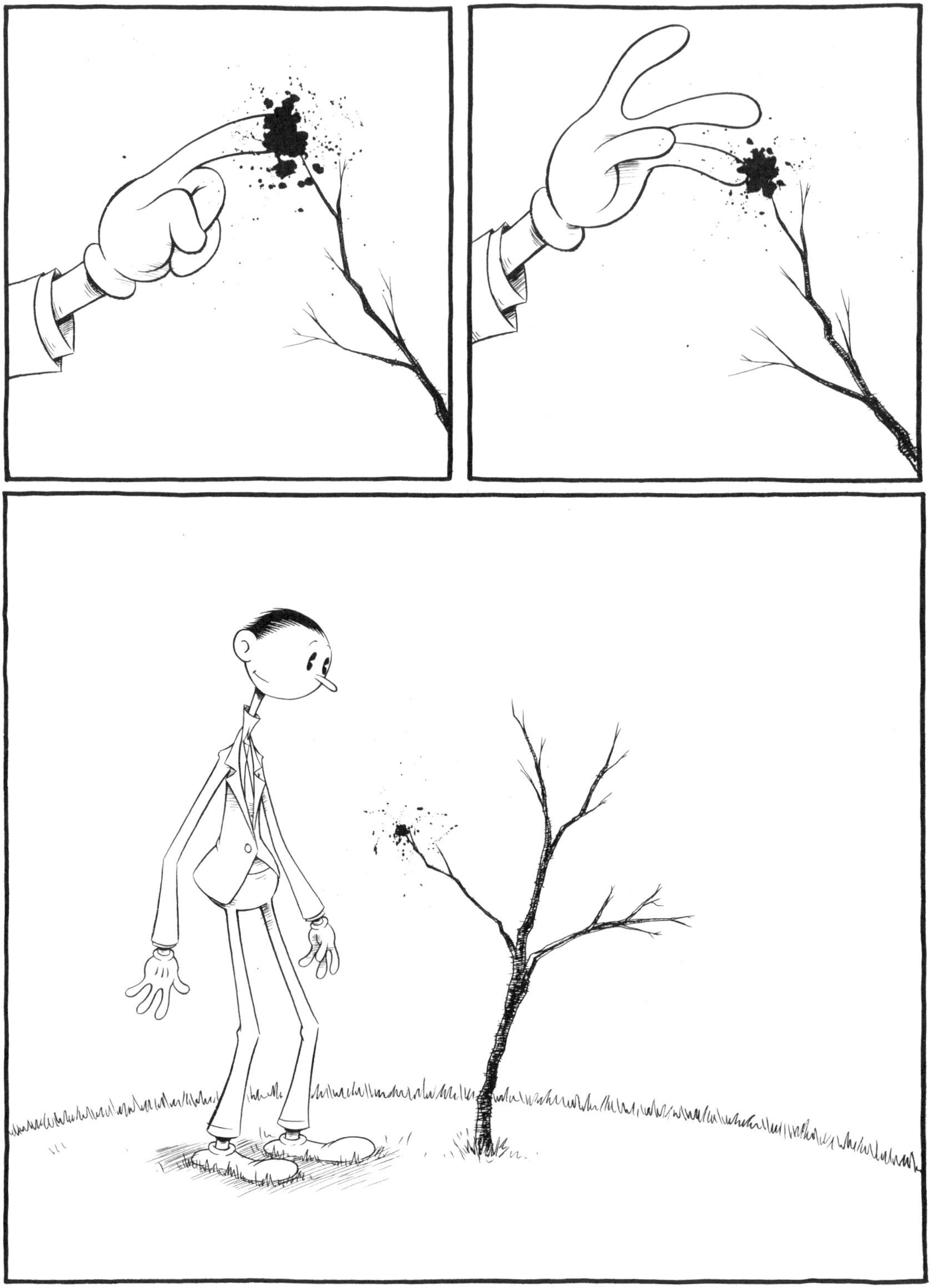

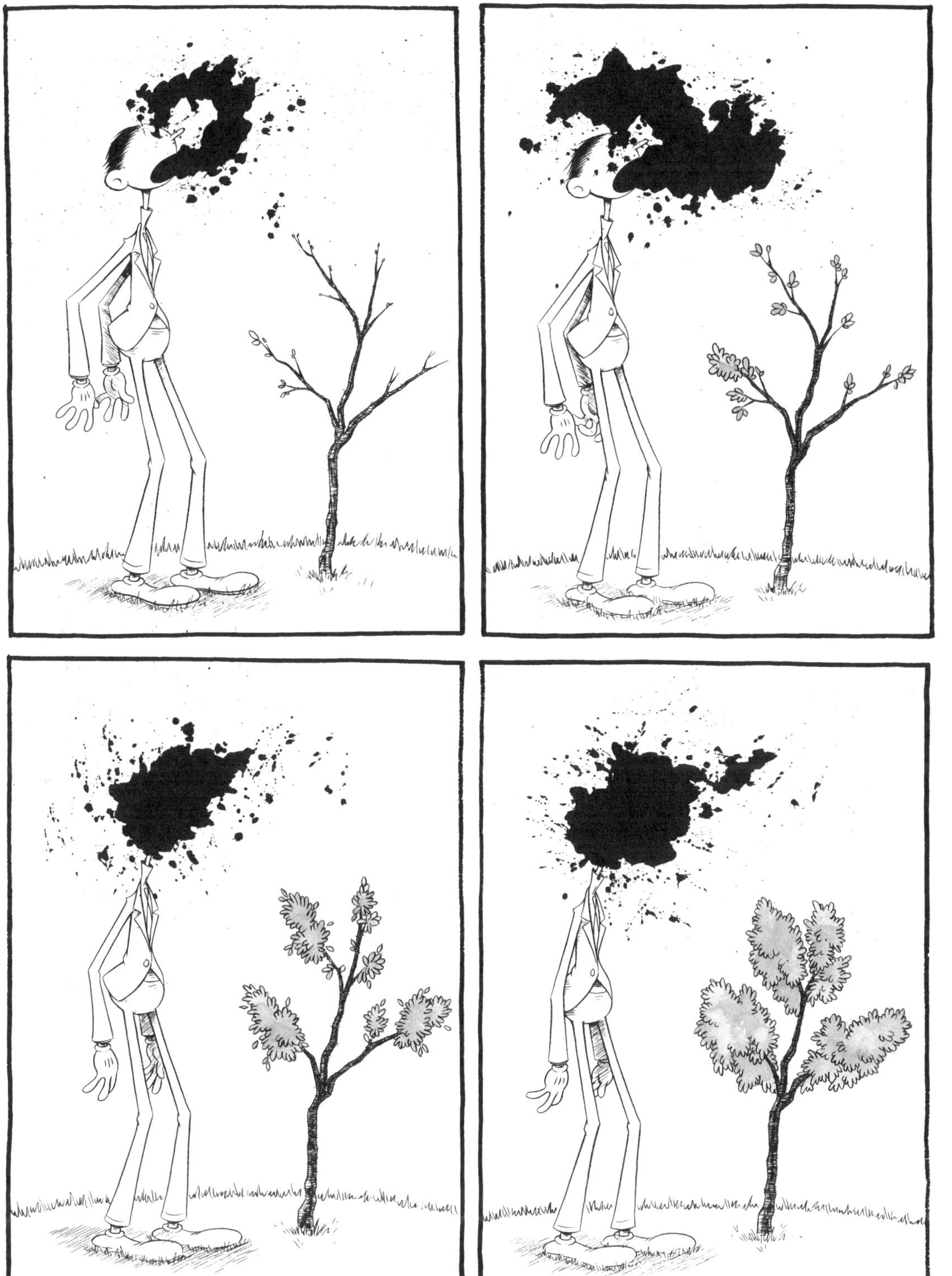

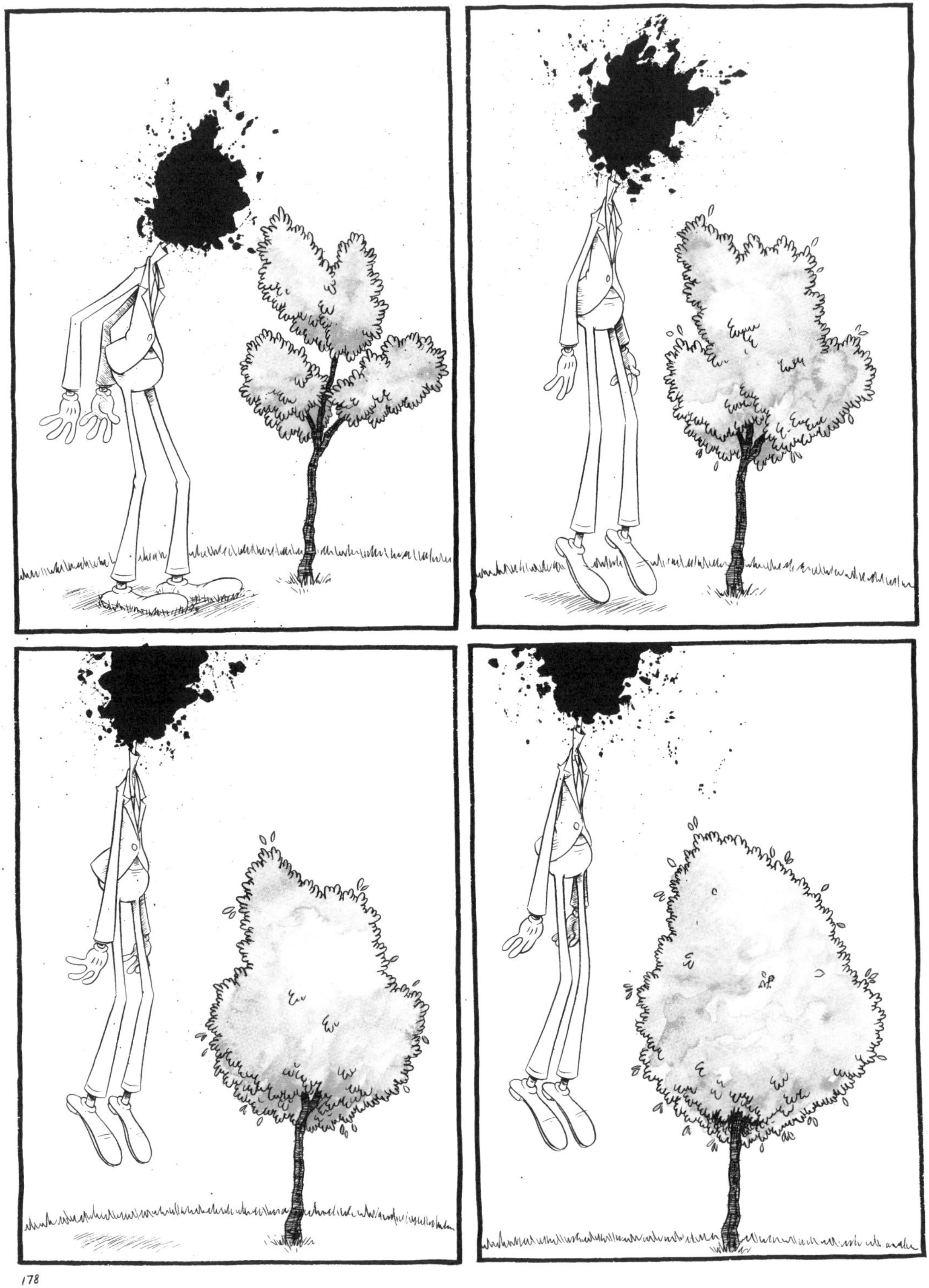

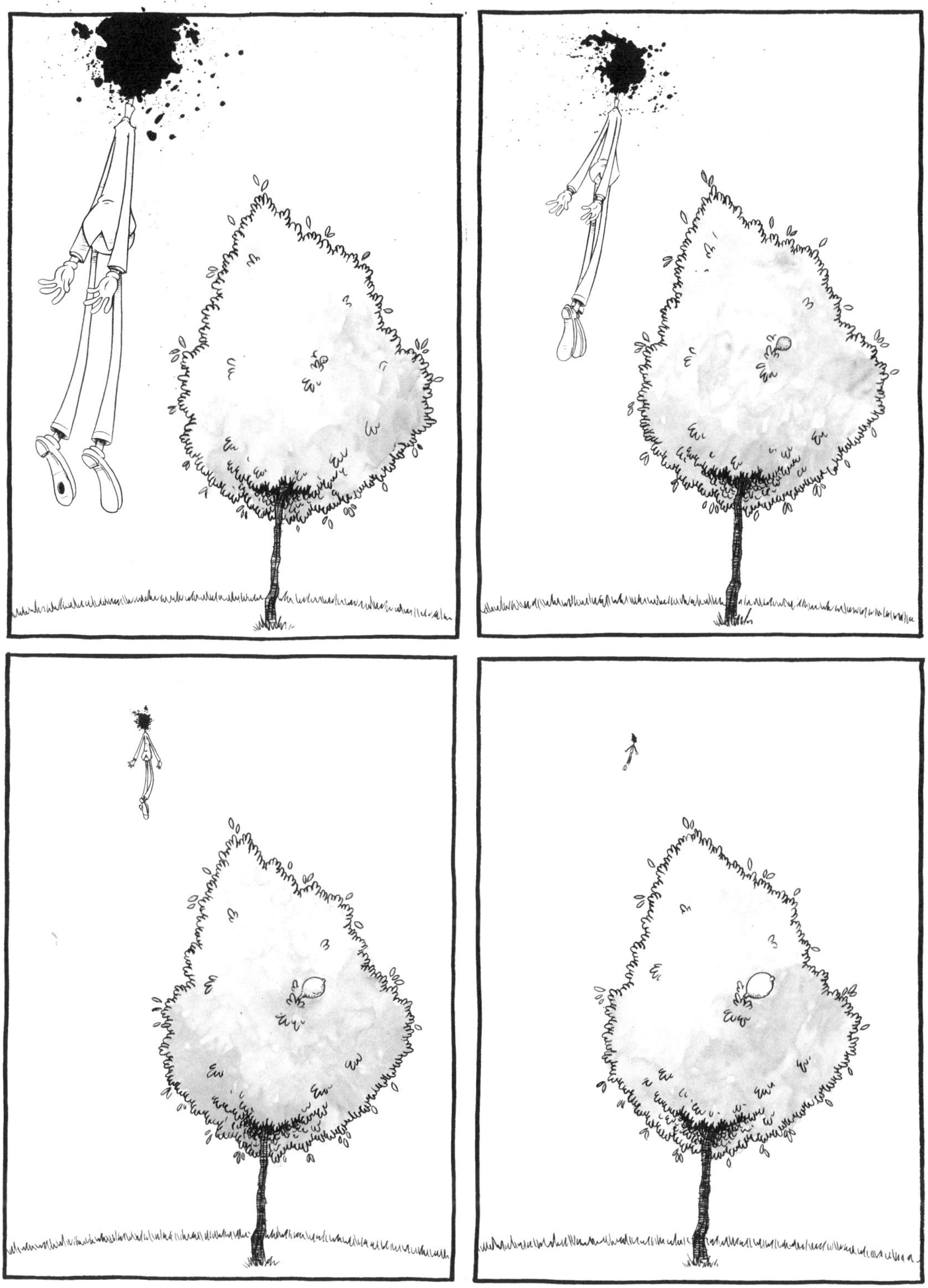

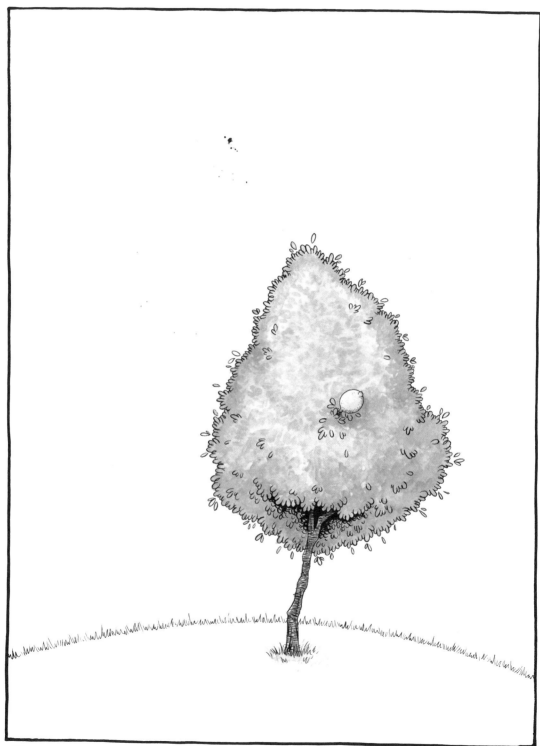

tomN!

thank you

greg & kristen, scot & lisa, matthew, levon & lila,
jesse & andrice, dylan, renée,
anthony & jennifer, wayne & patricia,
ross, josh, keith, monica, brian, kyle,
david, zara & sam, jordan, janet,
brett, virgil, glenn, mrs. hogue, trent,
everyone who has supported, encouraged,
inspired or helped me along the way,

and especially anna and barky.

special thanks to

the igloo tornado for beer, critiques and encouragement
david king for all the scanning
and brett and chris for wanting to publish me.

tom neely was born in 1975 in paris, texas.
when he was 6, his grandmother gave him a bunch of mickey mouse comics
drawn by floyd gottfredson and the smithsonian book of comic book comics.
pretty soon, tom figured out he wanted to be a cartoonist. a few years later,
he discovered renée magritte and got sidetracked into "fine art."
while studying painting at the san francisco art institute,
tom rediscovered his love of comics and began drawing his own
while making paintings that involved the same comic characters.

seven years later, this is his first graphic novel.

tom now lives in los angeles with his girlfriend, anna, and his dog, barky.
he continues to paint and his work can sometimes be seen in galleries
or on his website: www.iwilldestroyyou.com

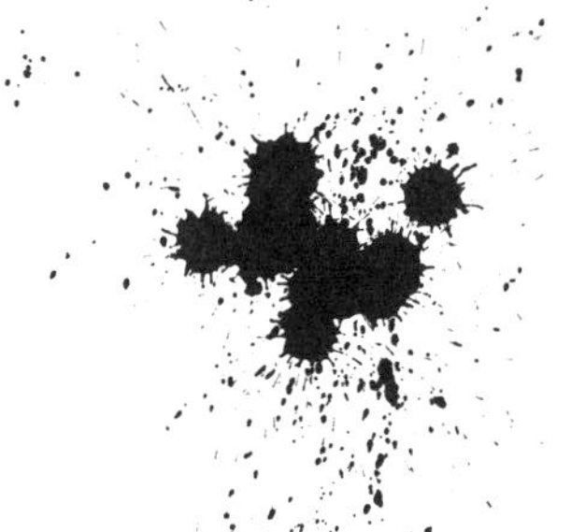